MULE EGGS
AND
TOPKNOTS

King Duncan

Seven Worlds Press
Knoxville, Tennessee

Copyright©1987 by King Duncan
ISBN: 0-936497-01-7
Library of Congress Catalog Card Number: 86-063997

Seven Worlds Press

Knoxville, Tennessee 37950

TABLE OF CONTENTS

MULE EGGS AND TOPKNOTS

I am assuming that you bought this collection of humor with the idea of putting it to work for you. There are many good laughs in this volume, but they are not intended simply for your private enjoyment. You can use this material to move people to action. As an evangelist and motivational speaker, I can speak from first-hand experience. "Just a spoonful of sugar *does* make the medicine go down." *Let me give you an example* (the most powerful six words in any speaker's vocabulary). The following story is one I have used to make the point that the major problem in our lives is that we do not really want to change:

Isn't it true that most of us are pretty contented with our lives as they are? There is nothing that we fear as much as a radical change.

There is a silly story about two Chicago men who had never been out of the city who decided that they had just about "had it" with urban living. So they bought a ranch down in Texas. They decided they were going to live off the land like their ancestors.

The first thing they decided they needed in order to ranch was a mule. So they went to a neighboring rancher and asked him if he had a mule to sell. The rancher answered, "No, I'm afraid not."

They were disappointed but they decided to stand around and visit with the rancher for a few moments. One of them saw some watermelons stacked against the barn and asked the rancher, "What are those?" The rancher, seeing that they were hopelessly city slickers decided to have some fun. "Oh," he answered, "Those are mule eggs."

The two city refugees were enthralled, "Mule eggs?" they asked. "Yes, mule eggs," the rancher answered. "You take one of those eggs home and wait for it to hatch and you'll have a mule." The Chicagoans were overjoyed at this and they offered to buy one of those mule eggs. They agreed on a fair price, put one of those watermelons in the back of their pick-up truck and headed down the bumpy country road toward their own ranch. Suddenly they hit an especially treacherous bump and the watermelon bounced out of the pick-up truck, hit the road and burst open. Seeing in his rearview mirror what had happened, the driver turned his truck around and drove back to retrieve his mule egg.

Meanwhile this big old Texas jackrabbit was hopping by and saw this watermelon burst in the road, and he hopped over to it. Standing in the middle of that watermelon, he begins to eat. Here comes the two city men. They spy their mule egg burst open, and there is this long-eared creature in the middle of it. One of the men shouts, "Our mule egg has hatched!"

Seeing those two men coming toward it, that jack rabbit takes off hopping with the two city fellows in hot pursuit. As is a jack rabbit's custom, it ran for a few minutes in a circle with the two men from Chicago giving everything they had to catch him. Finally they could go no farther. Both men fell wearily onto the ground gasping for air while the jack rabbit hopped off into the distance. Raising up on his elbow, one of the men said to the other, "Well, I guess we lost our mule." The other man nodded grimly. "Yes, but you know," he said, "I'm not sure I wanted to plow that fast anyway." Isn't that the real question when we come to Christian discipleship — whether we really want to plow that fast anyway?

I follow that story with one about my grandfather, the Reverend G. F. Cox who was a Supply Pastor in the Methodist Church. *Please do not be put off by the fact that many of the stories in this collection are by and for preachers. Many of the most sophisticated users of humor are pastors. Remember, pastors have to come up with good fresh material week after week. A good story is a good story.* To appreciate this story you have to understand that East Tennessee, where my grandfather preached and where I live, is Baptist country. Even the dogs and cats are Baptists. In the early days people would join the Methodist church but the Baptists had told them that a person could not go to heaven unless they had been baptized "all over" (i. e. "immersed"). A little bit of Methodist sprinkling would not open the Pearly gates.

A rather tall lady came to my grandfather one day wanting to join the church, but first she wanted to be baptized by immersion "just in case the Baptists are right." My grandfather agreed. They scheduled a time to gather the church down by the river for what generally must have been a most beautiful and meaningful occasion. What happened on this ocassion, however, was more ridiculous than sublime.

The river was quite shallow that summer, and, as I have already noted, the lady was rather tall. To make matters worse, she wore her hair in a topknot. For our younger readers that was once a rather fashionable hairdo in which the hair appeared to spiral upward upon milady's head for another eight to twelve inches. This particular lady must have approached seven feet tall, topknot and all. My grandfather was a man of rather modest height. For the uninitiated, immersion is performed by cradling the convert backward into the water as if being buried in the ground and then lifting him forward as if being raised to new life. This is, of course, the significant symbolism. Immersion is not as easy as it looks. I nearly drowned one young man who was much heavier and more compact than he looked.

My guess is that my grandfather must have labored mightily as he eased this rather tall lady with the topknot backward into a shallow river. As she made her entry into the chilly waters, she did what most of us would do under similar circumstances. She jerked her head forward until her chin nearly rested on her chest. This, in turn, kept her topknot from going under the water. Triumphantly my grandfather lifted her from the water and stood her upright as the choir sang the last verse of "Shall We Gather at the River." He had already started for the bank of the river, when she stopped him. "My hair is still dry," she said plaintively. "I'm sorry, Brother Cox. ·You will have to try it again." I guess she did not want to go into heaven without her topknot.

With a prayer for patience my grandfather braced himself to lower her into the water again. Speculation ran through the congregation gathered on the shore as to why the process was being repeated. Gently he lay her back into the water. Again, as soon as she entered the chilly liquid tomb, she pulled her head forward until the topknot stuck defiantly out of the water. My grandfather raised her to her feet only to hear her sputter that her hair was still dry. He would have to do it again. A third time he lowered her into the water. This time he took his left hand, placed it determinedly on her forward and thus insured that she could not bring her head and her topknot forward out of the water. At last she was satisfied. The people watching from the bank had finally deduced what was happening and were in stitches. They would never forget the woman with the topknot who wanted to be baptized all over.

The tag line I add to this story, if you have not already guessed, is that most of us are not like that lady. We do not want to be baptized that completely. We want to leave something out—our money, our habits, our moral inclinations, or whatever. Then I repeat the punchline to the mule egg story, "We are not certain in our commitment to Christ whether we really want to plow that fast anyway."

There are hundreds of quips, quotes and stories in this collection that can be used in just this way to pose serious questions or to make serious points in a totally non-serious way. In this way we help people deal with issues about which they might be defensive if we had used a more straightforward approach.

I am grateful to many persons who made this volume possible, but especially to pastors who have shared their sermons with me and from whom most of the best material is taken. I am also grateful to my staff at the Christian Communications Laboratory—Patti Sines, Janice Barbich, Lisa Raby and Jeanne Floyd who, by the outstanding performance of their duties, give me the time to do what I love best—collect stories like these and share them with others. Finally, and most especially, I am grateful to my wife Selina who strives to keep not only our work but also the really important parts of our lives running smoothly. I hope you find these stories as helpful in your work as I have in mine.

King Duncan

I like the story about the soldiers who were being trained to parachute. After receiving instructions on how to operate their chutes, they were given one last instruction:

"Now, in the one in a million case," said his sergeant, "that main parachute shouldn't open, just bear in mind, you have a reserve parachute, and pull the hook on the right side. It will open gradually. Relax when you hit the ground. There will be no pain. There will be a station wagon there to take you back to barracks."

But one soldier still wasn't convinced. However, the sergeant got him to the door and pushed him out gently. Our hero yanked the cord, and nothing happened. Then he yanked the reserve hook and looked up, but again nothing happened. As he was plummeting down with lightning speed to the ground, the soldier said to himself, "Now I'll bet you that station wagon won't even be there."

Along a Kentucky highway was parked a mammoth motor truck van. The driver was standing by the tractor from which a front wheel had been removed. A pastor stopped to see if he needed any assistance, but the trucker thanked him and said he had already sent for help. He had burned out a wheel bearing, and another one was on its way. As the pastor pulled away, his eyes caught the lettering on the side of the van: Standard Oil Company of Kentucky, Lubricants Division. He had burned out a bearing–hauling grease.
– John W. Lawrence, *Life's Choices* (Portland: Multnomah Press, 1975).

Brickman's "the small society" cartoon has a fellow look at the U. S. Capitol and say, "Hoo-boy! What this country needs is a credit card for charging things to experience."

Or as the writer Heine once put it: Experience is a good school, but the fees are high.

A certain wife always tried to give her husband a cheerful welcome home from a trying day at the office. On one day she really had to strain: "Guess what, dear," she said as he entered the door. "Of our five children, four of them didn't break an arm today."

A football coach gave this advice on how to deal with failure: "When you're about to be run out of town, get out in front and make it look like you're heading a parade."

In Georgia Methodism's **Wesleyan Christian Advocate,** James R. Webb passes on a story he heard in Savannah about a well-known lady of that coastal city who invited quite a few guests to dinner. As the main dish she prepared a huge crab salad. Just before her guests were due to arrive, our hostess set the crab salad on the dining table.

Upon entering the room the next time, she was horrified to discover the family cat engrossed in feasting on crab salad! Jerking him away, she was heartsick to realize that she had no time to redo the salad before the guests arrived. Throwing the cat from the house, she raced back to carefully scoop away the meat around the cat's feeding place. Smoothing it down, she resolved not to divulge her secret to the banqueters.

Duly arriving and beginning the meal, the guests dined heavily on the delicious crab salad. All went well until the hostess glanced out the kitchen window after dinner. Seeing her cat stretched out stiffly on the lawn, she felt her heart seemingly to fail. She checked to make sure, and he was dead.

Groaned the unlucky one, "Oh, it's that crab salad! It's poisoned this cat. All my guests have eaten it, and so have I and we'll be next! All I can do is tell my friends the whole story."

Rushing back into the living room, she unburdened her secret. As they all rushed to the hospital where the doctors quickly operated stomach pumps, they all appeared "rather green around the gills."

After the excitement died down somewhat, one of the next door neighbors dropped by to say, "I have a confession to make. As I was pulling into my driveway tonight, your cat ran in front of my car; I ran over him and killed him. I'm awfully sorry!"

Stifling the urge to kill — and her deepseated chagrin — she managed to mumble, "So am I."

"The meanest job I ever undertook," mused a cowboy," was that of apologizing to a widow, on behalf of a vigilance committee, which hanged her husband by mistake. It was hard to find just the excuse that would satisfy her."

Henny Youngman says, "If at first you don't succeed, so much for skydiving."

I like the story about a crew that was unloading a tank car of highly explosive chemicals when it exploded. Two men were killed and half a dozen were knocked unconscious. As the ambulance attendants were carrying one of the men on a stretcher he regained consciousness. Just as he did, his hand fell over the side of the stretcher. Feeling nothing but air, he let out a great moan and said, "Oh, no! I haven't even hit ground yet."

In the early days of luxury oceanliners, the evening entertainment was often chosen from the special talents of the passengers. On one night, the program featured a remarkable parrot which was followed by a skillful magician. The parrot was placed in his cage off to the side of the stage as the magician performed. The man first secured a bouquet from a nearby table which he covered with a black cloth, waved his wand, and pulling away the cloth, revealed that the flowers had disappeared. The parrot noticed and cocked his head to one side. Next, the man covered a china plate which, upon removal of the cloth, had disappeared also. The parrot inquisitively scratched his head with his claw. Pulling up a chair, the magician covered it, waved his wand, and presto, it was gone. The parrot hopped up and down at the growing excitement. Suddenly the ship struck a line of rocks, the airholds exploded, splitting the vessel in two; the lights went out, people screamed and cried out, and soon there was nothing left on the black night sea save the parrot clinging to a floating rafter. Blinking about at the dark emptiness a moment the parrot cried out, "Okay, I give up. What did you do with the ship?"

As a couple arrived by taxi at the airport and carried their luggage toward the check-in-counter, the wife said, "I think we packed everything for our trip, but I wish we'd brought the kitchen table."

"What?" said her husband. "Why in the world do we need the kitchen table?"

"Because I left our tickets on it."

A ticket agent in the bus station of a mountain town kept a pet parrot for company in the ticket office. At rush times, the ticket agent was overwhelmed with impatient masses of people, pushing to get up to the window and purchase their ticket. Frequently, the ticket agent had to remind them–"One at at time, gentlemen, one at a time." Apparently the parrot absorbed all this.

One day, the ticket agent carelessly left the parrot's cage door open. The parrot flew off into the nearby woods. Searching through these woods, the ticket agent was attracted to a large tree where a flock of noisy crows were dive-bombing. Nearing the tree, the agent spotted his parrot cowering among the swollen roots of the tree. As the ebony sheets of screaming crows swooped down towards the parrot, it called out "One at a time!"

I know how that parrot felt. I wish all of our problems could come one at a time. But usually they all come at once . . . . .

There is an old western legend about a rancher who was out riding and came upon an Indian friend lying flat on the ground with his ear pressed against the earth. Without looking up the Indian said in broken English: "Wagon . . . wagon pulled by horses . . . two horses . . . man driving wagon . . . long beard . . . wearing buckskin . . . woman in wagon . . . dressed in calico . . ." The rancher was amazed. "You can tell all of that just by pressing your ear to the ground?" he asked, "No," grunted the Indian. "Wagon run over me thirty minutes ago."

Clarence Forsburg tells a story about a preacher who went out to make some house calls in the afternoon. He knocked at one door where no one answered. He kept knocking, louder and louder. Finally there was a tiny voice from within which said, "Come in. Come in." He tried the door and found it open and stepped inside the living room. He heard the voice again, "Come in. Come in." He followed the sound down the hallway and entered the kitchen. From inside the kitchen he heard the voice saying, "Come in. Come in." He looked around and found himself face to face with an enormous, ferocious, growling German Shepherd police dog. The dog lunged at the preacher, pinning him against the wall with his enormous paws on his shoulders, snarling and breathing fire and brimstone. At that moment the preacher saw a parrot sitting in a cage over to one side of the kitchen. The preacher, realizing that it was the parrot beckoning him to come in, said, "You stupid parrot! Don't you know any other words?" The parrot said, "Sic'-em, sic'-em!"

It has become a cliche, but the ability to take a lemon in life and make lemonade is still the main determining factor in successfully coping with life's most difficult circumstances. Somewhere I read a story about an American serviceman who was stationed deep in the Sahara Desert. Finding himself with a few hours to kill, he put on his swimming trunks and began trudging merrily through the desert sand. One of his buddies asked in astonishment, "Where do you think you are going?" The carefree soldier replied, "Well, I've got a few hours leave and I thought I would take a dip in the surf." His buddy laughed at him and said, "Are you crazy? We are 500 miles from the ocean." His undaunted friend replied, "I know—but isn't this the biggest, most beautiful beach you have ever seen?"

Two western cowboys are talking about a third cowboy. "He's a real tough character," one of them says, "and quick on the trigger. He can shoot before his pistol clears the holster." His friend was impressed. "That is fast," he says, "if he can shoot before his pistol clears his holster. By the way, what's his name?" His friend answers with a smile, "Footless Frankie."

In the cartoon, *Broom Hilda*, Broom Hilda stands beneath a tree and says, "What a miserable day! Everything has gone wrong."
Then, she suddenly shouts at the top of her voice:
"I DEMAND A REPLAY OF YESTERDAY"

A second grader recited for the teacher the story of David using a sling-shot to kill the giant Goliath.
"What does that teach us?" the teacher asked.
The boy replied, "Duck."

A rookie in the cavalry was told to report to the lieutenant.

"Private," said the officer, "take my horse down and have him shod."

For three hours the lieutenant waited for his horse. Then, impatiently, he sent for the private.

"Private," he said, "where is that horse I told you to have shod?"

"Omigosh!" gasped the private, "Did you say *shod*?"

Xerox is a copying device that can make rapid reproduction of human error, perfectly.

The great pianist Rachmaninoff tells this story on himself. He said that when he was very young, he was giving a piano recital. He began with a Beethoven sonata that had several long rests in it. During one of those long rests, a motherly lady leaned forward, patted him on the shoulder, and said kindly: "Honey, play us something you know."

Stopped by a policeman for driving without a taillight, the driver became quite distressed.

"Don't take it so hard," consoled the officer, "it's a minor offense."

"That's not the point," replied the troubled driver. "What worries me is what's happened to my wife and my trailer?"

Alonzo Stagg once told about a football team of the agricultural college in a midwest state that was green and immature. As a matter of courtesy, the powerful university team played the "aggie" team each year, and regularly won by a terrific score. On one occasion the drubbing had been unusually severe. In the third quarter, the score stood at something like 119 to 0. About the middle of this quarter, a lean, lanky lineman for the Aggies rose suddenly from his position. He threw his headgear as far as he could throw it. He started off the field. Someone shouted, "Get back there. The game is not over." The bruised and beaten youngster continued to walk off the field, yelling, "It is over for me. We came down here to get 'experience' and I've got it."

Dr. John Bardsley reminded us of the classified ad that read like this:

"Lost—one dog. Brown hair with several bald spots. Right leg broken due to auto accident. Rear left hip hurt. Right eye missing. Left ear bitten off in dog fight. Answers to the name 'Lucky'."

Have you had days when you simply could not win? We heard about one fellow who was driving home from work listening to the radio announcer suggest that his listeners surprise their mates. "When you arrive home for dinner this evening," the announcer suggested, "instead of growling something like 'When will dinner be ready?', why not surprise your wife with a little gift?" The man thought to himself that that sounded like a good idea, so he stopped along the way for a bouquet of flowers and a box of candy. Instead of driving into the garage, he went to the front door and rang the bell. His wife opened the door, saw him standing there wearing a radiant smile, holding out his gifts and declared crankily, "Listen, buster, the baby had colic. The washing machine has broken down. Junior and another boy got into a fight today at school and were expelled. And now, as I might have expected, you make my day perfect by coming home drunk!"

—"Just the same" exclaimed Noah's wife, "I'd feel much safer if those two termites were locked up in a metal box."

Some needs are immediate. They cannot be put off. The story is told of a group of boy scouts who were taking a course in first aid. They were learning to bandage and make splints. One little boy was to pretend that he was badly injured and to lie on the ground and wait until they discovered him so that they could give him attention. The boy lay on the ground and waited. But somehow the other scouts got diverted and were slow getting to him. When they did, all they found was a note: "Have bled to death and gone home."

The passengers seated in the plane in flight heard this over the intercom system: "Sit back and relax. This plane is entirely automatic. Automatic pilot, automatic food servers, and automatic landing devices. You are perfectly safe. Enjoy your ride. Nothing can go wrong . . . nothing can go wrong . . . nothing can go wrong . . ."

Time after time the duffer would hit his brand new balls where they couldn't be found.

Finally, one of the members of his foursome said, "Why in the world don't you use an old ball on those difficult shots?"

"An old ball?" asked the duffer. "Can't you tell from the way I play that I never had an old ball?"

Sometimes we are better off if we do not ask too many questions. For example, a man indignantly asked the waiter why he had his thumb on his steak. Replied the waiter, "So it won't fall in the floor again."

9

One of those new-fangled jet planes was delivered to a Texas air base. The Commanding Officer examined it gingerly, called on his most experienced test pilot to test it. "Remember, Captain," he cautioned, "nobody knows how fast this fool thing can go. Besides, all the instruments aren't in it yet. So take it easy, boy!"

The captain promised and took the plane aloft. It was easy for him to manage and he couldn't resist letting it out. As he roared through space, he contacted the ground and asked, "How fast am I going?" Someone responded, in German, "Twelve hundred miles an hour." The pilot gasped and said, Are you certain?" The reply "Of course, we're certain," was in Russian! The pilot said, "Good Lord!" A voice nearby answered, "Yes, my son . . . ?"

—Bennett Cerf

Whatever happened to good news? Nowadays you pick up the morning paper and right away you're filled to the brim—with grim.

—Robert Orben

"Are there any alligators in this river?" asked the man in the water. "No, not a single one," assured his friend who was standing near. The swimmer was still disturbed. Again he asked: "If there are no alligators, what are those gray forms I see? Are you sure there are no alligators?" "Certainly," replied this newly made friend who was standing on the bank. "There are no alligators down there. Those gray forms you see are sharks that have chased the alligators away."

There is the tendency for persons nowadays to think that modern technology, education, psychology, medicine, etc. can solve all of our problems. So often, though, all we do is swap sharks for alligators.

Somewhere I read recently about a woman out in Oklahoma who stopped her car on a busy road to scrape the ice off of her windshield. For some reason she did not pull off on a shoulder, but probably thinking she had adequate time, stopped in one of the traffic lanes. A car coming over a bridge behind her saw her car and the driver instinctively hit his brakes which is the wrong thing to do on an icy bridge. He slid sideways, and before he could get his vehicle straightened out in the road, was struck by another vehicle. That car was struck by another vehicle. That car was struck by another and a chain reaction took place, in all involving 36 vehicles. The unidentified woman who stopped to clean the ice off of her windshield was not involved in the multi-car collision at all.

I've known people like that. Even more importantly, we live in a complicated world, where our lives are constantly colliding with those of others.

You may have seen a sign that reads, "Eat a live frog the first thing every morning and that's the worst thing you'll have to face all day."

10

The scene is a four engine airliner. The pilot's voice comes across the intercom: "Those of you on the left side of the plane have probably noticed that one of our engines has failed. Do not be alarmed. We can still fly on three engines, but we will probably arrive about 15 minutes late."

A few minutes later the pilot's calm voice was heard again: "Those of you on the right of the plane are probably aware that a second engine has failed. Do not be alarmed. We can make it on two engines, though we will probably be at least 30 minutes late now."

A few minutes later the pilot again spoke to the passengers: "It has just come to my attention that a third engine has failed. Please do not be alarmed. We can make it to the airport on one engine. However, we will arrive approximately 45 minutes late."

One passenger turned to another and said, "Boy, I hope that fourth engine doesn't fail. We could be up here all night."

Hagar, in the comics, was trying to pick up his depressed friend.

"Today the world dumped on you . . . today the world humilated and abused you . . . but remember . . . tomorrow is another day!"

With that, his little friend falls down and sobs!

I like the spunk of a beggar who asked a well-dressed man, "Mister, do you have a dollar for a cup of coffee?" "Of course not," replied the well-dressed man, adding, "If you are that bad off, I should think you would be humble enough to ask for a dime or a quarter instead of a dollar." The irritated beggar replied, "Look, forget about the dollar—but don't try to tell me how to run my business."

I like the story of the defense contractor who designed a revolutionary new aircraft. It was a fantastic plane. The only problem with it was that everytime it got into the air, the wings broke off next to the fuselage. The engineers were baffled as to how to solve this problem. Finally they listened to a janitor in the building who said he knew how to solve the problem. "Drill a line of little holes, " he said, across the wing where it breaks off. The engineers had tried everything else, so they thought to themselves, "Why not?" They drilled the holes and the plane flew perfectly. They went to the janitor and asked him, "how did you know?"

He replied wisely, "one of the lessons life teaches you is this—nothing ever tears on the dotted line."

Someone has said that middle age is when you pick the temptation that gets you home earlier.

In the cartoon, "For Better or Worse," the mother looks into the mirror and thinks:

"My face is changing. It's not the same--definitely not the same--different. It's older.

Maybe if I parted my hair on the side. Maybe if I were to rub a little more moisturizer around each eye. A little different colored blush perhaps?

Nope, This is it. I look older and there's nothing I can do about it.

I remember my mother's face looking like this. I remember how the lines crept around her mouth and her eyes. Yes. It's my turn now to take on that look of the mature older woman."

She gazes intently into the mirror and shouts for all to hear, "And I'm not ready!"

In the cartoon, HAGAR, Hagar is asked:

"Do you believe there's life after death?"

Hagar, with his ever-present tired look answers:

"Hey! I'm not sure I believe there's FUN after forty!"

You know you are getting older when:
- --Your back goes out more than you do.
- --Your knees buckle, but your belt won't.
- --You get winded playing chess.
- --You sit in a rocking chair and can't make it go.
- --You turn out the light for economic rather than romantic reasons.
- --Dialing long distance wears you out.

--Source Unknown

We feel like we've missed something somehow. We identify with the old lady who was celebrating her one hundredth birthday. She sat rocking on her front porch, her glasses perched on her nose.

"Grandma," said one of the visiting kin, "you must have seen a lot in the last hundred years."

"Not much," snapped the old lady. "Everything was always over by the time I could find these durn glasses!"

To celebrate their 50th wedding anniversary, the couple returned to their honeymoon hotel. After retiring the wife said, "Darling, do you remember how you stroked my hair?" And so he stroked her hair. She reminded him of the way they cuddled and so they did. With a sigh she said, "Won't you nibble my ear again?"

With that the husband got out of bed and left the room.

"Where are you going?" cried the upset wife.

"To get my teeth!"

The 80-year-old man, although still spry and in excellent health, felt it necessary to resist the determined advances of a widow some 20 years his junior.

"Mother and Father are both against it," he explained.

"You're not going to tell me that your parents are still living?" cried the woman.

"Quite the contrary. I'm referring to Mother Nature and Father Time."

– *Modern Maturity*, August-September, 1982.

"I went to my high school's twentieth reunion recently," said one man. "How was it?" asked a friend. "Oh, it was awful," the man replied. "All my friends are so old, fat and bald that none of them recognized me."

"The speaker was really getting into his message and so was his audience. "We must forever rid the earth of the scourges of capitalism, elitism, and political favoritism." One little lady raised her hand and said, "Could you possibly add rheumatism to that list as well?"

"To what do you attribute your great age?" asked the reporter. "I don't rightly know yet," replied the old-timer, puffing lazily at his pipe. "I'm still dickering with two breakfast-food companies."

Claude Pepper, eighty-year-old congressman from Florida, is now chairman of the U.S. House Committee on Aging. He says, "You have reached old age when you need glasses to find your glasses, or when people say you're looking good, but not that you're good-looking, or when you think today's policemen look like kids."

Patricia Leimbach, writing in *Woman's Day*, gives some humorous insight into the dilemmas of growing maturity in a column entitled, "Life at Midstream":

"Middle age," she remarks, "is when you find out where the action is so you can go someplace else."

Little girl in *Family Circus* cartoon to her brother: "Know why God hasta take some old people? They've used up all their birthdays."

A reporter was interviewing an old man who was celebrating his 100th birthday. "What are you most proud of?" he was asked.

"Well," said the man, I've lived 100 years and haven't an enemy in the world."

"What a beautiful thought. How truly inspirational," commented the reporter.

"Yep," added the centenarian, "outlived every last one of them."

Cary Grant grew exceedingly tired of reporters trying to ascertain his exact age. Once a fan magazine sent him a telegram that asked succinctly, "How old Cary Grant?" Grant wired them back, "Old Cary Grant fine. How you?"

Several years ago my wife received a birthday card which illustrated the difference between a kind of advice we need and the advice we so often get. The card bore an arresting message on its cover. It presumed to tell, "How to Live to Be a Hundred." The inside of the card contained this magnificent bit of innocuity, 'Get to be ninety-nine and be very, very careful!'
—E. Stanley Williamson, *Faithful to the Lord* (Nashville: Broadman Press, 1973).

The story is told about the mountain couple. The man was ninety-eight years old and the wife was ninety-five. They were returning to their home in the hills after attending the funeral of their seventy-six year old son. The mountain woman turned to her husband and said: "I knew we would never raise that young 'un."

David Berg has a *Mad* cartoon (October, 1977) showing a father telling a kneeling child with hands clasped beside the bed: "Please, darling! Don't talk so loud! I have a splitting headache!" "I was only saying my prayers!" "Oh, well . . . as long as your're talking to the Good Lord, ask him to make my headache better!" "Okay, Daddy . . . And Dear God, please make my daddy's headache go away! He was boozing it up all day . . . and now he's terribly hung over!" "Why'd you tell him THAT FOR? Why couldn't you just say I had a toothache or something?"

Bugs won't never bother a drinking man. It's a scientific fact that a muskeeteer'll buzz up to a whiskey drinker and take one look er one smell and fly fer his life.

—Poor H. Allen Smith's Almanac, p. 112.

A clergyman was being shaved by a barber, who had evidently become unnerved by the previous night's dissipation. Finally, he cut the clergyman's chin. The latter looked up at the artist reproachfully, and said:
"You see, my man, what comes of hard drinking."
"Yes, sir," replied the barber consolingly, "it makes the skin tender."

As a fourth grader turned in his drawing lesson, the teacher chided, "Why, Johnny, this looks as if that cowboy is going into a saloon!"
"He is, Teacher. But it's OK. He's not going to drink anything. He's only going to shoot a guy."

Pity the little boy watching his Dad squeeze into a new dinner jacket. "Please don't wear that suit," the little boy pleaded. "It always gives you a headache the next day."

An Irish priest, a very good man, was disturbed by the inroads which strong drink was making on his flock. He preached a strong sermon against it. "What is it," he cried, "that keeps you poor? It's the drink. What is it that keep your children half-starved? The drink! What is it that causes you to shoot at your landlords–and miss them? The drink."

Imagine a fine spring day. A man is driving cheerfully along a country road. Suddenly, from around the curve ahead, a car comes lurching toward him in his lane. He brakes hard, and as it swerves past, the woman driver screams at him, "Pig! Pig!" Furious, he shouts back at her. "Sow! Sow!" Pleased with himself, he drives around the curve and runs smack into a pig.

Forgiveness is such a rare phenomenon in our world. Pastor Dan Emmitte tells that his youngest brother for some time made his living selling printed checks for their depositor's use. Some of them were personalized to the point of printing the picture of the individual on the check rather than some scenic portrait of floral designs or backgrounds. His brother tells of a certain bank where the most unusual order was placed. It seems that one man wanted a very special picture printed on his checks. He was from California where the divorce laws require the payment of alimony as well as child support. It seems he wanted his order of checks to be printed for the sole purpose of making these alimony payments to his former wife. Guess what picture he had printed on the check? It was a picture showing him beautifully kissing his new wife!

In a television message, Dr. Robert Schuller told of a man with whom he had shared an auto mishap. The man used foul and abusive language and Dr. Schuller looked him straight in the eye and said, "Mister, God loves you—and I'm trying."

A saintly-looking old fellow was running to catch the bus. Just as he appeared to be winning the race, the bus driver with a fiendish smirk, pulled away from the curb and the wheels splashed muddy water over the old man.

Softly, the old gentleman murmured, "May his soul find peace." Still, more softly, he added, "And the sooner the better."

—The Lion

Victor Borge told a friend that he could tell time by his piano. His friend was incredulous, so Borge volunteered to demonstrate. He pounded out a crashing march. Immediately there came a banging on the wall and a shrill voice screamed, "Stop that noise. Don't you know it's 1:30 in the morning?"

A tramp looking for a handout in a picturesque old English village stopped by a pub bearing the classic name Inn of St. George and the Dragon.

"Please, Ma'am, could you spare me a bite to eat?" he asked the lady who answered his knock on the kitchen door.

"A bite to eat? For a no-good bum, a beggar? No!" she snapped. "Why don't you work for your living like an honest man? Go away."

Halfway down the path the tramp stopped, eyed the words "St. George and the Dragon," then turned back and knocked again.

"Now what do you want?" the lady asked angrily.

"Please, Ma'am," he replied, "If St. George is in too, may I speak with him this time?"

I've always enjoyed the story about the high-school student who asked his father to help him write a composition on how wars start. "Well, now, let's suppose we got into a quarrel with Canada," his father began.

"That's ridiculous," his mother interrupted. "Why should we quarrel with Canada?"

"That's beside the point, her husband said. "I was merely using an example . . . ."

"If you had an ounce of brains you wouldn't make such stupid . . . ." replied the mother.

"Who do you think you're talking to?" shouted the father. "I want to teach my son . . . ."

"YOUR son!" the mother screamed. "I suppose I had nothing to do with his being here. You just found him someplace . . . ."

"Please, folks," the boy pleaded. "Forget it. I just figured it out for myself."

I got a chuckle over this story:

"Perturbed over the absenteeism of his parishioners at the worship services a minister handed his secretary some church stationery, a list of ten members who were absent the most often and asked her to write each of them a letter concerning their absence.

Within a few days the minister received a letter from a prominent physician who apologized profusely for having been absent so often. He enclosed a check for $1000 to cover contributions he would have made had he been present those many times, promised to be there the following Sunday at church services and further to be there every Sunday thereafter unless providentially hindered. The usual complimentary closing with his signature was given. However, the following note was at the bottom of the page: 'P. S. Please tell your secretary there is only one "t" in dirty and no "c" in skunk.' "

One daughter borrowed the family car for a date and wrecked it. Later, her boyfriend asked, "What did your father say about our car accident?"

"Do you want me to leave out the bad words?"

"Yes."

"He didn't say anything."

The comic strip *Nancy* has Sluggo say: "That new kid on our block is a big FAT HEAD." Nancy remonstrates: "You shouldn't call people names like that." She adds, "I never call people nasty names." Sluggo explains: "Well, I got mad when he said you were silly looking." Nancy angrily demands: "What else did that big FAT HEAD have to say?"

It's an old story but we have never published it before. Anybody who has ever been a radical young pastor will appreciate it. A young pastor came in to a staid, conservative church and immediately started making changes. He brought more contemporary music in the worship service, he began a very lively youth ministry, and he began involving the church in the life of the community in a very dramatic way. Unfortunately, this brought some negative reaction from some of the church officers. They invited his District Superintendent to come for a meeting. The Superintendent immediately sided with the young pastor's critics and publicly chastised this young pastor in front of the entire congregation. It was all very humiliating. The entire room was quite hushed as the pastor stood slowly to his feet to respond, The younger man hung his head and said softly, "I'm sorry. I can make mistakes." Then looking at his congregation he said, "Each of you can make mistakes. Even our Superintendent can make mistakes." He continued, "I can sin, each of you can sin, the Superintendent can sin. Why, I could even go to hell, each of you could go to hell, and our Superintendent can go to hell."

"An itinerant preacher one night read a passage to a small group of listeners wherein they are admonished to turn the other cheek. Then, closing the Bible, he began his interpretation.

"Now, brethren and sisters, the Good Book tells us that if an enemy smacks you on one cheek, you turn the other cheek and let him smack you on that. But, brethren and sisters, the third lick, *the third lick*, I say, *belongs to you*."

– *Coronet*, April, 1958.

I guess we have all had times when we could echo Adlai Stevenson's words on national television after his defeat in a presidential election: "I am too old to cry and it hurts too much to laugh."

DEFINITION OF AN OPTIMIST: As he passed the 12th floor after falling off of a skyscraper, horrified onlookers heard him shout, "So far, so good!"

Robert Brault said it: "The average pencil is seven inches of lead, and a half inch of eraser — just in case you thought optimism was dead."

A New York City cab driver said with unknowing candor, "It's not the work that I enjoy so much, but the people I run into."

You simply cannot satisfy some people. Said one lady: "I much prefer the moon to the sun. The moon shines at night when we need it. The sun shines all day when we have plenty of light!"

There are some people who are impossible to please. One ill-tempered husband was sullen and silent at the breakfast table. "How do you want your eggs cooked?" asked his wife gently.

"One fried and one scrambled," he answered gruffly. When she placed the eggs before him, he was furious.

"What's wrong?" asked his wife.

"You fried the wrong egg, " he snapped.

Have you heard about the little old lady who must be one of the most thankful souls on God's green earth? She says she has so much for which to be thankful — she has only two teeth, but luckily they meet!

I like the attitude of the Californian who was asked if it were true that his native state had 365 days of sunshine. "That would be a conservative estimate," he replied.

H.L. Mencken once said that some people are so pessimistic that when they smell flowers, they immediately look for a coffin.

I like the story about the middle-aged man who was seeing his mother off at an airport. She was taking a trip to visit some old friends. "Have a good time, Mother," the man said. To which she replied, "Now, John, you know perfectly well that I never enjoy having a good time."

A man was justifiably proud of his lawn until one year a heavy crop of dandelions appeared. He tried everything imaginable in an effort to get rid of them, but without success.

Finally in desperation, he wrote to an agricultural college, listing the remedies he had tried, and concluded with the appeal, "What shall I do now?"

Several weeks later, he received this reply: "We suggest that you learn to love them."

You may know the story about a traveling salesman who talked with an old timer on the road. "I'm not doing too well," said the younger salesman, "every place I go I get insulted." "Too bad," sympathized the old timer, "I can't understand that. In more than forty years of traveling the road, I've had my samples tossed out the window, I've been thrown out myself, I've been kicked down the stairs, and I've even been punched in the nose. But I guess I'm lucky, I've never been insulted."

Every Christian should be like the little boy who ran into a man who was lost on a country road. The man stopped his car and approached the boy to ask, "Son, do you know where Fairview is?" The boy said, "No," The man said, "Do you know where Interstate 40 is?" He answered, "No." "Then do you know where the intersection of Bear Wallow Road and Grinder's Switch is?" "No," the little fellow replied. "Well," the man said, "You are about the most ignorant person I have ever met. You don't know much of anything, do you?" The small boy looked into his eyes and said, "Mister, I know one thing, I know I ain't lost."

—Dan Emmitte

There are some people who never let anything get them down. They are like the little boy who kept bragging to his father about what a great hitter he was. Finally the father said, "All right, son, show me!"

So the little boy got his softball and his bat and they went out in the back yard. The father stood over to the side while the boy tossed the ball up into the air and then swung the bat with all his might. "Strike one," said the little fellow after he had missed the ball completely. "Strike two," he said as he missed the ball again. "Strike three," he said as he missed a third time. Then he turned to his father with a determined glow on his face. "Boy, am I a great pitcher!"

I heard a story recently about a little boy who went to a grocery store and asked the clerk for a box of Duz detergent. The clerk said, "Son, what do you need detergent for?" The little boy said, "I want to wash my dog." The clerk said, "Well, son, that Duz detergent is pretty strong for washing a little dog." The little boy said, "That's what I want." The clerk said, "Alright," and he sold him the Duz and he said, "Now, you be careful when you wash your dog. That detergent is very strong; it might kill him." The little boy said, "I'll be careful." He took the box of detergent home. About a week later the little boy came back to the store and the clerk recognized him and said, "Son, how's your dog." And the little boy said, "I'm afraid he's dead." And the store clerk says, "Oh, I'm sorry, but I did try to warn you that the Duz was pretty strong to wash your dog with." And the little boy shook his head and said, "I don't think it was the Duz that did it. I think it was the rinse cycle that got him."

Sometimes we feel like we have been through the rinse cycle, don't we?

Ex-pro football quarterback Bobby Layne was a colorful character. For one thing, he had more than his share of self-confidence. Bobby was known to boast: "I never lost a football game, I just ran out of time." No wonder Bobby Layne was a winner. Some people simply will not accept defeat.

You may be familiar with Robert Schuller's famous story about the father who bragged to his son about what a great hunter he was. The son joined his father on the next hunting trip to see for himself. They sat in the duck blind for a time when one lonely waterfowl winged its way through the sky. The father took aim, fired and missed. "Son," he said, "you have just witnessed a miracle. There flies a dead duck."

An irate person asked a telephone operator, "Am I crazy or are you?" She softly said, "Sir, I'm sorry, but we do not have that information."

Regardless of what happens, there's always someone who knew it would!

Listening to prayers and giving a gold star for each correctly given one, a third grade parochial school teacher lost her grip on the box. Like confetti flew gold stars in all directions. On hands and knees, she tried to get her fingernails under the wee gold stickers while realizing what a ludicrous figure she appeared to be.

Caustically she said, "Isn't anyone going to give me a hand?"
Instantaneously all 24 students earnestly applauded.

There is good advice in a *Peanuts* cartoon. Lucy wears her fiercest frown. Linus, with an uncertain expression says to Charlie Brown, "Oh, Oh! Lucy's got her mad face on! No matter what I say or do today, I'm going to get slugged . . . I might as well get it over with . . . In the next frame Charlie Brown winces as off to the side we hear an awful, "Slug!" A dazed but relatively cheerful Linus, with stars circling his head, comes back into the frame and says, "Now I have the rest of the day to myself."

We allow ourselves to be tyrannized by our fears when we refuse to face them. We experience their destructiveness much more when we procrastinate. Face your most unpleasant task first thing in the day and then the rest of the day is yours.

In a sermon there is a variation on a very popular piece of humor that is particularly appropriate for those of us who believe in the providence of God.

The danger is always present that we will judge before all the facts are known to us. A few years ago "good news, bad news" stories were going around. A man meets a friend and says, "I won a thousand dollars in a contest." The friend replies, "That's good." "No, I spent it on a skiing trip to Switzerland and broke a leg." "That's bad." "No, while I was in the hospital I fell in love with an attractive nurse and married her." "That's good." "No, it turned out that she didn't like the United States and insisted that we had to live in Europe." "That's bad." "No, we set up a home in Paris and I got a job with an export firm." "That's good." "No, the firm went bankrupt and we were soon reduced to poverty." "That's bad." "No, under those difficult circumstances I examined my goals and values and discovered that I was living for the wrong reasons." "That's good." The dialogue goes on and what we discover is that the good and the bad grow side by side. Our judgement at a certain moment often does not take into consideration all the facts.

There is a beautiful example of the good news/bad news principle in the story of a young man who applied for the job as a sexton at a nearby church. The minister of the church knew the young man to be a hard worker and dependable. He was concerned, however, that the young man could neither read nor write. There were several duties around the church for which this would be a severe handicap. So he awarded the sexton's job to someone else.

The young man found another job, worked hard, saved his money, invested it wisely and became a quite wealthy man. It came as quite a shock to many people that he was illiterate—since he had attained such a high station in life. One of them said to him one day, "You have done so well in life. Just think where you would be, however, if you could read and write." The man thought for a moment, answered, "I know where I would be. I would still be a church sexton."

When life overwhelms us we may be like the intoxicated man who walked into a telephone pole, backed off, circled around, and hit it again. . . then again. After the fourth try, he stopped. "Trapped," he said, "in an impenetrable forest."

Hear about the two pessimists who met at a party? Instead of shaking hands, they shook heads!

A man stopped at a cafe and ordered a cup of coffee. When the waitress brought it, he tried to make conversation. "Looks like rain, doesn't it?" he ventured.

"I can't help what it looks like," she snapped, "It's still coffee!"

One poor fellow felt his education was a waste. He declared one day, "You've heard of the rambling wreck from Georgia Tech? Well, I'm a total loss from Holy Cross."

We need to encourage one another. It is kind of like the old man who had an old mule that didn't know his own strength. He had the mule hitched to a two-horse turning plow. He was always hollering, "Get up Will. Get up John. Get up Kate. Get up Bill."

A fellow hearing all those different names, asked him, "How many names does that mule have?"

"Oh," he said, "He just has one. His name is Pete. But I put blinders on him and call out all the other names and he thinks other mules are helping him, and he does the work of two."

A newcomer to the mountain country was a bit apprehensive about his neighbors. He noticed on every barn were painted "Bull's eyes." In the center of every bull's eye was a mark. One day he asked one of his neighbors about it: "Folks around here must be awful good with guns," he said. "I notice that every-one of these bull's eyes have a mark in the very center." The neighbor smiled, "It's not hard to understand," he explained. "We draw the circles after we shoot the guns."

The soldier had been sentenced to be flogged. He did not seem to take the matter seriously, but marched away with a broad grim, and he laughed con-tinuously during the flogging.

When the painful ordeal was over, the sergeant demanded, "What's so funny about being flogged? I don't think it's a joke."

"Why," the soldier chuckled, "the joke's on you. I'm the wrong man."

A farmer was having a hard time filling out a railway claim sheet for a cow that had been scooped up by the cow-catcher on a steam locomotive and had expired in the process. The puzzled man came down to the last item: Disposition of the carcass." After wrinkling his forehead and screwing up his eyes a few moments, he wrote, "kind and gentle."

A drunk was lying on the bar-room floor and begin to come to. Some joker in the room saw that he was starting to wake up and he put a little limburger cheese on the poor man's upper lip. Soon the drunk got up and walked out the door. In a few minutes he returned. Then he left again, and in a little while he wobbled back in, finally shaking his head in disgust, he shouted, "It's no use the whole world stinks!"

Some people are like the ship captain who, the story goes, saw one night at sea what looked like the lights of another ship heading toward him. He had his signalman blink to the other ship: Change your course 10 degrees south." The reply came back: "Change your course 10 degrees north." The captain answered "I am captain. Change your course south." To which the reply was, "I am seaman first class. Change your course north." This infuriated the captain, so he signaled back: "I am a battleship. Change course south." The reply came back: "I am a lighthouse. Change course north."
--Charles Garfield, *Peak Performers,*(New York: William Morrow and Co., 1986).

I live next door to a bully.   Last month he came up to me with hand extended. As I reached to shake hands, he grabbed me forcefully and threw me over his shoulder. "That's Judo," he said, "Picked it up in Japan."
I went into my garage and came back out and cracked him over the head. "That's crowbar," I said. "Picked it up at Sears."

A humble but friendly beggar used to ply his trade in our town.   A rather affluent man came toward the beggar one day. In his most solicitous tone the down-and out-one said, "May the blessing of God follow you all the days of your life." But the affluent gentleman walked on by without acknowledging the humble man's existence--leading him to finish his sentence: "And may the blessing never overtake you."

"There is only one Bible at our house," said the little girl, "and that is the reversed version."

You can't beat the story of the little old Sunday School teacher who visited the Holy Land and saw her first fig tree. "Ahem. . . uh, surely there must be a mistake," she told her guide. "I thought the leaves would be a little bigger than that."

So few people know the Bible nowadays. I was standing downtown waiting on a bus. It was raining cats and dogs (I know I stepped in a poodle). A lady was standing next to me so I tried to be friendly and make conversation. "If it keeps this up, we'll all have to buy an ark," I said. "What's an ark?" she asked. "You mean you haven't heard about Noah and the great flood and all those animals?" I asked increduously." "Look, mister," she replied, "I've only been in town for four days. I've scarcely had time to read a paper."

A little boy was asked what St. Paul called the Word of God. He remembered that it was something sharp, so he guessed, "The Axe of the Apostles."

A lot of us could confess the wisdom in one little boy's jumbled version of the Old Testament verse — "A lie is an abomination unto the Lord, and a very present help in trouble."

Gerald Kennedy tells about an old lady who heard the implications of evolution explained to her and said, "God grant that it may not be true, but if it is true, God grant that not many people will hear about it."

Cecil B. DeMille was once asked why he made so many biblical motion pictures. He answered, "Why let 2,000 years of publicity go to waste?"

When Gene Fowler, a friend of W. C. Fields, caught Fields reading a Bible during a siege of illness, he expressed amazement. Fields squelched his friend's concern about any sudden burst of piety by exclaiming, "I'm only looking for loopholes."

In his very fine book **The Becomers** (Waco: Word Books, 1973) Keith Miller tells about a group of graduate students visiting a regional computer bank. One of the students, having been invited to sit at a typewriter which fed information into a computer, typed out, "Howdy — hello!" Immediately the computer began to type back "Hello, there, welcome to the University of Texas." When the machine had concluded responding, the graduate student remarked wistfully, "That's the warmest thing that's been said to me around here in three years."

Having just entered a parochial school which had several Black families, Gail was asked at dinner by her mother, "Are there any colored children in your class?"
Uncertainly the child asked, "What color?"

I am free of all prejudice. I hate everyone equally.

—W. C. Fields

Arriving in town by mule-drawn wagon, a couple inquire of the knight in *The Wizard of Id*, "Is there any PREJUDICE in this kingdom?" "Why do you ask?" "Emma is an Irish Catholic and I'm a Polish Jew . . . but the kids are all Protestant." "You're welcome to stay, but you won't hear many jokes."

A student one time asked a professor, "Would it be possible for all the people of the world to live in the state of Texas?" The professor thought for a little while, estimated the size of the state and the number of people in the world, and answered: "Yes, it would be possible if they were all friends."

On a bus in a large city one day an elderly gentleman, full of spirits, suddenly shouted out, "I love the world and everyone in it! I love the world and everyone in it!"
"But," another passenger interrupted, "think what it will cost you in Valentine cards."

Christ didn't come into the world to die for the Church—He came into the world to die for the world, and so the other half of our responsibility in loving God is that we should love the world for which Christ died. That means all people everywhere, regardless of race. Hopefully we have come a long way in the last few years in our sense of brotherhood with persons of different color of skin, or nationality. "All in the Family" may have helped us. Sometimes we wonder if Archie Bunker didn't hurt the cause as much as he helped it, but there are some unforgettable scenes in that program, particularly when George Jefferson used to be Archie Bunker's neighbor. One day they were discussing the appearance of God, and Archie Bunker, of course, is convinced that God is white because man was created in the image of God. Archie Bunker is white, so God must be white. And he goes on to remind George that every picture he's ever seen, including those my Michelangelo, show God as being white. George Jefferson looks at him and says, "Maybe you just saw the negative."

Surely we've come a long way in our understanding of how God has created all of us, as the larger family of God, including persons of all races and all nationalities and all faiths. There is a story about a first grader who went on her first day to a newly integrated school in the South at the height of the segregation storm. An anxious mother met her at the door to inquire: "How did everything go, Honey?" "Oh, mother, you know what—a little black girl sat next to me." Her mother knew this was a new experience for the child, and didn't know how she should respond to it. Finally she said, "Well, what happened?" And the little girl said, "Oh, Mommy, we were both so scared that we held hands all day." I believe that scene would warm the heart of God.

When a closed mind reopens, it's usually under the same old management.

— Caroline Clark

We are God's own family, and so above all people on earth we ought to love one another. Dr. Dan Poling tells about trying to entertain his children one day by telling them the story of their family. He said to them, "Geographically we Polings are very representative. Your mother was born in the Midwest. I was born in Oregon. Some of you were born in Ohio, one in Massachusetts and one in New York. Little Jane, who had been listening very intently spoke up and said, "Isn't it wonderful how we all got together?"

Children are wonderful — especially the little girl who raised her hand at the revival meeting when she thought she heard the evangelist ask for all those to do so who "had family commotions at home each night."

The little boy was punished for saying he saw a lion in the backyard. A friend asked him if he prayed about it. "O, yea," he said, "and God told me it was all right. Sometimes he mistakes that big yellow dog for a lion himself."

"Children are the 'whys' guys."

One little boy refused to take his sister fishing with him. Said he, "She eats all the bait."

Eight-year-old Susie was crazy about school, while her six-year-old sister was less enthusiastic.

"Let's play school," suggested Susie one day.

"All right," agreed the younger one grudgingly, "but let's play I'm absent today."

A little boy was telling the story of the prodigal son. "He sold his shirt to buy food," said the boy. "He sold his undershirt to buy food. Finally he came to himself." That is what conversion really is. It is a return to who we really are — persons created in the image of God.

I like the explanation one little boy gave as to why Mary and Joseph took the baby Jesus to Egypt. "They couldn't get a sitter," he concluded.

Sometimes we need to combine firmness with our love, else it becomes sloppy. A little boy climbed on a huge rocking horse in a department store.

"Come on, son," the mother whined. "I must go home to get dinner ready." The lad refused to budge for love or money. Without success the department store manager also coaxed. Finally in desperation they called the store's psychiatrist. Gently he walked over and whispered a few words in the boy's ear. Immediately the child jumped off the rocking horse and ran to his mother.

With disbelief in her voice, the mother asked in awe, "What did you say?"

The psychiatrist hesitated before answering, "All I said was 'If you don't get off that rocking horse right now, I'll knock the stuffing out of you, son!'"

One lady wrote in *Reader's Digest* many years ago this powerful little paragraph:

When my second daughter was born, my mother came to help me with the new baby and my 14-month-old toddler. On one occasion, when both girls were fussing and wet, my husband remarked, "At times like this I think God should have made mothers with four arms." "He did," replied my mother with a smile. "But two of them are on the fathers."

A little daughter entered her parent's room saying, "In my room there aren't any good dreams. May I sleep here?"

A four-year-old boyish imp surprised the congregation one Sunday when most of the service had passed and he had barely moved, much less made any noise.

But the nearby parishioners heard him softly say, "Daddy," just as the pastor began his sermon.

A little later he repeated it a little louder, but the father continued to ignore him.

The audible but not disturbing "Daddy" kept up as the sermon continued.

When his patience was exhausted, the boy shouted, at the top of his voice, "Daddy! Daddy, I'm being good!"

Make no mistake about it, the father rejoices when the little boy is good. But what will really mold that young man's character is the knowledge that even when he was bad, he was still his father's son. He was still loved.

A young father pushed the shopping cart carrying the screaming baby through the super market muttering gently under his breath. "Easy, Freddy, calm down now. Everything's all right, boy. Come on, Freddy, don't get upset." A lady customer commented approvingly to him, "You are very patient with little Freddy." The young father looked up glumly, "Lady, I'm Freddy."

A young child was bugging his mother all day long, and finally he settled on the sofa and said, "I wish Daddy would come home and make me behave."

You may have heard the story about the mother who returned home to find her older son beating on his younger brother. "What is going on here?" she demanded. "Aw, he fell in a mud puddle," replied the older boy. "I was trying to do mouth-to-mouth resuscitation on him like they taught us at school, but he kept getting up and walking away."

One comedian explained today's youth like this:
When we were kids we were very disciplined. My father was very strict, but along came the electric razor and took away the razor strop. Then furnaces took away the woodshed. And along came taxes and the worries of it took away my Dad's hair and with that the old hair brush disappeared. And that's why kids today are running wild, the old man has run out of weapons!

You all undoubtedly recall the oft-told story of the young ten year old boy who answered the door bell at his home one day. When he opened it there stood a strange man on the porch. The man said "Son, you don't know me, do you?" The lad said no he did not. The man replied, "Well, I am your uncle on your father's side." To which the lad replied, "Well, I am glad to know you sir, but you are certainly on the losing side."

On one occasion when a precocious six-year-old displayed her aversion to a proper diet, her father exasperatedly asked, "Child, you don't care for meat, vegetables, salad, or milk — what do you like?"
Turning her wide brown eyes on him, she demurely answered, "Why, I like you, Daddy!"

A five-year-old lad was watching his mother change the baby. When she overlooked sprinkling the tot's back-side with talcum powder and hurried him into his diaper, the five-year-old reproved her sharply, "Hey, Mom, you forgot to salt him!"

Reminiscing about his childhood, Sam Levenson recalled a visit to a museum. A string of little Levensons moved too slowly to please their father, who said, "Look, kids, if you have to stop and look at everything, you're not going to see anything.

Mother's little darling returns from his first day of school. "Oh, I hope you didn't cry," his mother says reassuringly. "I didn't," he says, but boy the teacher sure did."

30

Her mother was trying to teach her manners: "If they ask you to dine, say, 'No, thank you, I have dined.' " But that isn't the way the question was phrased: "Come along, dear, and have a bite of lunch." The little girl's response: "No, thank you, I have already bitten."

Some little fellow put it right: "Some boys is brave because they always play with little boys, and some boys is brave because their legs is too short to run away, but most boys is brave because somebody's looking."

A father was somewhat irritable with his lively children and scolded them harshly as he put them to bed. The next morning he found this note pinned to his bedroom door:
"Be good to your children and they will be good to you.
                                        Yours truly,
                                        God"

A teacher was quizzing her pupils on natural history. "Now, Bobby, tell me where the elephant is found."
Bobby struggled for the answer. Finally his face lighted up as he replied, "The elephant is so big that he is never lost."

One mother was concerned that her twelve-year old daughter was growing up too quickly until she saw her wetting her hair rollers with a water pistol.

"How do you do, my dear?" said the old lady to the little girl.
"Quite well, thank you," was the polite reply.
After a long pause the old lady asked, "Why don't you ask me how I am?"
"Because," said the child calmly, "I'm not interested."

Taking some cookies without permission, a little boy was caught by his mother.
"Son, don't you know God saw you take those cookies?"
"Yes," replied the boy, "but He didn't see me eat them. I ate them under the table."

When a schoolmate telephoned, an enchanting eight-year-old girl requested, "Please call back in ten minutes. I'm in the middle of a tantrum."

31

A new Sunday school teacher had to iron out some problems with the *Lord's Prayer*. One child had to be corrected after repeating, "Howard be thy name." Another youngster prayed, "Lead us not into Penn Station." Still another surprised the teacher with, "Our Father, who art in heaven, how'd you know my name?"

—Modern Maturity

It has been said of children that they are "the world's greatest recorders but the world's worst interpreters."

"Billy, get your little brother's hat out of that mud puddle." "I can't ma, he's got it strapped too tight under his chin."

A little boy who went to the ballet for the first time with his father was amazed watching all the girls dancing on their toes. He turned to his father and asked, "Why don't they just get taller girls, dad?"

One mother reports that she and her children were out for a ride when her four-year-old daughter suddenly asked their five-year-old son, "Where do babies come from?" The parents were silent while the little boy thought it over and finally answered. "Babies come from heaven." This explanation didn't quite satisfy his little sister who then asked, "If babies come from heaven, why do people go to the hospital to get them? The little boy answered, "Because that is where they get their skins put on!"

One dear lady hadn't seen her grandson in many years. When she learned he would be spending the summer with her, she was so delighted she put five dollars in the collection plate that Sunday at church.

The Sunday after her grandson went home she put in ten dollars.

Art Linkletter reminds us that "kids say the darnedest things." He remembers a three-year-old girl with big, brown eyes whom he asked, "What do you do to help your mother?" "I help my mom cook breafas," she replied eagerly. "And what do you do to help you mom with breakfast?" Art asked. She didn't hesitate: "I put the toast in the toaster, but she won't let me flush it!"

–Denis Waitley

The teacher was making her pupils finish each sentence to show that they understood her.

"The idol had eyes," the teacher said, "but it could not —"

"See," cried the children.

"It had ears, but it could not —"

"Hear," was the answer.

"It had lips," she said, "but it could not —"

"Speak," once more replied the children.

"It had a nose, but it could not —"

"Wipe it," shouted the children; and the lesson had to stop a moment.

One day a teacher in a kindergarten school preparatory to giving out an exercise said, "Now children I want you all to be very quiet, so quiet that you could hear a pin drop." Everything had quieted down nicely and the teacher was about to speak when a little voice in the rear of the room said, "Go ahead, teacher let her drop."

The family was seated at the table with a man who was a business acquaintance of the father, when the six-year-old blurted out, "Isn't this roast beef?"

"Yes," said the mother, noting his surprised look. "What of it?"

"Well, Daddy said this morning that he was going to bring a big fish home for dinner."

A little boy caught in mischief was asked by his mother, "How often do you expect to get into heaven, acting like that?"

He thought for a moment and then said, "Well, I'll just run in and out and in and out and keep slamming the door until somebody says, 'For heaven's sake, come in or stay out.' Then I'll stay in."

There's a story about a little girl who climbed up on the lap of Dr. Dewitt Talmage and looked at his white hair and wrinkles and then asked, "Did God make you?" "Yes," he said.

Then she asked, "Did God make me too?"

Dr. Talmage said, "Yes."

"Well," said the little girl, "Don't you think He's doing a better job now than he used to?

I like the attitude of the little six-year-old when her mother asked how it went on her first day at school: "Fine, except for some older lady who kept interrupting us."

33

A clergyman was telling his Bible class the story of the Prodigal Son. Wishing to emphasize the disagreeable attitude of the elder brother on that occasion, he laid especial stress on this phase of the parable. After describing the rejoicing of the household over the return of the wayward son, he spoke of one who, in the midst of the festivities, failed to share in the jubilant spirit of the occasion.

"Can anybody in the class," he asked, "tell me who this was?"

A small boy, who had been listening sympathetically to the story, put up his hand.

"I know," he said beamingly. "It was the fatted calf."

A little girl was shown her newly-arrived baby brother. Looking at him lovingly she said, "When will he talk mother?" "Oh, not for a long time yet," said the mother. "Yes, but when?" persisted the child. "Well, not for a year or so." After thinking for a minute the child exclaimed, "How funny. Miss Clark read out of the Bible this morning that Job cursed the hour he was born."

Listening to his 7-year old scratch away on his violin while the dog howled dismally nearby, a father finally asked, "Can't you play something the dog doesn't know?"

Some third graders were asked to draw pictures of what they wanted to be when they grew up. One little boy turned in a picture of himself as an airplane pilot. Another drew himself driving a fire engine. But one little girl turned in a blank piece of paper.

When the teacher asked why, she explained: "I want to be married – but I don't know how to draw it."

Little Johnny was having a terrific time on his first plane trip. He pushed every button in sight, ran throught the aisles at top speed and finally crashed into the stewardess as she was serving a tray of coffee.

Picking herself up, the stewardess grabbed young Johnny by the arm and cooed as gently as she could force herself to. "Son, why don't you go outside and play?"

Somebody has noted that you can always tell an eight-year old – but you usually have to tell him more than once.

Boy to friend on school bus: "This morning I woke up with chills, sore throat, headache, and an upset stomach."

Friend: "So what!"

Boy: "Nothing, I guess, except that it didn't work."

A member of one church I served taught Agronomy at the University of Georgia. Another member of the church taught first grade and asked one of the professor's daughters what her father did. Quick as a wink the lassie replied, "He teaches grass!"

When my oldest daughter was in kindergarten, she came home one day and asked, "Daddy, what do you study in college?" "O, you study English and math and history and science, " I replied. "Science? That's nothing!" "Debbie, what do you know about science," I asked in amazement that she would consider science "nothing." "Well, when the teacher wants us to be quiet in kindergarten, she says, "Science!"

—Norman Kimsey

My young son Tommy brought home a note from his teacher saying that he had been fighting during recess. When I asked him about it, he protested. "Ricky and I weren't fighting." he said. "We were just trying to separate each other."

—Parents Magazine

A student timidly handed his report card to his father. His grades were very low. "Do you reckon," the boy asked his father, "it's heredity or environment?"

I believe Sam Levenson said it first. "Insanity is hereditary; you get it from your children."

If you have children at home, about this time of the summer your wife is discovering why they give teachers twelve week vacations.

One day when Francis Xavier, weary from his arduous missionary labors, went to his room to rest, he gave strict orders that under no circumstances was he to be disturbed. But before long his door opened and he reappeared long enough to say, "If it is a child that comes, awaken me."

The little girl was walking in the garden. She happened to see a peacock, a bird she had never seen before. After gazing in silent admiration, she ran into the house and cried out, "Oh, Granny, come and see. One of your chickens is in bloom!"

A five-year-old, visiting a farm for the first time, was looking at a fat sow lying in a pen. Said the farmer, "She's mighty big, isn't she?"

"You bet," said the youngster. "I just saw six little piggies blowing her up a few minutes ago."

"We had a new teacher and she wanted to know if I had any brothers and sisters and I told her I was an only child."

"What did she say?" the mother asked.

"She said, 'Thank goodness!' "

A small boy, told not to go swimming in a nearby pond, came home with his hair wet. He told his mother he had fallen in the water.

"Then why aren't your clothes wet, too?" she asked.

"Well," he replied, "I had a hunch I might fall in, so I took off my clothes and hung them on a limb."

One five-year-old couldn't figure out how people got holes in their tummies. He explained it this way. "You see, when God finishes making babies, he lines them up in a row—and then he walks along in front of them and pokes each of them in the tummy with his finger and says, 'You're done! You're done! You're done.' "

"Good by, Aunt Jane," said one little girl, "I hope I'll be a great big girl before you come to make us another visit."

"Oh, I sure am happy to see you," the little boy said to his grandmother on his mother's side. "Now maybe Daddy will do the trick he has been promising us." The grandmother was curious. "What trick is that?" she asked. "I heard him tell Mommy," the little boy answered, "that he would climb the walls if you came to visit."

One little boy said he was attending the wrong school. "I can't read and I can't write." he complained, "and they won't let me talk!"

Before I got married I had six theories about bringing up children now I have six children and no theories."

–Lord Rochester

"Don't take up a man's time talking about the smartness of your children, he wants to talk to you about the smartness of his children."

—Edgar Watson Howe

Although there were only enough cookies for each child to have three at a party for little folks, young Bobby took four.

"You're supposed to get only 3 cookies, Bobby," said the hostess. "You ought to put the fourth one back."

"Can't," exclaimed Bobby. "I ate that one first."

"Children are a great comfort in your old age — and they help you reach it faster, too."

—Lionel M. Kaufman

A little girl was on her first train ride, and she was getting a chance to ride in a sleeper in a Pullman car. On the first night out she was a little scared, and every once in a while she'd call out, "Daddy, are you there? Mama, are you there?" After a while his gruff voice replied, "Yes, Daddy is here. Mama is here. I am here. We are all trying to sleep. Now settle down, and for heaven's sakes, stop making that noise." After a great silence the little voice asked: "Daddy, was that God?"

Christmas is my favorite time of the year. It is a time of giving and receiving love and good cheer. Of course, there are those who don't get all that excited about Christmas. I heard about one wealthy husband who gave his wife a cruise around the world for her Christmas present. "Oh, Charles," she sighed with evident boredom, "we've already been there."

Said one lady to her husband: "Why don't we give only sensible gifts this Christmas — like ties and mink coats!"

We remind our readers of the dangers of fires from Christmas trees. We heard about one dear lady just a few weeks before Christmas who phoned the Fire Department excitedly. "My tree is on fire," she yelled into the telephone. "Quick," said the fireman on the other end of the line, "How do we get there?" "Oh, dear," exclaimed the lady, "Don't you have those large red trucks anymore?"

Christmas is a strange time of the year. That's when we celebrate the Prince of Peace by buying toy rockets, submarines, artillery, and hand grenades for our children.

A little boy in a Christmas program had but one sentence to say, "Behold, I bring you good tidings." After the rehearsal he asked his mother what tidings meant. She told him tidings meant "news." When the program was put on, he was so scared before the large congregation that he forgot his line. Finally the idea came back to him and he blurted out, "Hey, I got news for you!"

A woman was telling her friend about Christmas at her house. "I was visited by a jolly fellow with a big bag over his shoulder. My son came home from college with his dirty laundry."

A Sunday School teacher asked her class to draw a picture of the Holy Family for Christmas. One little boy turned in a picture of a mother, father, and a baby in an airplane with a pilot. "Who do you have here?" asked the teacher. "That's Mary, Joseph, the baby Jesus," answered the little boy, "and Pontius the Pilot."

38

Charles Schultz in his *Peanuts* cartoon shows us in our need. Lucy and Marsha are walking to school. Lucy says, "I'm going to ask the teacher if I can be Mary in the Christmas play this year."

Marsha answers, "She's already asked me, sir."

Lucy continues, "I think I'll be great in the part."

Marsha says once more, "She asked me yesterday."

Ignoring her, Lucy declares, "I like the part where the angel Gabriel talks to me."

With exasperation, Marsha says, "Why would Gabriel talk to you? You never listen."

To show what family life is like these days, the seven-year-old daughter of a correspondent was shown a reproduction of Leonardo da Vinci's famous "Virgin and the Christ Child." "That is Jesus when He was a baby." explained the mother. "Who's that holding Him?" asked the youngster, "A sitter?"

There is only one reason that God sent us the greatest Christmas gift, the gift of his son. It was his way of saying, I love you. Charles Schultz in his sensitive and entertaining way summed it up in a PEANUTS cartoon strip. Charlie Brown is reading the Christmas story. "In those days a decree went out from Caesar Augustus that all the world should be enrolled." Charlie pauses and turns to Marcie to explain, "Caesar Augustus was the Emperor of Rome and the most powerful person on earth! One night in the little town of Bethlehem, a child was born, but no one paid any attention. . . After all, he was born in a common stable. Who would have thought that this child would someday be revered by millions while Caesar Augustus would be almost forgotten?" Marcie interrupts and says, "No one paid any attention when I was born either, but now everyone loves me, and I'm gonna get so many presents for Christmas, it'll make you head swim."

Charlie Brown turns to leave, Bible closed, and Marcie says,"Hey! Aren't you gonna finish the story?" Charlie Brown replies, "I think you finished it. . . " Marcie may have had no idea about the deeper implications of the Christmas story, but she knew she was loved. That is the greatest gift of all.

Someone has stated that the three phrases that best sum up the Christmas season are: "Peace on Earth." "Good will to men," and "Batteries n included." Some of you who are parents of small children know the meani of this statement.

In his book, *Faith, Hope, and Hilarity*, Dick Van Dyke tells of a little girl who finished a church school class project of coloring a picture of "The Infant Jesus." She took it home and proudly told her mother, "There he is--instant Jesus."

God could have done it that way. He could have given us instant Jesus. Instead he gave us the infant Jesus.

Artist Wright had a cartoon in *The Miami News* sometime ago showing a motel manager informing the couple from Nazareth: "I'm sorry, but without any cash, credit cards or credit references the computer has rejected you!"

We don't want to be like the little girl who was on Santa Claus' lap. She gave him a whole list of expensive toys which she wanted for Christmas and then without a word of appreciation, she jumped off Santa's lap and started toward her mother. Her concerned mother spoke quickly, "Honey, haven't you forgotten something?" The little girl thought for a moment, then said, "O, yes." Then turning back toward Santa, she shouted, "Charge it."

We got our teenaged daughter a stereo for Christmas. Before daybreak a the next morning the whole family was awakened by the deafening sound of rock music. "Do you know it is 4 o'clock in the morning?" I shouted into her room. "Not off hand," she replied. "But if you'll give me a few minutes, I'm sure I have it somewhere in my record collection."

I don't get along with my brother-in-law. But I tried to find him something appropriate for Christmas. Finally I hit upon the perfect gift — a down payment on a Rolls Royce. That may sound cruel — but I had to do something to get back at him for giving our kid a set of drums last Christmas.

I heard about a lady who was Christmas shopping with her daughters. The crowds were awful. She had to skip lunch because she was on a tight schedule. Now she was tired, hungry, her feet were hurting, and she was more than a little irritable. As they left the last store, she asked her daughter, "Did you see the nasty look that salesman gave me?"

Her daughter answered, "He didn't give it to you, Mom. You had it when you went in."

At Christmas, the kids would like something that will separate the men from the toys.

You are familiar with the ancient tale of the slightly inebriated man on his hands and knees underneath a streetlamp searching the sidewalk. A friend came by and said, "Sam, what in the world are you doing out here on your hands and knees?"

"I'm hunting my house key." Sam replied. "I lost my house key." The friend got down on his hands and knees, too. "Show me where you lost it and I'll help you," he said. "Oh, I lost it way over there in the grass," Sam said. "Then, why in the world are you looking for it out here on the sidewalk?" the friend asked. Sam replied, "Because this is where the light is."

I have a feeling that a lot of people come to church because somewhere they have lost something. They're not sure what they've lost or where they lost it, but they are convinced that this is where the light is.

Cartoon golfer misses his putt as the church bells are ringing in the background and says, "It's hard to keep your head down anywhere but in church on Sunday mornings!"

There is a lesson for the church in this old story.

There was a sailor and a land lover who went out fishing one day. The land lover hooked a great big fish. As he reeled it in, it was so heavy that it began to pull the ship itself. All of a sudden the fish made one last surge for freedom, and it pulled the land lover overboard. Being a land lover, he couldn't swim a stroke. As he was trying to hold on to the fish, and coming up for air, he began to scream for help. "Help! I can't swim." The sailor wanting to get him back into the ship, reached over the side, and grabbed him by the hair of his head and wouldn't you know it, he wore a wig. The wig came off, down he went, and the sailor grabbed an arm. You guessed it — an artificial arm — it came off. So he reached out and grabbed the land lovers leg, and it too was an artificial leg. It came off. The guy came up for the last time, crying "Save me, I'm drowning." The sailor replied, "I would if you would stick together."

A minister was visiting in London. The guide showed him through Westminster Abbey, where so many of the nation's renowned are entombed. The guide said, "England's great sleep within these walls." The minister murmured, "I feel right at home."

Could it be that too many church members are singing "Standing on the Promises," while they are sitting on the premises?"
— *The Circuit Rider*, First United Methodist Church, Appalachia, VA, September 17, 1984

I ran across a subtle piece of humor this week that will either make you laugh, or it will make you cry. A man was reading the morning paper and said to his wife, "Hey, listen to this. The cashier at the bank has absconded with $100,000. Not only that, he stole one of the bank's executive limousines and ran off with the bank president's wife."

"My, that's awful," said his wife, "I wonder who they will get to teach his Sunday School class next week?"

Remember the story of the Methodist preacher who called his Bishop and told him that Jesus Christ was visiting his church in person that day and asked what he should do. "Look busy," was the immediate reply.

A few years ago Snoopy, the loveable beagle in the *Peanuts* cartoon, broke his left leg. Hundreds wrote letters to Snoopy or sent sympathy cards. Snoopy himself philosophized about his plight one day while pearched on top of his doghouse and looking at the huge white cast on his leg. "My body blames my foot for not being able to go places. My foot says it was my head's fault, and my head blamed my eyes . . . My eyes say my feet are clumsy, and my right foot says not to blame him for what my left foot did . . . ." Snoopy looks out at his audience and confesses, "I don't say anything because I don't want to get involved."

Could that be a parable of what sometimes happens within the church? We read in the letter to the Ephesians that we are like a body. "The eye cannot say to the hand, "I have no need of thee."

One pastor got up one Sunday morning in the pulpit extolling the virtues of teamwork, and he used a football team as an example. He said, "We have in our church quarterbacks, and halfbacks, and fullbacks, and then we have a few drawbacks."

No wonder there is so little enthusiasm in the church today.

Billy Graham tells the amusing story of a fire which broke out in a small-town church. When the fire brigade, siren wailing, arrived on the spot the minister recognized one of the men. "Hello, there, Jim—I haven't seen you in church for a long time," he chided.

"Well," answered the sweating man, struggling with the hose, "there hasn't been a fire in church for a long time."

Someone noted that because of a freak geological phenomenon, St. Paul's Cathedral in London was moving down Fleet Street at the rate of one inch per hundred years. Someone commented that the church ought to be moving faster than that.

We in the church can sympathize with the way one man described the major preoccupation of Professional Football today: "And when the Great Maker writes your name.

He won't ask who won or lost the game,
But what was the attendance?"

The most expensive piece of furniture in a church is an empty pew.

Our congregation offered to send their beloved pastor on a six month vacation. He declined saying: "On the one hand I am afraid that such a long absence might affect attendance in worship. On the other hand, I am afraid that my absence might not affect attendance in worship."

"Whenever I go past our church,
I stop to make a visit,
For fear that, when I'm carried in,
The Lord might say, 'Who is it?' "

Ever find it hard to find the right words to say to a backsliding parishioner? One minister, walking to his church on Sunday morning, came upon one of his members testing out his rod and reel out in the front yard. The man was obviously not dressed for church. "The Lord is coming," said the pastor cheerfully, and that was all. As the first hymn was being sung, he noticed the parishioner slip into the back pew. "I don't guess it will hurt me to be an hour late in going fishing," he said meekly following the service, "just in case."

Why is it that parents will take children to a circus but send them to Sunday School?

The Sunday School teacher was holding the class spellbound. "Think, children," she said, "in that far-off land there are millions of square miles of land without a single Sunday School where little boys and girls can spend their Sunday mornings. Now what should we all try and save up our money to do?"
One little fellow shouted, "Go there!"

From a church bulletin: "Ushers will swat late-comers at these points in the service."

–Vermont Churchman

Coming home one afternoon a man noticed something strange about the way his children were gathered on the front steps. When he inquired as to what they were doing, he was informed, "We're playing church."

On inquiring further, the puzzled father was told, "Well, we've already sung, prayed and preached, and now we're outside on the steps smoking."

Dear Church Member:

This chain letter is meant to bring happiness to you. Unlike other chain letters it does not cost money.

Simply send a copy of this letter to six other churches who are tired of their pastors. Then bundle up your pastor and send him to the church at the bottom of the list.

In one week you will receive 16,436 pastors, and one of them should be a dandy!

Have faith in this letter. One man broke the chain and got his old pastor back.

From a Church Newsletter

A Methodist church was trying to help a needy family in the neighborhood. The family claimed that they did not have clothing fit to wear to church. So the church collected enough money to buy the entire family beautiful new clothing. When they still did not show up at the little Methodist church, someone went to see them, "We thought," he said, "after we bought you those new clothes you might come to church." The mother answered, "Oh, we really like the clothes. In fact, they were so fine that after we put them on we decided that we looked so good, we ought to go to the Episcopal church."

The old drunk in the corner didn't know the owner of the frontier town saloon had given the church permission to hold services there while a church was being constructed. "Aha," said the drunk as the pastor stepped up to lead the service, " A new bartender." The choir stepped forward to sing. "O, great," he thought, "a new floor show." Then he peered out at the congregation: "Heck! same old customers."

I was in the hospital for three weeks. For a while it looked quite serious. The Chairman of my Church Board tried to cheer me up. "Preacher," he said reassuringly, "we don't want you to worry about a thing. Last night at our board meeting, we voted 10-9 to pray for your recovery."

Have you ever heard of *Divers Disease?* No? Well, I had not either until Dr. Harold Buell told of a country preacher who was warning his congregation about a deadly disease mentioned in the Bible which could only be cured by Jesus. His text was taken from Matthew 4:24 (KJV): "They brought to Jesus all sick people with divers diseases."

The following is the interpretation that preacher made of this scripture. It may not be exactly correct from New Testament scholarship, but it certainly has a piercing point!

He said, "Now the doctor can look you over and sometimes cure your ills, but when you have 'divers disease', only the Lord can cure you. And brethren, there is a regular epidemic of 'divers disease' among us!

Some dive for the door just as soon as Sunday School is over. Some dive under the cover and just sleep instead of being in the Lord's house on His day. Lots of others dive for the television set on Sunday and don't ever come to worship. Some others just dive into a bag of excuses about work that needs to be done for Jesus Christ, whom they are supposed to love.

Lots of other folks dive for the car and take a trip over the weekend. Still some more dive for the lake so that they can tell everybody that they are 'skiing.' We have a few that dive for the lawn mower and work on the back yard instead of assembling in the Lord's house to hear His Word. Then a few dive into a flurry of fault-finding every time the church takes up a special project or new work program. Yes, it takes the Lord and the love of His Church to cure 'Divers Disease.' "

—From A Church Newsletter

You heard about the golfer named Jones who was twenty minutes late at the first tee one Sunday morning, and the other three members of the regular foursome were almost ready to drive off without him. "I agreed with my wife," explained Jones, "that this Sunday I'd toss a coin to see whether I played golf or went to church. And you know, fellows, I had to toss that coin forty-three times before it came up heads."

A stranger came to church and the minister was pleased to see him come forward to sit in one of the empty seats. Afterwards he greeted the newcomer and said, "I'm glad you felt free to sit well forward, even though you are a visitor."

"Well," said the man, "I'm a bus driver and I just wanted to see if I could learn how you can get everyone to move to the rear all the time."

A lady contributed to *Reader's Digest* her experience of locating in her Episcopal church a prayer book which obviously had been used by a novice server for Holy Communion prompting. At the appropriate places he had written "sit," "stand" and "go to the altar." For one stage of the ritual he had added and underlined "Incense the people."

45

Vance Havner writes about people who come to church to be entertained. In his own inimitable way he tells about a church that brought in a performing horse. They asked the horse how many commandments, and he stomped ten times. How many apostles, and he stomped twelve times. Some nitwit in the crowd asked how many hypocrites there are in this church, and he went into a dance on all fours.

A certain preacher recently gave an endless discourse on the prophets. First he dwelt at length on the minor prophets. At last he finished them, and the congregation gave a sign of relief. He took a long breath and continued: "Now I shall proceed to the major prophets."

After the major prophets had received more than ample attention the congregation gave another sigh of relief.

"Now that I have finished with the minor prophets and the major prophets, what about Jeremiah? Where is Jeremiah's place?"

At this point a tall man arose in the back of the church. "Jeremiah can have my place," he said; "I'm going home."

Do you remember that old, silly story of the minister who was exhorting his congregation to become more active in church affairs, to get the church on it feet?

"Brothers and sisters," he proclaimed, "What this church needs is the energy to get up and walk." One of his deacons said, "Let her walk, brother, let her walk!" The preacher raised his voice a little and added, "But we can't be satisfied with walking, we've got to pick up speed and run." The preacher was really getting into his message now. "But running's not enough either. One of these days this church has got to fly!" That same deacon echoed, "Let her fly! Let her fly!" The preacher paused for a moment and said solemnly, "But if this church is going to fly, we are all going to have to work harder and give more money!" The deacon said softly, "Let her walk, brother, let her walk."

A confirmed horse player hadn't been in church in years even though his wife attended every Sunday. One Easter, with a bit of nagging and persuasion, he went to church with her.

On the way home, he said to her, "It wasn't bad. The church was airconditioned, the pews were cushioned and the singing was great. Did you notice people looking at me when I joined in with my deep baritone voice?"

"Yes, I noticed," his wife said. "But when we go next time, and you sing, be sure you sing Hallelujah, Hallelujah and not Hialeah, Hialeah."

I know that all of you were saddened to learn this week of the death of one of our church's most valuable members--Someone Else. Someone's passing created a vacancy that will be difficult to fill. Else has been with us for many years, and for every one of those years, Someone did far more than the normal person's share of the work. Whenever leadership was mentioned, this wonderful person was looked to for inspiration as well as results. Someone Else can work with that group. Whenever there was a job to do, a class to teach, or a meeting to attend, one name was on everyone's lips, "Let Someone Else do it." It was common knowledge that Someone Else was among the largest givers in the church. Whenever there was a financial need, everyone just assumed that Someone Else would make up the difference. Someone Else was a wonderful person, sometimes appearing super-human, but a person can only do so much. Were the truth known, everyone expected too much of Someone Else. Now Someone Else is gone. We wonder what we are going to do. Someone Else left a wonderful example to follow, but who is going to follow it? Who is going to do the things Someone Else did? Remember, we can't depend on Someone Else anymore.

There are many other churches that are doing quite well statistically. The sanctuary is moderately filled on Sunday morning. The choir is well trained. The minister well educated. And yet there is something missing. They very much resemble a dog I once heard about. This particular dog--a dachshund--long of body and short of legs has been memorialized in a poem:

> There was a dachshund,
> Once so long
> He hadn't any notion
> How long it took to notify
> His tail of his emotion;
> And so it happened, while his eyes
> Were filled with woe and sadness,
> His little tail went wagging on
> Because of previous gladness.

There is a sense in which many congregations today are still "wagging their tails" because of a previous gladness.

We expect so little out of church nowadays. One pastor was asked, "Do your people come to church expecting something?" He replied, "Yes, they expect to be out by twelve."

Bishop Kennedy told of a little boy who flatly refused to go back to church. His mother asked him why. The lad replied, "I don't want to go back because the preacher said he was going to preach about, 'The zeal of thy house hath eaten me up' –and that scares me!" "Honey," said his mother, "you go back to church and don't worry. There's not enough zeal in that church to hurt a fly!"

I was just not cut out to be a minister. I was on an airplane once that was about to crash. Everyone was in a state of panic. Someone looked at me and asked, "You're a minister, aren't you?" "Do something religious!" So I took up an offering.

The chairman of the pulpit committee was at least honest: "We don't want someone who's either too liberal or too conservative. We just want someone who's mediocre."

I always say the wrong thing. I was trying to comfort a man who was going to the electric chair. It was time for me to leave. I couldn't find anything appropriate to say. Finally I blurted out, "Well, John, more power to you."

I served one church in which a "Newcomer" was anyone who had been in the church less than 30 years. A 93-year-old man in town passed away. "Though not a native of Jonesville," read the obituary, "He did move to the town at the age of two."

Trying to sell Rev. Henry Ward Beecher a horse, the owner said, "Now here's one that is gentle and well behaved. Stands anywhere without kicking. He does anything you ask him. He hasn't a bad trait, won't kick, and listens carefully to everything you say."
"Ah," replied Beecher wistfully, "If that horse were only a member of my congregation."

"Church pews never skid into a ditch, smash against a telephone pole, or get tagged for speeding. They are a safe place to be on Sunday!"

In the church as everywhere else . . . When all is said and done, there will be more said than done!

Some time ago someone asked a quaint old Georgia preacher if he thought that the chairman of his Board was a Christian. He thought for a moment and then he said sadly, "Well, he jes is." We have too many Christians who "jes is."

A LETTER TO AN ASPIRIN COMPANY

Dear Sir:

You manufacture aspirins that relieve suffering, colds, and fevers. The mixture used in your tablets makes it possible for people to get out of bed and fight off headaches, bad nerves, and muscle spasms. I have noticed these tablets work wonders on Mondays, Tuesdays, Wednesdays, Thursdays, Fridays — and especially well on Saturdays. BUT people who take them on Sundays seem to get no relief. They cannot get rid of their aches and pains and are not able to attend Sunday School and Church.

Is it possible for you to examine your tablet and put in it an ingredient that will work on Sundays?

–Copied

Dr. Joe Harding tells a humorous story about a man who injured his thumb on the job. He was told by his foreman to go to the clinic. He stepped inside and saw an empty room with only a desk and two chairs. Toward the back of the room there were two doors--one marked "Illness" and the other marked "Injury." The man thought to himself, "I am not sick, I have just hurt my thumb." He walked through the door marked "Injury." He found himself in a second room. It was empty except for a desk and two chairs. Toward the back door were two doors--one marked "Internal" the other marked "External." The man thought to himself, "It's my thumb that is hurt not something inside." He walked through the door marked "External." He found himself in still another room. It was empty except for a desk and two chairs. Toward the back of the room there were two doors, one marked "Therapy" and one marked "Treatment." He thought to himself, "I don't need counseling or therapy. What I need is to have this thumb treated. He walked through the door marked "Treatment." He found himself in still a fourth room. It was empty except for a desk and two chairs. Toward the back of the room there were two doors--one was marked "Major" and the other marked "Minor." He thought to himself "This isn't a major illness, it's just my thumb that is hurt." He walked through the door marked "Minor." He found himself outside the clinic on the street. He walked back to the building and went to work. The foreman saw him and said, "Were they able to help you?" The man said, "I'm not sure–but I will tell you one thing, that is the best organized outfit I have ever seen!"

Wow, that hurts! Oraganization is a wonderful thing. An effective church needs to be well organized. But the best organized church in the world might as well be torn down if it is not truly helping people.

Dr. Edward Bauman tells the story about a fellow who was injured in an automobile accident and taken to a hospital. As it happened, it was a Catholic hospital. For several days it was touch-and-go for this fellow. The sisters gathered at his bedside, lit candles, placed a rosary in his hands and a missal on his chest, and waited to hear his last words. His lips finally began to move, and as the sisters leaned forward, this is what they heard: "Lord," the man whispered, "I hope you aren't fooled by all these gadgets; I'm still the same ornery Methodist I've always been."

–**David Rogne**

I like the story about the cowboy who went to church for the very first time in his life. He was really enthusiastic about the experience. He was telling a friend of his about what had happened. He said, "I rode up on my horse and tied up my horse by a tree in the corral." The friend said, "You don't mean corral, you mean the parking lot." "I don't know, maybe that is what they called it," he said. "Then I went in through the main gate." "You don't mean the main gate, you mean the front door of the church." "Well anyway, a couple of fellows took me down the long chute." "You don't mean the long chute, you mean the center aisle." "I guess that is what they called it — Then they put me in one of those little box stalls!" "You don't mean a box stall you mean a pew!" "Oh yes! Now I remember!" said the cowboy, "That's what that lady said when I sat down beside her!"

Pointing to the stained glass windows, a church going child of "The Family Circus" queries: "Who finger painted the windows, Mommy?"

Someone sent this one to us. I hope no one's offended, but it is simply too good not to print:

A little old lady planning a camping vacation wrote a letter to a particular campground to inquire about its toilet facilities. She couldn't bring herself to write the word "toilet," though, so she finally settled on the term "B. C.", meaning "bathroom commode."

The initials baffled the campground owner, who showed the letter to the other campers. They didn't understand, either, until one of them suggested the woman might be referring to a Baptist church. The owner agreed and wrote his reply:

"Dear Madam: Thank you for your inquiry. I take pleasure in informing you that a B. C. is located two miles north of our campground, and seats 250 people. My wife and I go quite regularly, but as we grow older, it seems to be more of an effort, particularly during cold spells. If you visit our campground, perhaps we could go with you the first time, sit with you, and introduce you to the other folks. Ours is a friendly community. Sincerely yours."

In a city-wide Sunday-school contest a Methodist minister remarked that his people would work harder to beat the Baptists than they would to beat the devil.

A father gave this piece of advice to a son leaving for boot camp: "Be quiet—and get in the middle." We know what he meant. Don't stick your neck out. Don't call attention to yourself.

You probably heard about the two sailors, adrift on a raft. They had just about given up hope of rescue. One began to pray, "O Lord, I've lead a worthless life. I've been unkind to my wife, and I've neglected my children, but if you'll save me, I promise . . . ."

The other shouted, "Hold it. I think I see land!"

Many people today seem incapable of making any kind of binding commitment. I am reminded of the sailor who brought his girlfriend to the local minister late on a Friday evening and asked that they be married. "That's fine," replied the pastor, "Do you have a marriage license?" The sailor hung his head. "We got to the courthouse too late," he replied. "It was already closed." The minister shook his head. "I'm sorry. I can't perform a marriage ceremony without a license." The sailor put a pleading expression on his face, "Couldn't you just say a few words to get us through the weekend?"

A traveler in Ancient Greece had lost his way and, seeking to find it, asked directions of a man by the roadside who turned out to be Socrates. "How can I reach Mt. Olympus?" asked the traveler. To this Socrates is said to have gravely replied, "Just make every step you take go in that direction."

A story is told about the great halfback, George Cafego, during the early days of pro football. Playing for the old Brooklyn Dodgers football team against the New York Giants one day, Cafego brought the ball upfield practically by himself. Just before the half ended, he broke away over left tackle.

First one man hit him, then another. But Cafego kept going. Finally, about five Giants ganged up on him, and still he plowed goalward. At last he started down—just as the timer's gun exploded.

"My gosh!" a spectator shouted. "They had to shoot him to stop him!"

Perhaps you may have heard about the mugging victim who had his watch taken, then his wallet, finally his assailants beat him quite fiercely. When he got home his wife asked him, "Why did you just stand there and let them do you that way? Why didn't you do something?" The man replied meekly, "Oh, I didn't want to get involved."

51

Thank you. Among those of us who wish to examine the state of the nation's economy and where we appear to be headed, a useful contribution we can make is to try to communicate clearly. Some people suspect that much of our trouble arises because those on "the receiving end" do not hear the same message sent out by those on the "transmitting end."

This is illustrated by the story of a wealthy noblewoman in Great Britain, who gave a very grand dinner party one evening. Among her guests was the Duke of Bedford, no less, a distinguished member of one of England's greatest families. At one point during the dinner, the hostess was horrified to note that her butle — a family servant of many years' standing and impeccable manners — was behaving very oddly, swaying on his feet, stumbling about, and nearly dropping dishes of food. Furious, she quickly scribbled a note to him and placed it on the butler's tray — it read, "You are drunk, leave the room immediately." Whereupon the butler, with a suavity and dignity born of years of service, moved down the table and gracefully laid the note on the plate of the Duke of Bedford.

-By E. M. Gershater, Communications Specialist, The Timken Company

A mountaineer of one of the back counties of North Carolina was arraigned with several others for illicit distilling. "Defendant" said the court, "what is your name?"

"Joshua." was the reply.

"Are you the man who made the sun stand still?"

Quick as a flash came the answer. "No, sir, I am the man who made the moonshine."

A vicar was asked by the choir to call upon old Betty, who was deaf, but who insisted in joining in the solo of the anthem, and to ask her only to sing in the hymns. He shouted into her ear: "Betty! I've been requested to speak to you about your singing." At last she caught the word 'singing,' and replied: "Not to me be the praise, sir; it's a gift."

The midget king in "The Wizard of Id" asks one of his counselors, "What's the latest news from the kingdom across the big bay?" When told, "They seem to be progressing in the arts and sciences a lot faster than us," the king retorts, "Send 'em some TV sets."

A commissar was rolling along in his car in the country near Moscow. Suddenly he noticed a man kneeling at the edge of a field, his hands folded, his eyes closed, his face up turned.

"Why aren't you working instead of doing that?" the commissar asked

"But, comrade, I am praying to God for our leader," answered the old man.

"That's something! I suppose in the old days you used to pray for the czar," inquired the commissar.

"Yes, comrade," replied the man.

"Well, look what happened to the czar!" said the commissar.

"Exactly!" answered the old man with a smile.

In the cartoon, *Beetle Bailey* is standing guard duty in knee-level snow and says to his sergeant:

"Guard duty is stupid! The army is stupid! War is stupid! I'll bet there's a soldier like me in Russia who's thinking the same thing!"

To which the sergeant replied, "With one small difference. He's THINKING it, not SAYING it!"

At a recent meeting, President Reagan and President Mitterand got into an argument about the respective merits of their country's computer systems. Says Mitterand, "I have a computer which knows the facts on any subject in the world. " Answers Reagan, "Our computer is better. It has all the current facts and the future facts."

Mitterand politely asked Reagan to test that premise by asking his machine, "What will the unemployment rate be in France in the summer of 1985?" Reagan tapped a few buttons and out came the answer: 'Zero percent unemployment." Obviously Mitterand was very pleased and asked if he could ask one more question: 'What will be the price of a loaf of bread in the summer of 1985 in Paris?" Mr. Reagan tapped the buttons on the console again. After a few seconds, out popped the answer. "Five rubles."

--E. Grady Brogue in *Vital Speeches*.

Someone has defined a quartet like this: The Moscow Symphony after it has toured the West.

I have never known a person who genuinely committed his or her life to God who was ever sorry. Chuck Swindoll has a humorous story in his book, *Growing Strong in the Seasons of Life* (Portland, Oregon: Multnomah Press, 1983) that illustrates this. A missionary was sitting at her second-story window when she was handed a letter from home. As she opened the letter, a crisp, new, ten-dollar bill fell out. She was pleasantly surprised, but as she read the letter her eyes were distracted by the movement of a shabbily dressed stranger down below, leaning against a post in front of the building. She couldn't get him off her mind. Thinking that he might be in greater financial distress than she, she slipped the bill into an envelope on which she quickly penned the words, "Don't despair." She threw it out the window. The stranger below picked it up, read it, looked up, and smiled as he tipped his hat and went his way.

The next day she was about to leave the house when a knock came at the door. She found the same shabbily dressed man smiling as he handed her a roll of bills. When she asked what they were for, he replied: "That's the sixty bucks you won, lady. **Don't Despair** paid five to one."

We need good Samaritans today. You may have heard about a woman who rounded the street corner and came upon an accident victim lying on the sidewalk. Suddenly, she was grateful for the first-aid course she had recently completed at the local YWCA. "I was going for a walk today," she told her husband later, "and saw this poor man lying on the sidewalk in pretty bad condition." "Then," she continued, "all my first-aid training came back to me, and I bent down and put my head between my knees to keep from fainting!"

In a delightful "Peanuts" cartoon strip, Lucy says, "Guess what...If you don't tell me that you love me, you know what I'm going to do? I'm going to hold my breath until I pass out!" Looking up from his piano, Shroeder informs her, "Breath-holding children is an interesting phenomenon... It could indicate a metabolic disorder... A fortymilligram dose of Vitamin B6 twice a day might be helpful...I think that's probably it... You need Vitamin B6...you might also consider eating more bananas, avocados and beef liver..." As he goes back to his piano, Lucy sighs, "I ask for love, and all I get is beef liver!"

A city fellow came to a fork in the road. An old farmer was standing in a field nearby. "Hey, old-timer," shouted the man, "does it make any difference which road **I take**?" The old man answered, "not to me, it don't."

I like the story about the man who went to his barber. The barber was one of those little people who is always cutting people down to size. The man mentioned that he was taking a trip to Rome. "I hear that Rome is overrated," said the barber. "The hotels are substandard and over-priced. The streets are a nightmare. Italians are rude to Americans. You really won't like it." The man protested, "But I've been saving for years to make this trip. Besides there is a good chance that I will be able to get an audience with the Pope."

The barber gave him a skeptical look. "I wouldn't count on that if I were you," he said. "The Pope only gives audiences to really important people."

A couple of months later the man returned to the barber shop. "How was your trip?" the barber asked diffidently. "Oh, it was great!" the man answered. "The city was beautiful, the hotel was fantastic, Italian people were so friendly, and I got to see the Pope." The barber couldn't believe it. "You got to see the Pope? What happened?" he asked. "That's right," said the man. "I bend down and kissed his ring."

"Wow!" said the barber. "Did he say anything?"

"Yes, he did," replied the man. "He looked down at my head while I was kneeling and said, 'What a lousy haircut!' "

The squeaky tenor had just concluded. The applause was less than warm.

But one member of the audience was exclaiming, "Extraordinary! Wonderful! Unbelieveable!"

"Pardon me," said a puzzled man sitting in the next seat. "You astound me. I think I may claim some knowledge of the subject, and I think his voice was very poor."

"Voice?" said the other man. "I wasn't thinking of his voice. I was praising his nerve!"

Pity the poor pastor who was delivering his sermon when a gentlemen in the back pew turned his head to one side, put his hand to his ear, and said, "Louder!" The preacher raised his voice somewhat and continued with his sermon, which was not too interesting. After a few minutes the man said again, "Louder!" The preacher strained even more and continued on, but by now the sermon had become quite boring. The man said again, "Louder!" At this point a man on the front row couldn't stand it any longer and yelled back to the man in the rear. "What's the matter, can't you hear!" "No," said the man in the back. "Well," said the man down front, "move over, I'm coming back to join you."

Somewhere I read about a Roman Catholic Church that was hosting a community Thanksgiving service. This was to be a first for the church and for the community. Naturally everyone was quite excited. With great dignity the priest led his three Protestant colleagues toward the chancel area when suddenly he realized that he had forgotten to put out chairs for his guests to sit in during the service. In a state of great agitation, he whispered in the ear of one of his elderly laymen, "Please get some chairs for the guest pastors." The elderly gentleman was quite hard of hearing, so he asked the priest to repeat his request. The priest did so a little louder: "Please get up and get three chairs for the Protestants." The old man had a puzzled looked on his face as he rose to his feet. Turning to the rest of the congregation, he said with a loud voice: "This seems highly irregular, but I've been asked to have you stand and give three cheers for the Protestants."

In his book *Let's Quit Fighting About the Holy Spirit*, Pete Gillquist tells of an imagined conversation between two men who lived in Jesus' day. Both men were healed of blindness, and they discovered that Jesus was the healer in both cases.

They discussed the method and technique of Jesus' healing, and to their dismay, they discovered that Jesus used an instant-type procedure to heal one. The other, however, was healed using a totally different mud-on-the-eyes approach.

Both men were frustrated, but positive of one thing: Jesus could not possibly have used the "other" method to heal. In great disbelief, one man said to the other man, "there's no way it could have happened like that!" And then Pete adds: "And there you have it, folks. The start of the world's first two denominations. The Mudites and the Anti-Mudites."

There is a piece of church humor that has been around for some time now in the form of a good news—bad news joke. The scene is the Vatican in Rome. A cardinal rushes in to see the Pope. "Your Holiness," says the cardinal excitedly, "I have some good news and some bad news." The Pope replies, "Well, give me the good news." The cardinal responds, "I have just received word that Christ has returned to earth." That's wonderful," replies the Pope, "but what is the bad news?" The cardinal answers dejectedly, "The call came from Salt Lake City."

A man addicted to walking in his sleep went to bed all right one night, but when he awoke he found himself on the street in the grasp of a policeman. "Hold on," he cried, "you mustn't arrest me. I'm a somnambulist." To which the policeman replied: "I don't care what your religion is — yer can't walk the streets in yer nightshirt."

One comedian hit the nail right on the thumb. Said he: "The world is changing. Jews eat pork, Catholics eat meat on Friday, Methodists drink in front of each other."

There has been some confusion of recent days about what constitutes "orthodoxy" and what constitutes "heresy." I have been asked to clear up the matter once and for all. "Orthodox" is my dox. "Heresy" — your dox, particularly if it disagrees with mine.

One little boy asking another about churches: "Which abomination do you belong to?"

The old Irishman was suffering from a severe case of flu. He was afraid of dying. "Call me a minister," he told his wife, "I need absolution."
"Why don't I just call Father Reilly?" she asked. "You surely don't want a Protestant?" The old Irishman answered, "Do you think I want to give this bug to our priest?"

A recent cartoon in a national periodical showed a Catholic Bishop singing the song, "Wedding Bells Are Breaking Up That Old Gang of Mine."

A *Sermon Builder* magazine cartoon (Aug. 1976) has two fellows standing on the street. One is saying to the other, "What denomination? Well, Mother goes to Central Church and Father goes to the Community Church . . . As for me, I'm Radio."

The story is told about a family that moved from the Methodist Church to the Episcopal Church. One of the children was asked why the family had changed churches. "I believe," said the little girl, "that my mother likes the Episcopal 'lethargy' better.
Lethargy is a major problem in our time.

Shortly after John Kennedy was elected the first Roman Catholic president, a Kansas woman went into her local post office. When she asked the clerk for 50 cents worth of stamps, he asked, "What denomination?"
She snapped angrily, "Well, I didn't know it would ever come to that. Baptist."

One frontier town wanted a minister but specified that he must not be a Baptist. It was not that they had anything against Baptists. It's just that they had to haul their water 15 miles.

Ross Phares tells of a Presbyterian home-missionary who came across an isolated cabin and asked the lady of the home if there were any Presbyterians there.

Never having heard of any such thing as a Presbyterian, she assumed the stranger was a hunter like her husband and explained, "Wal, I just couldn't say about thet. These woods is full of most every kind of varmet, but I ain't paid much attention to 'em. You might take a look around there on the back side of the cabin where my husband keeps his varmet (sic) hides, and see if he's got any Presbyterian hides nailed up. If there's any Presbyterians in this country, he's bound to have caught one by now."

A similar true story is told of a young Welshman in 1761 who arrived at the busy port of New York. Being of the Baptist faith, he decided to seek out some fellow-believers. He saw an old man on a porch step who had the look of a seasoned inhabitant about him. "Good morning, sir," the young Welshman began. "Can you tell me where any Baptists live in this city?" "Baptist? Baptist?" repeated the old man, straining his memory, "I don't really know as I ever heard of anybody of that occupation in these parts."

One little girl was quite disturbed to learn that Jesus was Jewish. "Hummph!" she said, "Jesus may have been Jewish, but God's a Baptist!"

A Methodist and a Baptist were discussing the question of how much water it takes to baptize a person. The Methodist asked, "If you were in water up to your waist, would you be baptized?" "No," said the Baptist, "that is not enough!" "Up to the shoulders?" he asked. "That is still not enough," replied the Baptist.

"Ahh!" said the Methodist, "so what is required is water on the very top of the head."

"That's right," said the Baptist. "Well, said the Methodist, "that proves we are right—because that is the part we baptize!"

When it comes to dieting most of us are like the overweight person who was seated one day in a restaurant with two slender friends. The friends drank unsweetened tea. In front of the overweight one was a seven-dip, hot fudge, marshmallow, whipped cream, nuts, and cherry covered sundae. Just before digging in, he explained, "I have tried calorie counting and I have tried crash diets; I have tried jogging and I have tried isometrics. Now I am trying for the heavyweight championship of the world."

I heard about another woman who was about 60 pounds overweight, and the doctor had been advising her for several months about her problem. No matter what sort of diet he would prescribe, she just wouldn't stick to it. Finally, one day he said to her, "We've tried everything I can think of to get your weight down, but you won't follow my directions. I have only one suggestion left. Why don't you forget about dieting and learn to be jolly."

Cartoon character *"Cathy"* smiles, "It's fun going to a party where you don't know anyone, isn't it, Andrea? You can be whoever you want. You can be vivacious and outgoing! Self-confident! Alive!"

"THAT'S the attitude, Cathy! Now what's the first thing you're going to do when you walk through that door?!" Cathy replied timidly: "Check around to see if I'm the fattest person in the room."

Some of us can identify with Robert Hutchins who wrote: "Whenever I feel like exercising, I lie down until the feeling passes."

I heard about one lady who joined a health club and was called upon to detail her daily routine. She said: "I eat moderately, I exercise moderately, I drink moderately and I live moderately."

"Is there anything else you would care to add?" she was asked.

"Yes," she said, "I lie extensively."

Our part of the country is so backward. It is said in the old days when they were interviewing teachers, if you could count to twenty without taking your boots off, you were hired.

A police officer stopped a senior citizen who breezed past him in her car while he was directing traffic. "Madam," he asked, "didn't you see my hand raised? Don't you know what that means?"

"Yes of course I do," she retorted. "I taught school for forty years."

The Romans would never have found time to conquer the world if they had been obliged to learn Latin first.

—Heinrich Heine

As Thaves *"Frank & Ernest* sit on a park bench, the reclining bum, Frank, smiles: "I didn't go to college. I figure a broader education would just help me discover more things to worry about."

The teacher required each student to sign an Honor System pledge at the end of their exams. One student wrote: "I didn't get no help on this here exam, and Lord knows I couldn't give none."

The boy, on receiving a poor report card, stopped after class to ask the teacher if she would reconsider his marks, adding, "At home I'm already on the list of endangered species."

A young man who had been hired by the personnel department of a large supermarket chain reported to work at one of the stores. The manager greeted him with a warm handshake and a smile, handed him a broom and said, "Your first job will be to sweep out the store."

"But," the young man said, "I'm a college graduate."

"I'm sorry," the manager said. "I didn't know that. Here, give me the broom and I'll show you how."

Art Sansom's "The Born Loser" smiles to the dog, Kewpie, "Let's see if they made you any smarter at obedience school! You'll have to admit you were pretty dumb before!" Having strung out most of his very long leash, he says, "Okay, girl, HEEL!" Tugging with all his might he screams, "HEEL, BLAST IT!" In total bewilderment he looks around to find the other end of his rope is tied around a light pole: "A little education can be a dangerous thing!"

After a lesson on digestion the teacher, anxious to know how much her instruction had been understood, questioned the class. The first answer was rather discouraging, as the girl called upon made this startling statement:
"Digestion begins in the mouth and ends in the big and little testament."
It was the same teacher who received the following note:
"Pleas teacher do not tel Mary any more about her incides it makes her so proud."

Scowling over a report card, a small boy told his dad, "Naturally, I seem stupid to my teacher; she's a college graduate."

My mother tells me that, when my first day of school, so long ago, was over, I ran home and burst into the house shouting, "I love school! I can write my name, I can count to 100, and I can draw a house. Do I have to go back?"

On the first day of school, each kindergartner arrived home with a note from the teacher. It read, "Dear Parents: If you promise not to believe all your child says happens at school, I'll promise not to believe all he says happens at home."

There are times when none of us want to face the world. "Get up and get ready for school," the little lady said to her son, "It's nearly 7:30." From under the covers came a plea. "Oh, Mom, it's awful. The kids don't like me. The teachers are against me. Even the janitor dislikes me." The mother persisted. "You have got to go to school. You're forty years old. You've got to go to school. YOU'RE THE PRINCIPAL!"

We heard about an old gentleman who said very cautiously, "When I were in school, they learned me figures, but not reading. So now when I see a sign by the road, I can tell how fur, but not where to."

61

A half-drunk Congressman once staggered up to Horace Greeley and exclaimed, "I am a self-made man." Horace replied that he was glad to hear it, "for," said he, "that relieves God of a great responsibility."

One of Disraeli's admirers speaking about him to John Bright, said: "You ought to give him credit for what he has accomplished, as he is a self-made man." "I know he is," retorted Mr. Bright, "and he adores his maker."

Here's to the man who is wisest and best.
Here's to the man who with judgment is blest.
Here's to the man who's as smart as can be—
I mean the man who agrees with me.

– Author Unknown

As one cynic said: "We would worry less about what others think about us, if we realized how seldom they do."

The story is told about General Robert E. Lee, who noticed that one of his officers had the habit of looking frequently with great satisfaction into the mirror. General Lee said to him: "Sir, you must be the happiest man in the world." "Why?" asked the officer. "Because you are in love with yourself, and you haven't a rival in the world."

I often think about the question that was asked the conductor of a great symphony orchestra. "What instrument do you think is the most difficult to play?" The old conductor thought for a moment, then said, "Second fiddle. I can get plenty of first violinists. But to find one who can play second fiddle with enthusiasm--that's a problem. And if we have no second fiddles, we have no harmony."

As someone once put it, "if we had our way, more of us would choose the front of the bus, the back of the church and the center of attention."

"Swelled heads," said one wise man, "are nature's way of filling vacuums."

Someone has described a most self-centered man like this: He always wants to be the center of attention. At a funeral he is sorry that he is not the corpse. Those who know him best are sometimes sorry for the same reason.

I will never forget my message last Sunday. Undoubtedly it was my finest hour in the pulpit. Unequalled eloquence seemed to roll off of my lips. Afterwards I commented I thought rather modestly to my wife. "I wonder how many great preachers there are in the world?" Replied she, "Well, there is one less than you think there is."

If you can't stand being outdone by others you sure won't enjoy heaven. One preacher up there preached on the Johnstown flood only to discover Noah was in his congregation.

EGOTISM: A drug administered by nature to deaden the pain of being a fool.

Henry Ford II once described a bore. He opens his mouth and out comes all his feats.

Good advice for preachers and other sinners: "He who falls in love with self has no rivals."

"What's worse than talking about others like being a gossip?
Talking about yourself and being a bore!"

A visitor entering the social room of a mental institution, came upon an odd sight. In the center of the room stood a young man, erect and haughty, with his hand thrust in the buttoned front of his coat. In a nearby corner stood an older man, apart from the rest, staring seriously at the ceiling. The visitor inquired as to the identity of the younger man. He replied, "I'm Napoleon." Amused, the visitor asked, "Who told you that?" The fellow replied, "God told me." At this, the older man in the corner retorted, "I didn't tell you any such thing!"

Coach Don Shula tells a priceless story on himself. He said that he wished to take his wife to a quite place for vacation. They chose a small seaside town in Maine, where they could relax without people recognizing them. When they arrived, it was raining só they decided to go see a movie. When they entered the theatre, the house lights were on and they were surprised that the small handful of people gave them a warm little round of applause as they took a seat.

Secretly pleased, Shula whispered to his wife, "I guess there isn't any place I'm not known."

A man came over with a friendly smile and shook hands with Shula and his wife.

"I'm surprised that you know me here," said Shula.

"Should I know you?" asked the man, puzzled. "We're just glad to see you folks-the manager said he wouldn't start the film until at least ten people came in."

I enjoy the story about the man who was short and fat, he was also bald and middle-aged. One morning he and his wife were walking down the street, when suddenly the man turned a beaming countenance to his wife and said, "Did you see that pretty girl smile at me?"

"Oh, that's nothing," said his wife, "The first time I saw you I laughed right out loud."

It is said that one night, after General De Gaulle and his wife had retired, he casually mentioned to her that he might run for another term. To which she replied, "Oh, my God!" And he said: "In our private chamber, Madame, you may call me Charles."

We are like the young man who invites a lady out to dinner. For the first hour, he talks non-stop about himself. Finally, he says, "I've been doing all the talking, it's time that you had a chance to say something. Tell me, what do *you* think of *me*?"

A rather conceited man was invited to dinner by a female acquaintance, but did not accept. A few days later, seeing her in passing he said in a gracious manner. "I believe you asked me to dine with you last week."

The lady looking thoughtfully at him a moment, answered: "And did you?"

The story is told of a private in World War I who shouted, "Put out that match," only to find to his chagrin that the offender had been General "Black Jack" Pershing. When he tried to stammer out his apology, General Pershing patted him on the back and said, "That's all right son; just be glad I'm not a second lieutenant."

Norman Vincent Peale tells about a former Lieutenant Governor of Pennsylvania who told about boarding a train for Harrisburg when in came a guard from the state insane asylum with twenty men who had been committed to that institution. They all sat down around the Lieutenant Governor. The guard didn't know the Lieutenant Governor, and before the train started he came down the aisle to count the people for whom he was responsible. He came along and said, "One, two, three, four, five, six, seven . . ." and coming to the Lieutenant Governor said, "Who are you?"

"I am the Lieutenant Governor of the State of Pennsylvania," answered the gentleman honestly.

The guard continued, counting him, . . . eight, nine, ten, eleven. . . ."

Somewhere I heard about a pastor who wrote a sermon on "humility," but he locked it away and never preached it. He wanted to hold it until a really big occasion when he could impress a lot of people.

When Woodrow Wilson was Governor of New Jersey, a very ambitious young civil servant called him at his home at 3:30 one morning and said urgently, "Mr. Governor, I'm sorry to wake you up, but your State Auditor has just died, and I would like to know if I can take his place."

Mr. Wilson thought that over for a moment and then replied dryly, "Well, I guess it's all right with me, if it's all right with the undertaker."

Samuel M. Crothers tells us that a young man once left with him a manuscript for criticism, and remarked in passing, "It is only a little bit of my work, and it will not take you long to look it over. In fact it is only the first chapter in which I explain the Universe."

Comic Sam Levenson is a short man, but does not brood about this fact. At a dinner he once attended he found himself surrounded by an unusual number of tall actors. "Don't you feel rather small among all these big men?" somebody asked him.

"Yes, I do," Levenson answered promptly. "I feel like a dime among a lot of pennies."

A society woman once went to consult a famous psychotherapist. He said at the first interview, "Now tell me all about yourself." She needed no second invitation. At the end of the hour the doctor said, "That will do now; I'll see you again tomorrow." The same formula was repeated several times a week for some weeks. Then one day the doctor said to his patient: "Madam, I can do no more for you now, I advise you to take the first train to Niagara Falls, and there take a long lingering look at something bigger than yourself."

—John Trevor Davies, *Lord of All*

Once in a saintly passion
I cried with desperate grief
O, Lord, my heart is black with guile
Of sinners I am chief
Then stooped my guardian angel
And whispered from behind
"Vanity my little man,
You're nothing of the kind."

—Author unknown

Intelligence has a lot to do with what folks believe — those with smart kids, for instance, are more likely to believe in heredity.

When a man starts singing his own praises it is pretty sure to be a solo.

"I wonder," remarked the vain young woman, "how many men will be miserable when I marry."

"It all depends," replied her friend, "on how many of them you marry."

Such lovely roses," remarked the lady as a man stopped his flower cart near her house. I don't need any now, but please come by Wednesday. I'd like to purchase several dozen to decorate the living room. My daughter is coming out that day, and I'd like everything to be perfect."

"Thanks, ma'am," he said. "I'll be here with the prettiest roses I can find. I know how you feel about your daughter coming out. What was she in for?"

I love a story Willsie Martin told on himself when he was pastor of the Wilshire United Methodist Church in Los Angeles. Willsie arrived early one Sunday morning to see an elderly woman struggling to get up the steep stairs to the large sanctuary, "Here, let me help you," said Willsie and, with a great deal of patience and love, he helped her to the top of the stairs. Reaching the entrance to the sanctuary, the elderly lady turned to Willsie and asked, "Can you tell me who is preaching this morning?" With a smile, Willsie answered, "Yes, Willsie Martin." Whereupon she said, "Would you mind helping me back down the steps?"

Most of us don't want to simply keep up with the Joneses–we want to be slightly ahead. There is a popular joke going around right now about a fellow named Pat who always wanted a telephone in his car. Finally he got one. He couldn't wait to tell his best friend Mike. Mike was enraged with envy. That very day he ordered a telephone for his car. He immediately called Pat. "Pat," he said, "I'm calling you from the telephone in my car." Imagine his feelings when Pat said, "Excuse me for a moment, Mike. my other phone is ringing."

Willard Scott of "The Today Show" remembers his radio days when he received his all-time favorite letter from a fan:
"Dear Mr. Scott–I think you're the best dis jockey in Washington. You play the best music and have the nicest voice of anyone on the air. Please excuse the crayon–they won't let us have anything sharp in here."
—*Willard Scott's Down Home Stories* (Bobbs-Merrill)

A mother whale once warned her son, "Remember, it's when you go to the top and start blowing that you get harpooned."

The Duke of Wellington once haughtily drew himself up to his full height and thundered to one of his staff officers, "God knows I have many faults, but being wrong is not one of them!"

Rufus Jones once told a tale about the daughter of a prosperous egg rancher who came into a village store in Maine. Wanting to be friendly, the storekeeper smiled and started talking with her. "Are your hens laying now?" he asked. "They can," the girl replied with her nose in the air, "but in our financial position they don't have to."

Stories about the monumental ego of the late French Premiere Charles DeGaulle are legion. My favorite--which could be attributed to any other strong personality as well--has DeGaulle calling the Vatican to inquire about the possibility of being buried in the Holy Sepulchre. "Yes, you can be buried there," replied the Vatican, "but it will cost you one hundred million dollars." DeGaulle replied, "One hundred million dollars--just to stay there for three days?"

That reminds me of another favorite. This would be a good one to tell on a well known pastor. We'll call him Rev. Smith.

One thing I have discovered about Rev. Smith is that he is well known. As you know, I traveled with him to the Holy Land and Europe last summer. Everywhere we went, Rev. Smith seemed to know everybody. We went to Rome. Rev. Smith even got an audience with the Pope. I was standing down in St. Peter's Square with the tourists when an Italian lady pointed to the two of them on a balcony where the Pope often greets visitors. The Italian lady turned to me and said, "Whose-a the nice-a looking fella on the balcony with Rev. Smith?"

Obviously, we much more appreciate the candor and humility of one politician years ago. A great crowd had gathered to hear him speak. One of his friends said, "You must get a great thrill to know this kind of crowd came out just to hear you speak."

The politician answered. "Yes, I am thrilled. But I always remind myself how much larger the crowd would be if I were being hanged."

Another politician, however, was speaking in another town. Before he arrived, he sent a four page report to all of the local papers detailing his address. On page 3 appeared this paragraph: "But the hour grows late and I must close (No, No! Go on! Go on!)"

Dr. Adler, the great psychiatrist who succeeded Freud, enjoyed telling his favorite joke. A group of people were crowded together, trying to sleep on the floor of a great auditorium during the war, but one woman kept them awake with her pitiful cries, "Oh, God, I'm so thirsty!" Finally, someone got up in the dark and brought her a glass of water. They could hear the woman gurgle the water down, but suddenly, they heard her again saying, "Oh, God, how thirsty I was!"

A visiting psychiatrist, wandering through the wards of a state asylum, was particularly intrigued by a patient who sat huddled in a corner all by himself, scratching himself for hours on end.

"My good man," the doctor addressed the patient gently, "why do you stay huddled in a corner all by yourself, scratching yourself?"

"Because," replied the man wearily, "I'm the only person in the world who knows where I itch."

No one is immune to distress. An emotionally disturbed man went to see a noted psychiatrist. He confessed he was frustrated, depressed, and desperate. The psychiatrist probed. Finally, after a lengthy consultation, the psychiatrist remembered there was a circus in town. He recommended the troubled man go see the circus clown. The psychiatrist said, "He will make you laugh, and you will feel better." The disturbed man blurted out, "But doctor, I am the clown!"

A little girl came running downstairs one morning, lighthearted as only a child can be. She rushed into the kitchen and noticed that her mother wore a glum expression.

"Mommy," she said, "aren't you happy?"

"Why certainly I'm happy," the mother replied.

"Well," said the little girl, "you certainly haven't told your face yet."

There is a humorous story about a man who was drafted into the army. While in the army he developed a quite disconcerting habit. As he walked along each day he kept picking up pieces of paper saying to himself aloud, "That's not it!" He would pick up one piece of paper after another and say, "That's not it!' That's not it! That's not it!" This went on for about six months. Such bizarre behavior was finally brought to the attention of his superiors in the military. They ordered him to report to the company psychiatrist. The psychiatrist asked, "What is wrong with you? What is the problem?" The man had a baffled expression on his face as he asked "What problem? I don't have a problem." The psychiatrist said, "Well, there's got to be something wrong with you. It has been reported to me that you keep going all over this base picking up pieces of paper and saying, "That's not it, that's not it! Now, tell me, just what is it you are looking for?"

The man said, "I don't know. I just don't seem to be able to find." The psychiatrist consulted with some of his colleagues, then said to the man, "I think your problem is serious, and I'm going to give you a medical discharge from the service." When the psychiatrist handed the discharge paper to him, the man shouted excitedly, "This is it! This is it!"

We are a bundle of anxieties concerning our health, our finances, our children, the safety of our world. Our constant anxiety reminds me of a story that Mark Twain once told about a friend of his who came to him at the races one day and said, "I'm broke. I wish you'd buy me a ticket back to town."

Twain said, "Well, I'm pretty broke myself but, I'll tell you what to do. You hide under my seat and I'll cover you with my legs." It was agreed and Twain then went to the ticket office and bought two tickets, without saying anything to his friend. When the train was under way and the supposed stowaway was snug under the seat, the conductor came by and Twain gave him the two tickets.

"Where is the other passenger?" asked the conductor.

Twain tapped on his forehead and said in a loud voice, "That is my friend's ticket. He is a little eccentric and likes to ride under the seat."

A man walked into a psychiatrist's office. On his head for a hat he had placed half a cantelope. Around each ear he had wrapped a piece of bacon. The psychiatrist rubbed his hands in glee, "I've got a live one this time," he thought to himself. Then the man with the cantelope on his head and the piece of bacon wrapped around each ear sat down. "I've come," he said to the psychiatrist, "to talk to you about my brother."

One out of four people in this country is mentally imbalanced. Think of your three closest friends. If they seem okay, then you're the one.
                                                              – Ann Landers.

A little girl fell down on the sidewalk and skinned her knee. She said to her mother, "Wouldn't it be wonderful if all the world were cushioned?"
                                              –Charles L. Allen, *Roads to Radiant Living*

You may know the story about the truck driver who was driving through a large city. There was nothing particularly unique about the driver or the truck except for one thing–at every traffic light the driver would get out of the truck, take a baseball bat and beat on the side of the trailer at the back of the truck with all his might. Then he would jump back in the cab of his truck and drive on to the next light where he would repeat this ritual.

A fellow following him in a car was puzzled by this bizarre behavior and asked him at one light why in the world he was beating on the side of his truck. "Oh," said the driver, "the answer is simple. I have a two-ton truck and I am carrying four tons of canaries in it. That means that I have to keep two tons of them in the air at all times."

Maybe you feel like you are carrying around an extra ton of canaries this morning.

You know, it's said that the human person is a rational animal. Okay, that's basically true. But don't count on people being *rational* animals all the time. Sometimes their animality takes over from their rationality. Not just sometimes—frequently. Nor just frequently—more frequently than not.

There was a man who had everything going for him. He was rich, he was smart—high I. Q.—he was well educated. There was only one thing wrong with him. He thought he was dead.

So his family and friend prevailed upon him to visit a psychiatrist. The psychiatrist recognized that this man was intelligent, educated, successful in business. He though, "Well, I'll *reason* him out of his illusion!"

So he asked him, "Listen, tell me, do dead men *eat*?" The patient said, "Well, as a matter of fact, maybe they *do*. In many cultures— in the Orient for example—they put food in the tombs so that the dead can come back and consume it. Apparently dead men do eat."

And then the psychiatrist asked him, "Well, do dead men *talk*?" And he said, "Well, maybe they do. You know, Houdini, for example, had a telephone put in his coffin so he could call back from the other world. And people apparently talk through mediums. Yeah, dead men do talk sometimes."

Next, the doctor asked, "Do dead men *walk*?" The man said, "Sometimes they do. There are documented cases, in England, for example, of haunted castles – the former occupant comes back and walks during the night, rattles chains. Yeah, dead men do walk."

In desperation, he finally asked, "Do dead men *bleed*?" And the patient said, "No, absolutely not. Dead men do not bleed."

The doctor said, "Roll up your sleeve." So he rolled up his sleeve and the doctor took a scalpel and made a small incision in the man's forearm. The blood began to roll down his arm and he put his finger on it and tasted it and he said, "What do you know . . . dead men *do* bleed."

The point? You cannot *reason* people out of any proposition to which they have a strong emotional commitment.

A man who climbed a flag pole and then began shouting at the top of his voice was arrested and charged with disturbing the peace. After hearing the charge, the magistrate peered over his glasses at the defendant.

"What have you got to say for yourself?" he demanded.

"Well, it's like this, Your Honor," replied the man sheepishly, "if I didn't do something crazy once in a while, I'd go nuts."

A psychiatrist received a postcard from one of his patients who was vacationing in Rome. The message went like this: "Having a terrfic time. Wish you were here to tell me why."

The pastor, the groom and the best man were out in the hall waiting for the ceremony to begin. The groom was unusually nervous and agitated. He kept pacing and wringing his hands. Finally, the minister became so concerned about him that he asked, "What's the matter, have you lost the ring?" The groom replied, "No, sir. I've lost my enthusiasm."

I love the story that was once told on Claire Booth Luce, the well-known playwright and later the U. S. Ambassador to Italy. Mrs. Luce became a Roman Catholic late in life. Like many late converts, her enthusiasm and zeal for her new faith knew no bounds. Once a reporter spied her in earnest conversation with the Pope. The reporter crept closer wondering what important issues they might be discussing. Finally he was close enough to hear the Pope saying to Mrs. Luce, "But you don't understand, Mrs. Luce. I already AM a Catholic."

An old Pentecostal grandmother used to say to her children, "Children, it doesn't matter how high you jump or how loud you shout. It's what you do when you come down that really matters. "

Those who say it can't be done are usually pushed out of the way by those who are doing it.

The man desperately needed a job. "Okay," said a potential employer, the manager of a large clothing store, "Here's the deal. I have this ugly, ugly suit. If you can sell it, you have a job." The man was ecstatic. "That's all I wanted was a chance," he said. An hour later he came back to the manager very excitedly, "I did it, I did it!" he shouted. "I sold that suit." The manager was quite pleased. "You must be a determined salesman," he said. "But tell me, where did you get all of those lacerations? Was the customer angry?" The man replied, "Oh, no, sir, but his seeing-eye dog nearly tore me to pieces."

The great missionary E. Stanley Jones once credited his zestful life to "grace and gumption."

Somewhere I read an amusing story about Bear Bryant—the legendary coach of the Alabama Crimson Tide football team.

In one game Alabama was ahead by just six points, and the clock had less than two minutes to run. He sent this quarterback in with the instruction to play it safe and run out the clock. The quarterback came into the huddle and said, "The coach says we should play it safe, but that's what the other team is expecting. Let's give them a surprise." So he called a pass play. He dropped back and threw, and the defending cornerback, a sprint champion, knifed in, intercepted, and headed for a touchdown.

Now if you know anything about Coach Bryant, you know that the Alabama quarterback had a problem. He had to catch that corner back or face Coach Bryant.

That quarterback was no runner but he took after that fleet corner back, ran him down from behind on the five-yard line, and saved the game. After the game the opposing coach came up to Bear Bryant and said, "What's this business about your quarterback not being a runner? He ran down my speedster from behind."

"Well," said Bryant, "your man was running for six points. My man was running for his life."

A story is told of a knight who returned to his castle at twilight. He was a mess. His armor was dented, his helmet skewed, his face was bloody, his horse was limping, the rider was listing to one side in the saddle. The Lord of the castle saw him coming and went out to meet him, asking, "What hath befallen you, Sir Knight?" Straightening himself up as best he could, he replied, "Oh, Sire, I have been laboring in your service, robbing and burning and pillaging your enemies to the west." "You've been WHAT?" cried the startled nobleman, "but I haven't any enemies to the west!" "Oh!" said the knight. And then, after a pause, "Well, I think you do now."

There is a moral to this story. Enthusiasm is not enough. You have to have a sense of direction.

There are a lot of folks who are out seeking to win persons for Christ. They are enthusiastic folk. They are committed folk, but some of them are also offensive folk. Some of them are making as many enemies as friends for Christ. That is because they have never fully understood what they are about.

I like the story of a fellow who stopped by his friend's store to buy a jar of mustard. The shelves were loaded with salt—bags and bags of salt. The storekeeper said he had some mustard, but that he would have to go down to the cellar to find it. The friend went down with him, and there to his surprise were still more bags of salt. Everywhere he looked he could see salt.

"Say," said the friend, "you must sell a lot of salt in this store!"

"No," said the storekeeper, "I can't sell salt. But the feller who sells me salt—boy, can he sell salt!"

73

Now admittedly, blind enthusiasm is not the sole answer. A story is told about Bob Zuppke, the former football coach at the University of Illinois. In this particular game, the University of Illinois was woefully behind at half-time. Bob Zuppke got up in front of his team and gave a stirring dramatic half-time speech, trying to enliven this dispirited and lackluster team. As he neared the conclusion of his speech, his voice became louder, his pleas more dramatic, and finally he pointed to the door at the other end of the room saying, "And now let's go through that door and on to victory!" The team rose as one man, tears welling in their eyes, their throats choked with emotion, and they ran through that door—right into the university swimming pool.

Did you hear about the minister who was waxing eloquent in his prayer and said, "And O Lord, if the spark of enthusiasm has been created here tonight . . . Lord, water that spark. Water that spark."

A story is told about a city man who was riding along at fifty-five miles an hour when he looked out the window. He couldn't believe his eyes for he saw a three-legged chicken running right alongside the car! He accelerated to sixty miles an hour but the chicken kept right up with him. At seventy miles an hour, the chicken took off and left the man in a cloud of dust. Dumbfounded the man pulled over and stopped in a farmer's yard. He rolled down his window and asked the farmer who was sitting there, "Did you see that?" The farmer said, "Sure, I saw it. I've seen plenty of them."
The man said, "What was it?"
"That was one of our three-legged chickens."
"Three-legged chicken! What do you mean a three-legged chicken?"
"Well," said the farmer, "there are three of us in the family: my wife, my boy, and myself. We all like drumsticks. So we decided to breed a three-legged chicken, that way we all get a drumstick.
"Well, do they taste good?" asked the city man.
The farmer shook his head and replied, "I don't know. We've never been able to catch one."

Fred Allen, the radio comedian of days past, said, "You only live once, but if you do it right, once is enough."

A comedian used to tell the story of a man who took Carters Little Liver Pills all his life. He said that when that fellow died, they had to take a big stick and beat his liver to death. That's what the life of devotion ought to do for our faith —make it so strong that somebody would have to take a stick and beat it to death.

74

Sometimes we fool ourselves into thinking we're alone in this world. A little girl was asked in Sunday School, "Who made you?" And she said, "Well, God made part of me." "What do you mean, God made part of you?" "Well, God made me real little, and I just growed the rest myself."

Dr. Earl Pierce used to tell the story of a city dweller who moved to a farm and bought a cow. Shortly after he did, the cow went dry. When he reported this fact to a neighbor farmer, the farmer expressed surprise. The city man said he was sruprised too. "I can't understand it either, for if ever a person was considerate of an animal, I was of that cow. If I didn't need any milk, I didn't milk her. If I only needed a quart, I only took a quart." Dr. Pierce tried to explain that the only way to keep milk flowing is not to take as little milk as possible from the cow, but to take as much as possible. Is that not also true of the Christian life? Those who only turn to God in need miss the real joy that is the rightful heritage of the Christian.

Here's a good story on commitment. The story is told of a hen and a pig that were making a journey. After a time they became hungry. They began looking for a restaurant. Finally they came to one that had a sign out front: "Ham and Eggs are our specialty." The hen wanted to go in, but the pig refused. When the hen became upset, the pig is said to have replied: "It's easy enough for you to say, my dear, all they expect from you is a contribution — from me they will expect total commitment."

The story is told about the early Methodist circuit rider and bishop, Francis Asbury, that he and a layman were making a horseback journey when they encountered some hostile Indians. After they escaped, the layman asked Asbury: "I'll bet you were feeling for your religion back there weren't you bishop?" Asbury replied, "To tell you the truth, I was feeling for my pistol."

How far have you moved from God?
There is a humorous story about a cowboy who was camping out on the prairie. When it came time to cook breakfast, he could not find any firewood. Smart as he was, he decided to light the grass and hold his skillet over the flame. A wind came up, so he moved along with fire — holding his skillet over it. This worked fine except that when his eggs were finally cooked, he was three miles from his coffee.

During the reign of Oliver Cromwell, the British government began to run low on silver for coins. Lord Cromwell sent his men on an investigation of the local cathedral to see if they could find any precious metal there. After investigating, they reported:

"The only silver we could find is in the statues of the saints standing in the corners." To which the radical soldier and statesman of England replied: "Good! We'll melt down the saints and put them into circulation!"

The late Archbishop Temple, when he was primate of England, once told this story. One morning, in a house where he was a guest, he heard from the kitchen a voice singing lustily, "Nearer, My God to Thee." He thought that was great that she should be singing hymns and he spoke of it to his host.

"Oh, yes," replied the host. "That's the hymn she boils the eggs to—three verses for soft boil and five for hard."

"What a let-down that must have been for the Archbishop. He thought she was expressing her faith. All she was doing was timing her eggs.

I heard of a Sunday school teacher who asked her class of small girls if one of them could quote the 23rd Psalm. A girl timidly raised her hand and said she could. She stood in front of the class and said, "The Lord is my shepherd. That's all I want."

An elderly lady had never ridden in an airplane. Her grandson finally persuaded her to take an air-flight. With fear and trepidation, she agreed.

After a short flight, the plane landed. As she deplaned, the grandson asked cheerily, "How did you like the flight, Grandma?"

"Well," she unenthusiastically replied, "I went up in the plane, but I never let down my weight during the whole flight!"

We are all too often like the little boy whose mother asked him to go into the pantry and get her a can of tomato soup. The little boy didn't want to go into the pantry alone, and he said, "Mommy, it's dark in there, and I'm scared." "It's all right, Johnny," she said. "You go in there and get a can of tomato soup. I need it for a recipe." He said, "But Mommy, it's dark, and I'm too scared to go in there by myself." "It's okay, Johnny," she said again. "Jesus will be in there with you. Now you go and get a can of tomato soup." Johnny went to the door and opened it slowly. When he peeked inside, it was dark, and he was scared. His hands began to tremble, but he got an idea. He said, "Jesus, if you're in there, would You hand me that can of tomato soup?"

An 86 year old woman flying for the first time heard the following announcement over the plane's intercom: "This is your captain speaking. Our number four engine has just been shut off because of mechanical trouble.

However, there is nothing to worry about. We will continue our flight with three engines and will land in Chicago on schedule. Also, I have some really reassuring news for you. We have four bishops on board."

The elderly passenger, who had been listening apprehensively, called the flight attendant. "Would you please tell the captain that I would rather have four engines than three bishops."

It's like the story of a fellow whose business had fallen on hard times. He was a devout person, and had given generously to his church for many years. He figured that perhaps there were accounts receivable he hadn't pursued. So he went to church and asked God to let him win the lottery. He waited, expectantly, but nothing happened. So he returned to church, somewhat upset. Once again he pled his case. And once again, nothing. The next time, angry, he shouted at the Almighty: "Why don't you give me a break?"

Suddenly, a great wind swept through the church, and a deep, powerful voice said, "Give *you* a break? Why don't you give *me* a break? At least buy a ticket!"

The story is told of a frightened citizen who lived in the days of President Monroe and was suspected of not being a true patriot. He protested to a mob that wanted to beat him up: "I didn't say I was against the Monroe Doctrine; I love the Monroe Doctrine, I would die for the Monroe Doctrine. I merely said I didn't know what it was."

A Buggy Conversion Experience! A certain man was gloriously converted one night during revival services. He began sharing the story of his conversion in churches throughout the area. During one of these sharing sessions someone suggested writing down the story of his conversion to prevent it from being lost. And so he did.

Years later someone asked him about the story of his conversion experience. "Well," he replied, "I have forgotten most of it, but I did write it down. Let me get it for you." He turned to his granddaughter and said, "Honey, please go to my desk and bring me the story of my conversion."

Later she returned with several sheets of yellowed, torn, and tattered paper and said, "Grandpa, I hate to tell you this but the roaches have gotten into your conversion experience."

—Bob Norton

A lady took a trip to Israel. In her later years she came back determined to learn the study of Hebrew before she died. She said, "I want to be able to greet my Creator in His native tongue."

Leslie Weatherhead once used a limerick to illustrate the shallowness with which many regard God's providence. The limerick went like this:
"There was a young lady from Ryde
Who was carried away by the tide
A man-eating shark
Was heard to remark
'I knew that the Lord would provide.' "

Cynic Oscar Wilde also had fun with the Christian idea of the infinite Goodness of the Almighty: "Don't you realize that missionaries are the divinely provided food for cannibals?" he asked. "Whenever they are on the brink of starvation, heaven, in its infinite mercy, sends them a nice, plump missionary."

We are like the rich man who was so proud of his beautiful lawn. "I had these trees moved right here to my lawn," he boasted. "Had them set up in perfect geometrical pattern this way."
"My, my," murmured the pastor, "it just goes to show you what wonders God could perform if only He had the money!"

One little fellow knelt at the side of his bed, closed his eyes and prayed, "God bless mom. God bless dad. God bless grandma." He said it the same way every time.
But one night he added, "And please take care of yourself, God. 'Cause if anything happens to you, we're all sunk!"

A mother, walking by her son's room, noticed that he was on his knees evidently in prayer. She could not help but notice, however, that he kept repeating one word over and over, "Tokyo," he prayed, "Tokyo, Tokyo." She wondered if this were some eastern chant he had picked up from some of his friends. Later she asked him about it. "Oh," he said with embarrassment, "we had our geography exam today and I was praying that God would make Tokyo the capital of France."

Very often the emphasis placed on various religious celebrations gets clouded by the emphasis placed on them secularly. Even children become somewhat confused over the meaning and importance.

In the cartoon *The Family Circus* the two children have found their Easter baskets and are enjoying them. One asked, "Who colored all these eggs?" To which his sister replied, "The Easter bunny."

"Who gave us the jelly beans?"

"The Easter bunny."

"And the chocolate rabbit?"

"The Easter bunny."

Obviously, there was nothing beyond the reach of the Easter bunny.

The family attended Easter services and heard the preacher say, "They came to the tomb and saw that the stone had been rolled back. Who could have done this?"

To which the little boy jumped up in the pew and said, "The Easter bunny?"

–Dr. John Bardsley

An old story from the South says that a police officer caught a bootlegger with a lot of jugs in his truck. The officer asked what was in them. The bootlegger said: "Water." The policeman didn't believe him. So he opened one of the jugs and took a gulp. He said to the bootlegger, "This looks like wine and tastes exactly like wine." The bootlegger exclaimed: "Praise the Lord. He done it again!"

Norman Vincent Peale tells about a business executive who had three boxes on his desk labeled INCOMING, OUTGOING, and UNDECIDED. The latter usually contained the most papers. Then he added a fourth box which he labeled WITH GOD ALL THINGS ARE POSSIBLE.

There is a conversation in Brecht's *Mother Courage*. The chaplain says to Mother Courage: "We're in God's hands now!" And her answer is: "I hope we're not as desperate as that, but it *is* hard to sleep at night."

On one of his visits home, a traveling salesman volunteered to give his wife a night out while he kept the kids. Having sent the children up to bed, he settled down to read. Like a yo-yo-, one kid kept bouncing to the bottom of the stairs, but Dad kept sending him back up.

At 9:30 the next-door neighbor inquired if her son were there.

Dad promptly informed her in the negative.

Over the bannister popped a little head and a voice shouted, "I'm here, Mom, but he won't let me go home!"

One man sent this bit of information and humor to a national magazine: The women of our church had a handsome 30-inch-tall paper-mache stork, which was used frequently for baby showers. The last time they got it out for one of these occasions, however, they couldn't use it—someone had wrung the bird's neck.

It's more difficult to have a family in this modern world. Once when the power went off at the elementary school, the cook couldn't serve a hot meal in the cafeteria. She had to feed the children something, so at the last minute she whipped up great stacks of peanut-butter-and-jelly sandwiches. As one little boy filled his plate, he said, "It's about time. At last—a home cooked meal."

A Sunday School teacher asked a group of children in her class, "Why do you believe in God?" In reporting some of the answers the teacher confessed that the one she liked best came from a boy who said, "I don't know, unless it's something that runs in the family."

Cecil Myers reports a definition of a happy home as given by a thirteen-year-old boy: "A happy home is like a baseball team, with Mom pitching, Dad catching, the kids fielding and everyone taking a turn at bat."

Two men began to talk about world problems, high taxes, the cost of living, and, finally, their families.

"I have three boys," one of them said proudly.

"That's a nice family," sighed the other man. "I wish to heaven I had three children."

"Don't you have any children?" the proud father asked with a touch of sympathy in his voice.

"Oh, yes," sighed the second man, "I have six."

Two high school students were discussing a classmate. "No wonder he's good in French," said one, "His father and mother talk French all the time at meals." To which the other replied, "If that's the case, I ought to be terrific in geometry. My parents talk in circles all the time!"

Mother: Every time you're naughty I get another gray hair.
Son: Gee, Mom, you must have been a terror when you were young. . . just look at Grandma.

Billy watched his new baby sister in the crib as she screamed and kicked. He finally asked, "Where did she come from?" "Heaven," was the reply. "No wonder they let her go," Billy responded.

Johnny was only four years old but he knew an important truth about our need for love. He appeared one day at the door of his father's study with a forlorn-looking chick that had apparently strayed from a neighbor's brooder. The father said rather sternly, "John, take that chicken right back to its mother."
"It ain't got no mother," Johnny replied.
The father, insisting that he be obeyed, said, "Well, take it back to its father then."
But Johnny protested, "It hasn't got no father either. It hasn't got anything but an old lamp!"

The other day my daughter came home from school and asked a question of my wife. My wife said, "Why not wait until your dad comes home and ask him." To which my daughter replied: "But, mom, I don't want to know that much about it!"

"Your mother-in-law needs a warm climate," said the doctor.
"How about Florida?" suggested the son-in-law.
"Not warm enough."
"How about Death Valley?"
"Not warm enough," muttered the physician.
For a moment the son-in-law looked at the doctor in silence, and then left the room.
In about a minute he was back with a pistol in his hand. He handed it to the doctor. "You shoot her, doctor. I can't."

We are told that Winston Churchill had a favorite story about mothers-in- law. A man once made a desperate call to his minister. His mother-in-law, a shrew of a woman, had just died. The minister needed to know what the man wanted done with the remains. It did not take the man long to decide: "Embalm, cremate, and bury — take no chances."

Father: "Get up, son. When Lincoln was your age, do you know what he was doing?"
Son: "No, Dad, I don't. But I know what he was doing when he was your age."

One man described mixed emotions like this: It's like watching your mother-in-law go over a cliff in your new Cadillac."

The frightening thing about heredity and enviroment is that we parents provide both!

One parent sent her son's teacher a note. "Dear Teacher, Please do not strike Willie. We never do at home except in self-defense."

His marital relations far from rosy, a husband returned home one evening to find his young son sitting on the porch step with head in hands and a forlorn expression.
"What's wrong, Ronnie?" asked the father.
After a minute of silence, the lad confesses.
"Just between me and you, Dad, I can't get along with your wife either."

TRANSPARENTS: Parents children can easily see through.

"My son has reached the stage where he runs around with his shirttail hanging out," one of the women said. "I have talked and talked to him about it, but somehow I just can't get him to tuck it in."
"Oh," said her friend, "that one was easy for me. When my boy started doing that I just sewed a bit of pink lace around the bottom of his shirts."

If you have more than one child in your family, you have probably faced a very familiar dilemma. A mother was telling about her three boys. "My boys are very loyal to each other," she said. When one of them mis-behaves, the others will not tell on him."

Her friend asked, "How do you know which one to punish then?"

"It's not too hard," she replied. "When one of them does something wrong, we send all three to bed without supper or TV. The next morning we spank the one with the black eye."

Screen door: Something the grandchildren get a bang out of.

A man walking across the street was almost run down by a car driven by a woman — the car overflowing with children. The red light was against the woman, and the man who had almost been hit walked over to the ancient bus and said, "Lady, don't you know when to stop?"

Glancing back at the many children in the car, she said icily, "They aren't all mine."

Some tip-offs that your child may have some flaws — even though you may think he or she is perfect.

1. Your child gets extra credit for being absent.
2. Neighbors always have their cement poured while you are on vacation.
3. You find the phone off the hook and the mailbox in his room.
4. You are shopping with your child/children and a clerk gives you a flyer from the store across the street.

Mary McBride, *Please Don't Call Me Collect on Mother's Day* (New York: Doubleday & Co., 1983).

Here's a letter written by a youngster: "Dear God, do you get your angels to do all the work? Mommy says we are her angels and we have to do everything. Love, Maria."

– Source Unknown

A little girl asked her daddy, "What's a slave?" He tried to explain. When he was finished, she asked, "Is that what Mommy is?"

In a *New York Times* cartoon, a mature executive sits in a plush office reading a letter which says, "Dear Sonny,

Thank you for the copy of your annual report. Your father and I are mighty proud of the good job you're doing as president of such a big outfit. However, we thought you looked tired in the picture of you opposite the president's report. Have you been getting enough rest and exercise? Are you taking your vitamins, and is that daughter-in-law of ours fixing you good nourishing meals?

Ken Friedman claims one of his uncles announced last week that his daughter (Ken's cousin, Lucille) was engaged to a husband who would be named sometime in the future.

A *Hi and Lois* cartoon has the little boy asking his sister, "How do you get an ulcer?" His sister answers smugly, "You get an ulcer when you lie and steal cookies and are mean to little girls." The little boy looks amazed and answers, "Dad thinks he has one."

Having raided the refrigerator and located some drumsticks, Dennis the Menace and his little friend decide they need pepper which causes Dennis to sneeze. His friend says, *"Gesundheit!"* Immediately Mrs. Mitchell appears to inquire who sneezed, Dennis is rushed upstairs and his friend sent away as Dennis' mother explains, "Dennis won't be able to play any more today, honey."

Rolling back the covers she orders, "Off with your clothes and into bed now." An exasperated Dennis gestures, "Will ya jus' LISSEN for a minnit?" His unyielding mother says, "Now STAY there. I'll bring you a nice, hot bowl of soup." "I DON'T WANT ANY HOT SOUP!" he yells as she departs. Sitting up in bed he says, "I'll bet GESUNDHEIT means, 'I hope your mother didn't hear you!' "

A woman rang up her insurance company and said she wanted to change the terms of her insurance policy. "I've just had twins," she informed her agent. The agent had difficulty in hearing her, and asked: "Will you repeat that again, please?

She shot back emphatically: "Not if I can help it!"

A little boy asked his mother where he came from, and also where she had come from as a baby. His mother gave him a tall tale about a beautiful white-feathered bird. The boy ran into the next room and asked his grandmother the same question, and received a variation on the bird story. He then scampered outside to his playmate with the comment, "You know, there hasn't been a normal birth in our family for three generations!"
—Howard G. Hendricks, *Heaven Help The Home* (Wheaton, Il.: Victor Books 1974).

A super-cautious mother always wore a gauze mask when coming near her baby and insisted that all visitors do likewise. Several older and wiser women tried to tell her tactfully that she was carrying things too far, but the young mother insisted that most parents were absolutely criminal in their carelessness about a child's health.

Then the mother mentioned that she thought the baby was beginning to cut a tooth and she wished she could find out about it in some way. A friend with more experience said, "Why, just put your finger in his mouth and ..."

There was such a horrified expression on the mother's face that the friend quickly added, "Of course, boil your finger first."

Visiting an Episcopal church for the first time, a kindergarten youngster was perplexed when the choir filed in, white surplices stiff with starch. "Mama," he demanded. "Mama, are all those people going to get their hair cut?"
—Webb Garrison in *Creative Imagination in Preaching*

Nearly every man is a firm believer in heredity until his son makes a fool of himself.

Children begin by loving their parents; as they grow older they judge them; sometimes they forgive them.

—Oscar Wilde

Two explorers met in the heart of the jungle. "I'm here," declared one, "to commune with nature in the raw, to contemplate the eternal verities and to widen my horizons. And you, sir?"

"I," sighed the second explorer, "came because my son has begun playing the saxophone."

A young mother had trouble with a small son who had locked himself in the bathroom, and either could not or would not open the door.

In desperation she finally called the fire department and explained their predicament. Told it was a little boy, the fireman called, "You come out of there, little girl!"

The door promptly flew open, and an indignant boy marched out. The fireman grinned, "Works nearly every time."

One father was trying to read the paper. He was asked by his little daughter a whole series of questions–difficult questions which children ask: "Where did God live before he created the earth? What makes the leaves green? Where do butterflies get their wings?" At the end of each question, the father would simply say, "I don't know." Finally the little girl said, "Am I bothering you with my questions?" The father smiled, "not at all, how are you going to learn if you never ask!"

A young father-to-be was pacing back and forth, wringing his hands in the hospital corridor while his wife was in labor. He was tied up in knots of fear and anxiety, and beads of perspiration dropping from his brow revealed the agony of his suffering. Finally at 4 a. m. a nurse popped out of a door and said, "Well, sir, you have a little girl." He dropped his hands, became limp, and said, "Oh, how I thank God it's a girl. She'll never have to go through the awful agony I've had tonight."

"What is it," asked the teacher who had been discussing the weather, "that comes in like a lion and goes out like a lamb?"

A small girl raised her hand and volunteered, "Father."

One little boy was crushed to learn the truth about Santa Claus. That next Sunday the Sunday School teacher was talking about the devil. Spoke up the little boy: "I'll bet it's just my daddy."

Small boy at piano: "Mon, I just wish you hadn't been deprived of so many things when you were a child."

86

The little boy asked his father, "Daddy, where do I come from?"

The embarrassed father gulped and proceeded to go into a long-winded explanation of the birds, the bees, the stork and anything else he could think of. Finally, the father turned to his son and asked, "Why do you want to know?"

"Oh," he replied, "there's this new kid in the neighborhood and he's from Nashville, and I just wondered where I came from.

Someone has noted that there are millions of women today who take birth control pills. These women are called liberated, modern, progressive. There are also millions of women who do not take the pill. These women are called "mama."

On the arrival of their sixth child, Mr. and Mrs. Cummings were perplexed as to how to send a unique birth announcement. Their pearl: "Announcing another of our short Cummings."

After reading a letter from the camp director stating her son needed disciplining, a mother replied, "Please don't slap Irvin, he is very sensitive. It would be much better to slap the boy next to him — that will scare Irvin."

They keep urging us to reach zero population growth as quickly as possible. How can people who are not having babies not have them any faster?

A first grader arrived home on the opening day of school. "Did you learn anything?" he was asked. "Sure did," he replied, "I learned that I'm the only kid in my class who doesn't get an allowance."

"I'm looking for adventure, excitment, beautiful women," said the young man to his father as he prepared to leave home. "Don't try to stop me, I'm on my way."

"Who's trying to stop you?" shouted his father. "I'm going with you!"

Blondie screams, "Dagwood!" Running into the room with arms akimbo, she exclaims, "It's terrible! Cookie and Alexander are having the biggest argument they've ever had!!" Soothingly putting his hands on her shoulders, he says, "Now, Honey . . . first of all you have to calm down. In order to help teenagers solve problems, it's really important for their parents to remain calm and in complete control. And then, after hearing both sides . . . we resolve the argument with the cool, calculated wisdom that only adults can provide." Approaching the embattled teenagers, he commands, "All Right! All Right! Let's hold it down for a minute!!" Stepping between them he asks, "Okay, now what's this all about!" Almost coming to fist cuffs, they begin:

"I'm Right. He's Wrong!!
Not this time! Yes, this time!
Flake off!! Not a chance!!
YES! YES! YES! NO! NO! NO!

Blondie intercedes, "Children! Stop it! Stop it! Listen to what your father has to say!" Sticking his fingers in his ears and flapping them, Dagwood says, "Abooga . . . Booga. . . Booga . . ." As they watch in mystified bafflement, he leaves bewildered, "Doggone it! That's the only thing I could think of right then!"

A father complaining to his neighbor: "Things were a lot different when I was a boy. In his room his son has a color TV, a home movie set, a stereo, several radios and his telephone. When I want to punish him, I have to send him to my room!"

Father and son spend a weekend camping out in the woods.
"There now, wasn't that fun?"Dad asked.
"I guess so," said the son. "Only next time, could we bring Mother and the catsup?"

I like the story of the mother who accompanied her son to registration. She wanted to make sure that he had the right kind of roommate. She also wanted to make sure that the college did not tolerate foul language, dirty movies, or alcoholic beverages. She wanted to make sure that her son was exposed to a totally Christian atmosphere, she told the registrar. After all, she said, this is the first time he's ever been away from home except for the three years he spent in the Marines.

"Another thing so simple a child can operate it is a grandparent."

When I was born, my grandmother said something wonderful about me — she called me a grand child!

"Did I ever tell you about my grandchildren?" a proud grandfather asked.
"No," replied the friend, "and you don't know how much I have appreciated it!"

"More children are spoiled because parents can't spank Grandma."

I like the story of the little boy, a first grader, who strutted up in front of his classmates and proclaimed, "When I grow up, I'm going to be a lion tamer. I'll have lots of fierce lions, and I'll walk in the cage and they'll roar." He paused a moment, looking at his classmates' faces, and then added, "Of course I'll have my mother with me."

A little girl stayed for dinner at the home of her first-grade friend. The vegetable was buttered broccoli and the mother asked if she liked it. The child replied very politely, "Oh yes, I loved it."
But when the bowl of broccoli was passed she declined to take any. The hostess said, "I thought you said you loved broccoli."
The girl replied sweetly, "Oh yes ma'am, I do, but not enough to eat it!"

Rotary Magazine

"Well, John, how does it feel to be a grandfather?"
"Oh, it's good news, of course, but I'll have to get used to the idea of being married to a grandmother."

Sam Levenson says that when he was a boy he used to have to do what his father wanted, and now he has to do what his boy wants. When can he do what he wants?

Looking at his 10-year-old pride and joy watching TV with a bored expression, a father remarked, "When I was your age, Son, I walked miles in blizzards, milked four cows early each morning, and rode a horse instead of riding in a comfortable car. What do you think of that?

Looking up at his father, the boy replied, "I wish we could have that kind of fun now."

"The child had every toy his father wanted."

—Robert E. Whitten

Fathers are people who give their daughters away to other men who aren't nearly good enough so they can have grandchildren who are smarter than anybody's.

Now I know it is difficult to be a parent nowadays. I can sympathize with the family who had three small children who were determined to have their own little puppy dog. Mother protested because she knew that somehow she would end up caring for the pup. The children solemnly promised that they would take care of it, if only she would let them have their own puppy. Finally she relented and they brought their little puppy home, named him Danny, and cared for him diligently—for about a month.

Time passed and Mom found herself responsible for cleaning and feeding the dog. She decided that the children were not living up to their promise so she resolved to find a new owner for Danny.

Mom was quite surprised to find that the children's reactions were mild. One of them remarked matter-of-factly, "We'll miss him."

"Yes," Mom answered, "we will miss him but he is too much work for one person and since I'm the one that has to do all the work, I say he goes."

"But," protested another child, "if he wouldn't eat so much and wouldn't be so messy, could we keep him?"

Mom held her ground, "It's time to take Danny to his new home."

"With one voice and in tearful outrage the children reacted, "DANNY? We thought you said Daddy!"

O. Dean Martin tells the story of a frog who fell into a deep rut and, try as he might, he could not get out. Mrs. Frog, standing above the rut, admonished, cajoled, beckoned, and belittled. "Get out, come on, let's go," she pleaded.

Mr. Frog, down in the deep rut, said simply that he couldn't. "I've tried everything and there is no way I can get out of this rut."

Mrs. Frog hopped on down to the pond, and in a few minutes Mr. Frog appeared beside her on their favorite lily pad. "I thought you said you couldn't get out," she exclaimed.

He responded. "Big truck came along and I had to."

The story is told in a different way about a fellow walking through a cemetery late at night who fell into an open grave. He didn't know that sometime earlier another man had fallen into the same grave. He felt around the walls of the grave and tried to climb out but he couldn't quite make it. Suddenly, behind him in that open grave he heard a voice, "You can't get out of here." But he did.

I like the story about the uncle who wanted to humor his little nephew who had a large balloon shaped like a lion. "I'm scared of that big lion of yours," he announced to the boy with the big balloon. "Don't be scared," said the boy. "You ought to see how small he looks when I let out the air!"

There is a story about Bishop Quayle, who must have had a keen sense of humor. He told of a time when he sat up late in his study, worrying over many things. Finally the Lord came to him and said, "Quayle, you go to bed. I'll sit up the rest of the night."

There is a story of a young boy who on sudden notice was called upon to have one line in a drama in his public school. He was to come at the indicated time and say these few words: "Fear not; it is I." The dreaded moment came. he was excited and frightened. He rushed on to the stage; but instead of saying what he had been taught, the old habits of speech rose up, causing him to blurt out in an excited manner, "Don't be scared—ain't nobody but me!"

Wilson O Weldon, **A Plain Man Faces Trouble** (Nashville: The Upper 1971).

One of the most famous of the *Peanuts* comic strip series has Linus giving Charlie Brown this sage bit of advice:

I don't like to face problems head on. I think the best way to
solve problems is to avoid them. This is a distinct philosophy of
mine. No problem is so big or so complicated that it can't be run
away from!

A joke is told about a young man who was dancing with his best girlfriend while another boy kept breaking in. Finally, he stopped, took off his glasses and said to his girl, "Will you please hold my glasses?" The girl became anxious and said, "Oh, you aren't going to fight him are you?" "No, I just can't stand the sight of him."

A nervous millionaire was interviewing an applicant for the post of chauffeur. "My last man," grumbled the millionaire, "took too many unnecessary chances. I want somebody who'll always play it absolutely safe." "I'm your man, sir." said the applicant cheerfully. "Can I have my first month's pay in advance?"
                                                                    – Bennett Cerf

Ten years ago in London, England, a pioneer BBC broadcaster told of sitting next to the great Winston Churchill as he gave a splendid oration to a small group. The broadcaster noted that what appeared to be notes in Churchill's hand was only an ordinary slip, and he commented on this later in private to the great statesman.
    "I know," said Sir Winston, "but it gave confidence to my audience."

My friend's house was destroyed by an avalanche. I said to him, "Do you have any insurance?" He said, "I got a piece of the rock!"

"That's a mean-looking dog you've got there," said a man to his friend.
"Mean as he looks too," replied the friend, "and a real fighter."
Just then the dog took off after another dog passing by and was thoroughly whipped in a brief scuffle.
"I thought you said your dog was a fighter."
"Well, he is. He's just a lousy judge of dogs."
                                                                    –Bits & Pieces

A rich woman from New York was touring the West and finally arrived in Santa Fe. She noticed an old Indian with a necklace made from curious-looking teeth.
    "What are those?" she asked.
    "Those are grizzly bear teeth, madam," replied the Indian.
    "Ah, yes," she nodded. "And I suppose they have the same value for you red men that pearls have for us."
    "Not exactly, madam," replied the noble savage. "Anybody can open an oyster."
                                                                    –Contributed

I like the story about the mountaineer who had been gone from home for over a week and when he came back home his clothes were torn, his shoes were worn thin, and it was obvious that he was exhausted. His wife put her hands on her hips and said with suspicion, "Where in tarnation have you been?"

"I went out in the woods to check the still," replied the mountain man, "and a giant bear stepped out in front of me. I took off running ahead of him and finally lost him. I never ran so fast in my life!"

"But that was a week ago," said the wife. "Where have you been since?"

"I've been walking back," he said.

Several old-timers were talking about old days in the West, "I'll never forget the time I killed my first Indian," one recalled.

"Shoot him?" asked another.

"Nope," said the old man.

"Kill him hand-to-hand with a knife?"

"Nope, nothing like that," was the reply. "Ran him to death."

"How far did you chase him?"

"Didn't," said the old-timer. "I was in front."

How much we put up with in life because we do not believe in ourselves.

I heard about one timid little fellow who went to his first movie theater. He bought his ticket and went inside. A few minutes later he came back to the ticket office and asked for another ticket. Then he returned a third time, visibly angry, and bought another ticket. He muttered softly to the cashier, "If that man inside the door tears up my ticket one more time, I'm going home."

Even when fear is not physically destructive, it adds a great burden to our lives.

Panting and perspiring, two men on a tandem bicycle at last got to the top of a steep hill.

"That was a stiff climb," said the first man.

"It certainly was," replied the second man. "And if I hadn't kept the brake on, we would have slid down backward."

One-time baseball great Joe Garagiola stepped up to the plate when his turn to bat came. Before assuming his stance, however, fervent Roman Catholic Joe took his bat and made the sign of the cross in the dirt in front of homeplate. Catcher Yogi Berra, also a devout Catholic, walked out and erased Garagiola's cross. Turning to the astonished Garagiola, Berra smiled and said, "Let's let God watch this inning."

I heard about a salesman who had been working in Virginia and was being transferred to California. The move had been the principal topic of conversation around the house for weeks. Then, the night before the big move, when his five-year-old daughter was saying her prayers, she said, "And now, God, I'll have to say goodbye forever because tomorrow we are moving to California."

For some, the fear of death is translated into a fear of God.

Woody Allen once quipped, "I don't want to achieve immortality through my work; I want to achieve immortality by not dying." He goes on to say: "It's very important to realize that we're up against an evil, insidious, hostile universe, a hostile force. It'll make you ill and age you, and kill you. And there's somebody—or something—out there who, for some irrational, unexplainable reason, is killing us."

I like the story about an officer in a police helicopter who spotted a car speeding down the Interstate. He radioed his partner on the ground and the patrolman in the car stopped the speeder and began writing a citation. "How in the world did you know I was speeding?" the man asked.

The patrolman didn't say anything, but pointed skyward. "Do you mean to tell me that he's turned against me, too?" the man moaned.

I saw somewhere a church bulletin miscue. The choir anthem was listed, "Hallelujah, the Lord God Omnipotent Resigneth."

Two little girls were once studying a portrait of Queen Victoria. "What's she doing?" asked the one little girl. The other gazed hard at the picture, then replied, "Oh, nothing. She's just reigning."

An explorer to an African village which practices cannibalism saw the following sign in a grocery store window:

SALE
Brains

Farmers $1/lb
Hunters 2/lb
Teachers. 3/lb
Doctors 4/lb
Fishermen 5/lb
Bureaucrats 100/lb

"Why so much for bureaucrats' brains?" the explorer asked the store-keeper.

"Oh sir," came the answer, "if you knew how many bureaucrats we had to catch to get a pound of brains, you wouldn't ask that question."

April is the month when the green returns the lawn, the trees, and the Internal Revenue Service.

We will never get anywhere with our finances until we pass a law saying that every time we appropriate something we got to pass another bill along with it stating where the money is coming from.

—Will Rogers

Remember this thought: Many of the political jokes you laughed at last year were elected.

When John Kennedy was President, he met a stockbroker. "If I were not president," said JFK, "I'd certainly be buying stocks." Answered the broker, "If you weren't president, I would be buying stocks."

According to Bill Cosby, our native Americans had the right approach after all. "Four hundred years ago the Indians were running this country. There were no taxes, no national debt and the women did all the work. It beats me how the white man thought he could improve on a great system like that."

95

JUST THINK how this country would be today if the Indians had stricter immigration laws.

Visit your money this year — vacation in Washington, D.C.

"I wouldn't vote for you if you were St. Peter, himself," I told one candidate with whom I was in particular disagreement. "Don't worry," he replied, "If I were St. Peter, you wouldn't be in my district."

Last week we were studying George Washington, our first president," said the teacher. "Does anyone remember the greatest obstacle that President Washington faced?" A little boy raised his hand. "Yes, ma'am, he replied, "he could not tell a lie."

During his third term campaign, Franklin Delano Roosevelt met an old neighbor and inquired, "Whom are you voting for this year?"
"The Republicans."
"How come? Third term issue bothering you?"
"It's not that at all, Franklin. It's just that — well — I voted Republican the first time you ran, I voted Republican the second time you ran, and I'm going to vote Republican again because I never had it so good."

Christopher Columbus has been called the forerunner of modern government. He didn't know where he was going when he started; he didn't know where he was when he got there, and he did it all on borrowed money.

A little boy wanted $100 very badly, so he decided to pray about it. After getting no answer, he wrote the Lord a letter. Not knowing what to do with it, the post office sent it to Washington. A congressman got hold of it and sent the boy $5. Then the boy sent the Lord a letter of complaint. He said, "You routed the letter through Washington, and they deducted 95%!"

The politician began his speech like this, "Ladies and gentlemen, please let me tax your memories for a moment." Someone in the crowd immediately spoke up, "Well, you've tried to tax everything else."

96

As Belgium's Paul Henri Spaak presided over the first United Nations General Assembly, he concluded: "The agenda is exhausted. The Secretary-General is exhausted. You are exhausted. I am exhausted. At last we have achieved unanimity."

It was a French revolutionary who supposedly said: "There go my people. I must find out where they're going, so I can lead them."

Winston Churchill once noted that "the Nation will find it hard to look up to leaders who keep their ears to the ground."

Harry Truman said that after winning his first election to Washington, he spent six months wondering how he made it to the Senate and the rest of his term wondering how the others made it.

The Presidential campaign reminded us of a gag back in 1964: Barry Goldwater is running for president and will campaign in all thirteen states.

DEFINITION OF "BULLDOZER": One who sleeps through a political address.

Some time ago a cartoon pictured the angel Gabriel, up in heaven, about to blow his horn and close the show. But the Almighty, looking down on the earth said, "Hold it, Gabriel. They're going to have another summit meeting."

A father took his small son to visit the U.S. Capitol. From the gallery they watched as the House of Representatives came to order and the Chaplain led in prayer. "Why did the minister pray for all those men, Dad?" asked the lad. "He didn't, son," the father exclaimed, "He looked them over, then prayed for our country!"

One of the wittiest men in American politics was Adlai Stevenson. One of his supporters said to him on one occasion, "Governor, you will have the support of every thinking American." Stevenson replied, "Madam, unfortunately that is not enough. I need a majority."

97

Woody Allen has said, "The government is unresponsive to the needs of the little man. Under five-seven, it's impossible to get your Congressman on the phone."

A young lawyer from Pennsylvania sought to locate in the South. He wrote to a friend in Alabama, asking him what the prospects seemed to be for "an honest young lawyer and Republican." The friend replied, "If you are an honest lawyer you will have absolutely no competition. If you are a Republican, don't be uneasy. The game laws will protect you."

There is a story about a bishop who advised a politician to go out into the rain and lift his head toward heaven. "It will bring a revelation to you," he said.

The next day the politician reported: "I followed your advice and no revelation came. The water poured down my neck, and I felt like a fool."

"Well," replied the bishop, "isn't that quite a revelation for the first try?"

I hope you can come, Senator, because all of us would like to hear the dope from Washington.

—*Quoted by Kenneth B. Keating*

"A billion here, a billion there; and it soon runs into real money."
—*Everett Dirksen*

Former Senator Eugene McCarthy once said, Being in politics is like being a football coach. You have to be smart enough to understand the game and dumb enough to think it's important."

Several years ago, during a debate in the British Parliament, a minister from the Labor Party got up to speak about socialism. "Under our Socialist government, more housing units have been built than ever before," he said, and continued: "Under Socialism, more hospitals have been built than ever before. And, under Socialism, we have witnessed the greatest population increase in the history of the island."

At that point, the great Winson Churchill had heard enough. He said: "Would the Honorable Minister perhaps concede that the baby boom is due to private enterprise?"

Since this is an election year, I'll tell a little story that one of our government officials recently told on himself. He said that on his first day in office he discovered that his predecessor had left three envelopes on his desk with the instructions that they were to be opened only in times of distress.

It was not long before this official got in trouble with the press so he opened the first envelope. It contained a note with three words printed on it: "Blame Your Predecessor." That, of course, will work in almost any field for a while, so that is just what he did, he blamed his problems on his predecessor.

A few months later this official got into trouble again--this time with a congressional committee. So he opened the second envelope. It contained a note with only one word, "Reorganize." Now, people who have dealt with the Federal Government tell us that reorganization rarely accomplishes anything, but it does buy you a little time. "I'm sorry, I can't answer your questions right now," said the official to the committee, "we are in the midst of a reorganization." Sometime later this same official got in trouble with the president. So he opened the third envelope. In it was a note that offered this advice: "Prepare three envelopes."

I like the rather pejorative story of the son of a wealthy Texas oilman who asked his father for an airplane, so the father bought him a Boeing 747. He asked him for a boat, so he bought him the Queen Mary. He asked him for a Mickey Mouse outfit, so he bought him the Department of Energy.

A citizen of America will cross the ocean to fight for democracy, but won't cross the street to vote in a national election.

You have probably heard by now about the elderly gentleman who took his Social Security check to the bank to cash. Although it was clearly marked, "Do not fold, staple or mutilate," the old gentleman had folded it and creased it pretty severely. The teller at the bank cautioned him, "You should be more careful with your check. The government doesn't like it when you mutilate your check like that." The old fellow shook his head and said, "There are some things that the government does that I don't like either."

No man's property is safe while Congress is in session.

--Mark Twain

An elephant is a mouse drawn to government specifications.

99

I like the little boy in Sunday School I heard about. His teacher had just finished her lesson, and wanted to make sure she had made her point. So she asked: "Can anyone tell me what you must do before you can obtain forgiveness for sin?"

The little boy's hand shot up: "You've got to sin first," he said.

One man told his doctor, "I've been misbehaving, Doc, and my conscience is bothering me."

"You want something to make your willpower stronger," the doctor deduced.

"Actually," the man said, "I'm more interested in something to weaken my conscience."

Anybody who doesn't cut his speed at the sight of a police car is probably parked.

Pittsburgh Green Sheet

Do you remember a cartoon a few years ago picturing a boy standing before the stationery counter in a bookstore? He was saying to the clerk, "Lady, do you have any blank report cards?"

You probably heard about the man who wrote the IRS the note: "I haven't been able to sleep because last year, when I filled out my income tax report, I deliberately misrepresented my income. I am enclosing a check for $150, and if I still can't sleep, I will send you the rest."

Elizabeth Brinton, 13-year-old Girl Scout, explaining how she sold 11,200 boxes of cookies: "You have to look people in the eye and make them feel guilty."

A wife asked her husband, "Honey, do you know what day this is?" He didn't, but to play it safe, on the way home from the office he bought a dozen roses. His wife said with mock surprise, "Why, dear, you shouldn't have. But this will be the best Groundhog Day I've ever had!"

There was a funny scene in the series "All in the Family" a few years ago when Edith was still part of Archie's household. Edith, in her own way, was kind of a saintly person. Archie is complaining, as Archie commonly did. He says to her, "That's you all right. Edith, the Good. You'll stoop to anything to be good. You never yell. You never swear. You never make nobody mad. You think it's easy living with a saint? Even when you cheat you don't cheat to win. You cheat to lose. Edit', you ain't human." Edith says, "That's a terrible thing to say, Archie Bunker. I am just as human as you are." Archie retorts, "Oh, yeah . . . then prove you're just as human as me. Do something rotten."

Or you might remember the story of the large metropolitan newspaper that was having a slow afternoon. "You mean," asked the editor to his top reporter, "this city has gone through one afternoon without a single newsworthy event—not a single robbery, murder or assault?" The reporter answered, "Don't panic, boss. The evening's still young. You've got to have faith in human nature."

We know what the trouble is. Something's missing in our lives. We are like the little boy that Ethel Barret tells about who wrote a letter to God:
"Dear God:
I'm taking violin, but you shouldn't listen yet, because I still squeak a lot.
Russell"

You may know the story of the butcher who cheated people by putting his thumb on the scales. Late one afternoon a lady came into the butcher shop and wanted a chicken. He had only one left in the meat counter. He put it on the scales and announced the price. She hesitated. She said, "I think I would like a little larger bird." He said, "That's no problem." He then reached into the meat counter, put the same chicken back in, shuffled around a little bit and brought out the same chicken, put it on the scale this time with his thumb on the scale and announced a heavier weight and higher price. She smiled and said, "Fine, I'll take it!—in fact, I think I'll take BOTH OF THEM."

A taxi driver, his garbage uncollected, tried leaving it in a neat package in his cab's back seat. Said he, "It works, I watched one woman through the mirror. She spent five minutes stuffing it into her shopping bag."

House Speaker "Tip" O'Neill tells a story about "Blameless Jake" Bloom of Boston who fed three generations of Irish, Jews and Italians on credit in his small variety store. In appreciation, his friends and neighbors sent him to London for a fling. Inspired, Jake came home, slimmed down, capped his teeth, bought a hair piece and hit Miami Beach. He met a beautiful blonde and just then, was struck by a bolt of lightning.

"God," Jake complained when he reached the Pearly Gates, "in the twilight of my years, I just wanted to have a little fun."

"Oh, it's you Jake," said God. "I'm sorry--I didn't recognize you."

Many of you know those feelings of inadequacy, do you not? Charles Schultz does a masterful job of capturing those feelings in the cartoon character, Charlie Brown.

Charlie Brown, Linus, and Lucy are lying on a hillside looking up at the clouds. Lucy says, "If you use your imagination you can see lots of things in the cloud formations . . What do you think you see, Linus?" Linus replies, "Well those clouds up there look to me like the map of the British Honduras on the Carribean . . . The cloud up there looks a little like the profile of Thomas Eakins, the famous painter and scupltor . . . And that group of clouds over there gives me the impression of the stoning of Stephen . . . I can see the Apostle Paul standing there to one side." Lucy responds, "Uh huh . . . That's very good . . . What do you see in the clouds, Charlie Brown?" And Charlie responds with his typical note of inadequacy: "Well, I was going to say I saw a ducky and a horsie, but I changed my mind."

I heard about a student at a university who signed up for a course in introductory ornithology. He didn't know what it was. He just like the sound of the course and he figured it would impress his parents. He heard it was a very easy course, taught by an old professor who gave everyone at least a C and gave a lot of A's and B's. After he had registered he learned it was a course about birds and that the professor had retired. Instead there was a young Ph.D. who was just waiting to demonstrate his brilliance to the students. It was an incredibly difficult course. On the final exam, there were 25 pair of bird legs, from the knees down, and the students were asked to identify them. "I quit! This is ridiculous! This is absurd." The professor said, "Young man, what is your name?" The young man calmly rolled up his trousers to his knees and walked out!

A man entered a donkey in the Kentucky Derby. He didn't expect to win, but he thought the association might do him good.

Dagwood, in the comic *Blondie*, is walking along the street when he is stopped by a man who says, "Don't tell me your name. I'll think of it."

"Isn't it Billy? . . . . What's your name?"

Dagwood replies, "Dagwood Bumstead."

The man lowers his head and says, "No, that's not it!" and walks away.

Dagwood says, "If I'm not me, then who am I?"

Don Bubna, in *Building People*, tells of an experience he had in his church. A man who had been to their worship service once, came back to visit, and the pastor felt awkward because he remembered his face and the earlier visit, but not his name. So, resorting to an old trick, he asked, "How do you spell your name, with an 'i' or an 'e'?" The man looked strangely at him before answering. "With an 'i', it's Hill, H-I-L-L!"

It is difficult to separate the person from the profession as this epitaph shows:

> Stranger, tread
> This ground with gravity:
> Dentist Brown is filling
> His last cavity.

There was a bachelor who loved the color yellow. He had a yellow rug on the floor of his apartment. Yellow furniture, yellow drapes on the windows. He had a yellow refrigerator and stove. He slept in bed with yellow covers and wore yellow pajamas. He got sick. Do you know what he came down with? You are right — yellow jaundice! He called the doctor. The doctor came to the apartment and asked for direction. The manager said, "You won't have any trouble finding his apartment. You just go down the hall and come to a yellow door. That is his apartment." In a very short time the doctor was back. The apartment manager said, "Were you able to help him?" The doctor replied, "Help him! I couldn't even find him!"

A man approached me on the street just last week. "Why Jim Jones," he said, "It's so good to see you. Why I hardly recognized you, you've put on so much weight. And you hair has so much gray in it—what hair you have left. What has happened to you. You're so pale. Have you been sick? Either that or you are not getting outdoors enough. Why, you look positively terrible. It is amazing that I recognized you at all."

Fianlly I interrupted. "Wait," I said, I've been trying to tell you that I am not Jim Jones."

"What" He said with much surprise. "You've gone and changed your name too?"

I got a chuckle out of a story that Tip O'Neill tells on himself. O'Neill had a chance encounter with a man while waiting in an airport not too long ago. After a few minutes the man said to O'Neill, "Say, you don't recognize me, do you?" "No, I really don't think so," said the senator. "You see, I'm so well known. I have this big shock of white hair and this large red nose, and I'm on the TV news two or three times a week. A lot of people recognize me, but I can't keep track of all the people I meet. Who are you?" The man answered. "We met at a dinner party about six weeks ago in Washington. My name is Robert Redford."

A little girl was asked to bring her birth certificate to school one day. Her mother wisely cautioned her about the important document and told her not to lose it. The child forgot; you guessed it—she did lose it. When she became aware of her loss, she started crying. When asked why she was crying, she answered, "I lost my excuse for being born!"

At the national prayer breakfast held in Washington, D.C. a few years ago Congressman Tribble told an interesting story from his own family. He said that wherever his little daughter went, she was constantly being associated with him. People would say, "Oh, you must be Congressman Tribble's little girl." She quietly explained to her parents that she wanted to be herself, not just known as someone else's daughter. Her father told her not to worry about it. Her mother, on the other hand, who was more understanding said to her, "The next time that happens, just stand right up and say, "I am Constance Tribble!" Sure enough a few days later, a group of people met her and when they heard her name, they said, "Why, Congressman Tribble must be your father!" The little girl looked right back at them and said, "Oh, no! That's not what my mother says!"

A woman got on an elevator in a tall office building. There was just one other person in the elevator, a handsome man. She pushed the button for her floor and then casually looked over at the man and suddenly had one of those moments of recognition shock. Could it be? The man looked exactly like Robert Redford, the movie star. Her gaze was almost involuntarily riveted on him. Finally, she blurted out, "Are you the REAL Robert Redford?" He smiled and said, "Only when I'm alone!"

"There's nothing radically wrong with this town," the booster said. "All it needs is a better type of citizen and a decent water supply."
"Come to think of it," a listener replied, "those are the only drawbacks to hell."

Here is a good story to use as a visiting preacher (assuming your host pastor is a good sport):

Last night I dreamed I died and went to heaven. St. Peter met me at the Pearly Gates. He looked over his records. "Hold on," he said. "You have some sins that you need to pay for. You see that lady over there." He pointed to the ugliest lady I have ever seen. "Your punishment is to spend the next 400 years with that lady."

Well, I knew I had not been perfect. Besides, what is 400 years in eternity? I could live with that. At least I thought I could. Then I saw your pastor. And he had on his arm the most beautiful, gorgeous blonde that I have ever seen. I couldn't believe it. I went to St. Peter and protested. "It's not fair! Here I have to spend 400 years with this ugly woman and Brother [host pastor's name] gets this gorgeous blonde."

St Peter was patient but firm. "I'm sorry," he said, "but that blonde must pay for her sins too."

Is it true that the first introduction was something like this: "Madam, I'm Adam?"

Good way to introduce guest speakers. It is said that:
1. Good teachers never die; they just lose their principals.
2. Good principals never die; they just lose their faculties.
3. Good doctors never die; they just lose their patients.
4. Good lawyers never die; they just lose their appeal.
5. Good preachers never die; they just go on and on and on.

I am always a bit uneasy about long introductions, much like Mark Twain. He wrote that he spent $25 to research his family background, and then $50 to cover it up.

The word leaped out of the page right between the eyes! "WILL YOU BE READY FOR JUDGMENT DAY?"

I quickly read on only to find out that it was an advertisement for the Abingdon Press' "Clergy Income Tax Guide!"

—Dr. John Bardsley

A mother, hearing a startling scream from her four year old son, rushed into the playroom to see what was happening. There he sat while his baby sister yanked his hair with all her might.

"Don't be upset," said his mother. She doesn't know that it hurts you."

Several minutes later, the mother again heard sharp screaming, this time from her little daughter. Once, more in the playroom, she asked her son, "what's wrong with the baby?"

"Nothing much," he said, "except now she knows."

Evangelist: There will be weeping, wailing and gnashing of teeth among the wicked who pass on to the next world.
Old Timer: What about those who haven't any teeth?
Evangelist: Teeth will be provided.

At the start of the holiday weekend, the service station was extra crowded. At last the attendant came up to the local pastor, who had been waiting in line for some time.

"Sorry for the delay pastor," apologized the attendant. "Seems like folks always wait until the last minute to get ready for a trip they know they're going on."

The pastor smiled. "I know what you mean," he said. "I have the same problem in my business."

A prison chaplain who was passing a group of inmates stitching mail bags, paused to look at one man's work.

"Sewing, I see." He remarked to one.

"No, Chaplain," the inmate remarked ironically. "Reaping."

There is an old story told about Dr. Werner Von Braun that you may have heard, while he was on the lecture circuit. He traveled by chauffeur-driven limosine.

One day, while on the road, the story goes, Von Braun's chauffer said: "Dr. Von Braun, I have heard you deliver that lecture so many times that I'll bet I could deliver it myself." Von Braun replied, "Very well, I'll give you that opportunity tonight. The people at the University where I am to lecture tonight have never seen me. So before we get there I'll put on your cap and uniform and you will introduce me as your chauffeur and yourself as me. Then you will give the lecture."

And for a while everything went according to plan. The chauffeur delivered the lecture flawlessly. But as the lecture concluded, a professor in the audience rose and asked a complex question involving mathematical equations and formulas. The quick thinking chauffeur replied, "Sir, the solution to that problem is so simple, I'm really surprised you have asked me to give it to you. Indeed, to prove to you just how simple it is, I am going to ask my chauffeur to step forward and answer your question."

Chuck Swindoll told about an elementary student who took a test in anatomy and failed it. This is what the little boy said, "The human body is composed of three parts, The brainery, the borax, and the abominable cavity. The brainery contains the brain. The borax contains the lungs and the living things. The abominable cavity contains the bowels of which there are five: a, e, i, o, and u."

The comedian Ed Wynn claimed that he landed his first job many years ago simply on the basis of a single test administered by two personnel assistants. One looked into his right ear while the other peered into his left. He qualified, Wynn said, "because they could not see each other."

On a large camp ground one morning while a beautiful testimony meeting was running and the saints were full of praises and the glory of God was on the multitude, a young man arose and began to testify, and he at once began to leap in the air. He thanked God that he had no education and that he was ignorant, and was glad of that. An old white-haired saint with a beautiful smile on his face said, "Young man, you have lots to be thankful for."

—Bud Robinson **Nuggets of Gold** (Louisville, Ky.: Pentecostal Publishing Co.).

A former Florida politician is credited with this bit of rhetorical genius to some backwoods constituents:

"It's well-known that my opponent is not married yet practices celibacy. He matriculated with several coeds while at the state university. He is a shameless extrovert who has practiced nepotism with family members in his business. And I happen to know that he has a sister who is a practicing thespian in New York City."

A member of the faculty of the University of Wisconsin tells of some amusing replies made by a pupil undergoing an examination in English. The candidate had been instructed to write out examples of the indicative, the subjunctive, the potential, and the exclamatory moods. His effort resulted as follows:

"I am endeavoring to pass an English examination. If I answer twenty questions I shall pass. If I answer twelve questions I may pass. God help me!"

In one of the memorable debates between Douglas and Lincoln in 1858, the former, who was an eloquent and practised orator, had delivered such an enthralling speech that his audience was spellbound, and Lincoln's friends felt that the victory was already won for his opponent.

When the cheers had died away, Lincoln got up, shed his long white duster, and, dropping it on the arm of a young man standing nearby, remarked, with his droll smile:

"Hold my coat while I *stone Stephen.*"
– A. C. Edgerton, *More Speeches and Stories for Every Occasion.*

Winston Churchill received a hot letter from an angry schoolteacher who was protesting Parliament's poor use of English in writing some of its laws. "Why they are even misplacing prepositions!" she wrote. "Madame," Sir Churchill agreed, "this is an outrage up with which we will not put!"

You remember the words of the famous announcer who was introducing the President of the United States—who was then Herbert Hoover. He said, "Now ladies and gentlemen, it is my pleasure to introduce to you the President of the United States, Hubert Heaver."

A TV sportscaster told this Yogi Berra story. The pudgy former manager of the New York Mets and present-day Yankee baseball coach has a distinctive way with words. Once he was talking about a restaurant that ball players went to: "Nobody goes there anymore," said Yogi. "It's too crowded."

Mark Twain used a lot of profanity in his speeches. This embarrassed his wife a lot. One night they were getting ready to go out for a speech. As she was tying his tie she uttered a long string of profanity at him. He just looked at her and said, "Livey, you've got the words, but you ain't got the music."

Somewhere I read about an evangelist who promised, "We're gonna fill you so full of the Holy Spirit that if a mosquito bites you, he's gonna fly away singing. 'There's Power in the Blood.' "

A nun who teaches in a Catholic high school has a reputation for perfectionism.

During the months preceding the College Board examinations, she administers a battery of mutiple-choice answers and then "chooses one of the above."

From these oft-repeated directions, she has earned herself a heavenly nickname — the students affectionately call her Nun of the Above.

—Contributed

A wise old sea captain stood on the bridge of his ship day in and day out, opening a box and peeking inside, never letting anyone else see the contents. The day he retired, the crew rushed to the bridge, cut the lock and looked inside the box. Hidden inside was a piece of paper that read, "Left — port. Right — starboard."

Oscar Wilde was noted for taking verbal potshots at his literary friend. He said of George Bernard Shaw, "He has no enemies but is thoroughly disliked by his friends." . . . "Do I know George Moore," he once answered somebody. "Why, I know him so well that I haven't spoken to him for ten years." And with Max Beerbohm he scored a happy bull's eye: "The gods," said Wilde, "have bestowed on Max the gift of perpetual old age."

British diplomat in speech: The gravity of this situation is impossible to exaggerate, but I'll try.

Newly commissioned naval officer: "Listen sailor, if the captian ever caught you calling the deck a floor, he'd throw you right out one of those little round windows over there."

A good story has turned up in the South Carolina Methodist *Advocate*, this time involving a bishop, and it goes like this:

"A newly appointed preacher wrote his first report to the district superintendent. It stunned the DS because it was obvious the new man was a blithering illiterate and had been pawned off on him by another DS. Here is what the newly appointed preacher wrote:

'Dear Super,

I sen you the report you ask for. I aint ben on this here new pointment but three month and the report aint so gud. I aint had but leven to jine the church on that there perfeshun of faith but I god six baptist and two piscopaleens. We dun paint the church inside and out and bout them purty new red song books you tole us about. We tuk all them portionments you give us and aim to pay em too. I am workin on a better report nex time. We gonna have some renuel in this Church.'

"Before the illiterate preacher could be called on the carpet by the district superintendent for his sloppy language, this note came from the brother:

'We don paid all them worl survice and bennevolunces and aim to get a passel of money for them missum specials. I got me one of them long black things to preach in.'

"Fearful if he did, and fearful if he didn't call the brother on the carpet, the district superintendent dumped the problem in the lap of the bishop.

"In the next edition of the conference paper, the brethren were amazed to see the two letters printed, and this notation from the bishop:

'We ben spending two much time trying to spel instead of trying to sel. Let's keep an eye on the mission of the church. I want all brethren shud read these letters from Gooch who is doin a grate job for the church, and you shud go out and do like he done.' "

– Contributed

A sign on a university bulletin board read, "Shoes are required to eat in the cafeteria."

Underneath, somebody had scribbled, "Socks may eat wherever they want to."

A store had this sign hanging on the front door:
IF WE'RE NOT OPEN
WE'RE CLOSED.

A teacher telling the story of Sodom and Gomorrah to her class explained: "Lot was warned to take his wife and flee out of the city which was about to be destroyed. They got away safely. Then Lot's wife looked back and turned into a pillar of salt. Now, children, do you have any questions to ask about this story?"

"Yeah, I have a question," announced one boy, raising his hand. "Could you please tell us what happened to the flea?"

Another goodie from an ancient text:

The following copies of advertisements have been collected and printed by club women:

Bulldog for sale; will eat anything; is very fond of children.

Lost-Near Highgate Archway, an umbrella belonging to a gentleman with a bent rib and a bone handle.

Mr. Brown, furrier, begs to announce that he will make up gowns, capes and so forth, for ladies out of their own skin.

Wanted — a herder for 500 sheep that can speak Spanish fluently.

For Sale — House in good neighborhood, by an invalid lady three stories high and heated with furnace.

I heard about a fellow who was having trouble with the problem of cursing. Seems like every time he got angry he let out a phrase that wasn't very nice. He went to his pastor for help, he was struggling to live a new life. His pastor said that every time you get angry why not try singing a hymn? That way you won't express your anger in an inappropriate way. So the fellow said he would try this, "but I don't know many hymns." So the pastor gave him a hymn book to use, and the man took it and tried it, and in a couple of weeks he came back to the pastor. The pastor said, "How are you doing?" The man says, "I'm doing pretty well." The pastor said, "That's great!" The man said, "There's only one thing." And the pastor said, "What's that?" The man said, "I'm ready for a new hymn book."

Psychologist Gordon Allport once told about a patient who was dying in a hospital. The attending physicians told him quite frankly that he could not expect to be cured since the diagnosis was unknown. The only hope they offered him was a distinguished diagnostician had been called in and was soon to give his expert opinion. The specialist arrived but needed only a little time to reach his conclusion. To the physicians in attendance and almost out of the patient's earshot he pronounced: "Moribundus." After some years, our patient, who did not die, called on the specialist to report on his good health and to thank the physician for saving his life. The ex-patient explained how the medical staff had told him that he could be cured only if the disease could be diagnosed. Therefore, he explained, he knew that he would recover as soon as he heard the consultant's diagnosis of "moribundus."

As the family sat around the dinner table one evening, Alan looked at his father very intently and asked, "Daddy, when are you going to stop practicing law and really do it?"

Once upon a time the fence between heaven and hell broke down. St. Peter appeared at the broken section and called to the devil, "Hey, Satan, since all the engineers are over in your place how about getting them to fix this fence?"

Replied Satan, "Sorry. My men are all too busy to bother fixing measly fences."

Answered St. Peter, "Well, then, I'll have to sue you if you don't."

Countered the devil, "Oh, Yeah, and where are you going to get a lawyer?"

Arguing a case in court, two lawyers began calling each other names.

Roared one, "You're a loop-brained shyster."

Shouted the other, "And you're an ambulance-chasing cockroach."

Rapping for order, the judge said, "Now that you two fellows have introduced each other to this court, you may proceed with the case."

A man, when tried for stealing a pair of boots, said he merely took the boots in joke. It was found that he was captured with them forty yards from the place he had taken them. The judge said he had carried the joke too far.

One lawyer drove his $10,000 Cadillac to Las Vegas and returned on a $150,000 Greyhound.

Have you heard about the lawyer's daughter who told her boyfriend, "Stop, and/or I'll slap your face"?

The story is told of a man on trial for murder who had bribed a member of the jury to hold out for the lesser verdict of manslaughter. After debating for several hours, the jury finally brought in the verdict: "We find the accused guilty of manslaughter." The murderer sought out the juror he had bribed to thank him and asked him if he found it difficult to influence the others. "Yes," replied the man, "I had a most difficult time. All the rest of them wanted to vote, 'Not guilty.' "

112

Of all the road construction projects you never hear about any need to widen the straight and narrow path so that it can accommodate more traffic. You don't have to worry about congested traffic on that road.

—Edward L. Friedman

A man who wants to lead the orchestra, must turn his back on the crowd.

At a dinner party, a woman said to Lord Northcliffe, "It is really quite surprising — Thackeray awoke one morning and found himself famous!" Lord Northcliffe answered, "When that morning dawned, Thackeray had been writing eight hours a day for fifteen years. No, Madam, the man who wakes up and finds himself famous hasn't been asleep."

THEY SAY THAT SOME MEN RISE TO THE OCCASION, WHERE OTHERS MERELY HIT THE CEILING.

A railroad agent somewhere in Africa had been bawled out for making decisions without orders from headquarters. One day his superior received the following startling telegram, "Tiger on platform eating conductor. Wire instructions."

A senior pastor was training his assistant and requested his presence on a rather serious counselling session between a husband and wife. The pastor listened to each person separately.

After the husband shared his side of the story, the pastor patted him on the shoulder and said, "You're so right. You're so right."

As the wife was leaving, having shared her side with the pastor, he also patted her arm saying "You're so right. You're so right."

Alone now with his superior the confused assistant said, "You first told the husband he was right, then you told the wife she was right. You know they can't both be right."

The senior pastor looked at his assistant and said, "You're so right. You're so right."

Police were so totally baffled by the latest string of burglaries that they brought in a clairvoyant. This man had professed to have had stunning success in locating kidnapped children, missing person, lost wallets, pets that had strayed off, etc. The police welcomed his assistence and told him to come on down to the station. Unfortunately the clairvoyant was not able to help them. He could not find the police station.

The crusty, old colonel gave his newly commissioned second-lieutenants a pop quiz. "You are out on maneuvers," he barked brusquely, "And you are going to put up a tent. What is your first order?" Each of the lieutenants stuttered and stammered around with answers such as "Get out the camping gear." None of their answerss satisfied the colonel. Finally one of the lieutenants who had been silent to this point stepped forward and said with confidence, "Sir, my first order would be my only order. I would say, 'Sergeant, pitch a tent!' "

The chairman of one of our great corporations was late for a meeting. Bolting into the room, he took the nearest available seat rather than moving to his accustomed spot. One of his young aides protested, "Please, sir, you should be at the head of the table." The executive who had a healthy understanding of his place in the company answered, "Son, wherever I sit is the head of the table."

A friend of mine used to spend summer vacations as a ranger at Lessen Volcanic National Park in California. He was on duty one morning when a tourist approached, gave a brief description of an unusual bird he had just seen and asked whether my friend could identify it.

"No," my friend replied, "I don't recognize it either, but I *can* help you. I have here a copy of Roger Tory Peterson's definitive *Field Guide to Western Birds*."

"That won't help," replied the disappointed tourist. "That bird's not in there. I'm Roger Tory Peterson."

—Stephen L. Brown, Sr., in *Smithsonian*

I like the way one comedian put it. He said, "I once rubbed a magic lamp–and got lead poisoning."

All of us identify with the born loser–the fellow who tries so hard but can't win. Like the fellow who wrote a card to his girlfriend on her twenty-fourth birthday: "Since you are as lovely as a rose I have instructed the florist to deliver a rose for each year of your life on this your birthday." The florist was in a generous mood that day. He had an extra dozen roses. He sent them along with the two dozen as a free bonus.

"If at first you don't succeed, welcome to the club."

A dejected basketball coach entered a telephone booth after losing out in a recent high school tournament. When he discovered he didn't have a dime, he called to a passing student, "Hey, lend me a dime so I can call a friend."

Grinning sourly, the student reached in his pocket and handed the coach two dimes. "Here's twenty cents, Coach; call all your friends."

I was with one of my parishioners at the funeral home. She asked how much the newspapers charged for running obituaries. "Thirty cents an inch," I told her. "Oh dear," she said, "It will be far too expensive. My husband was six feet tall."

Someone told me that chewing gum would keep my ears from popping while flying. They were right. Now if I can figure a way to get the gum out of my ears.

Like Rodney Dangerfield, I don't get any respect at home. I was sick in bed last week. Our five-year-old got worried. "Is Daddy about to go to Heaven?" he asked his mother. "Not a chance," she replied.

A small town paper reported that a newcomer, who had moved there to escape the traffic and congestion of the city, was run over by the Welcome Wagon.

115

A *Punch* cartoon is captioned, "I'm sorry, Mr. Mellowane, but we can no longer insure your car. It's accident prone." (May 25, '77, p. 981).

As his surprised wife looks on, a fellow reads from the collar tag of a large, mangy-looking mutt: "It says, 'If found, don't bother to return.' "

I'll try to keep my comments brief this morning but I can't approach the all-time record for short speeches. That belongs to a psychologist who had to speak on the subject of sex. He said, "Ladies and gentlemen, I've been asked to speak to you about sex, it's a pleasure" — then he sat down. Well for different reasons, it's a pleasure to be here this morning with the distinguished business and commercial leaders of Oak Brook. I know none of you are affected by the recession but hardly a day goes by without a report of some hard luck story.

The last I heard concerns an auto salesman named Joe. When automobile sales went to pot, he started gambling at Arlington Park, hoping to make ends meet. He lost all his money, his car and his house. Then his wife left him, and in desperation, he started drinking. He became one of those street people spending the night on Lower Wacker. Well, one night, as Joe drained the last drop from a bottle of muscatel, there was a puff of smoke and a geni rose out of the bottle and said, "Master, I am your genie. I have come to grant you one wish." Joe grinned and said, "If I can have anything I want. I'd like a foreign car agency." There was a flash of light and when Joe opened his eyes he was standing in his new showroom — a Chrysler-Plymouth dealership in downtown Tokyo!

— Introduction to an address by Robert T. Powers in *Vital Speeches*

Newton's Seventh Law according to broadcaster Paul Harvey: "The other line always moves faster."

Have you heard about the group of men who went mountain climbing? They had just scaled their way to the top when one of the men fell over a cliff. His companion climbers tried to rescue him. Ever so carefully they leaned over the cliff and yelled, "Joe, are you all right?" Back came Joe's voice, "I'm alive, I'm alive, . . . but I think my arms are broken."

"We will toss a rope down to you and pull you up," yelled the rescuers. "Hurry, please hurry!" cried Joe.

Withing a few minutes the men began to pull Joe up. When they had him about three-fourths of the way up, it suddenly dawned on them that Joe had said he had broken both his arms. "Joe," one of them yelled, "if you broke both of your arms, how are you holding on?" Joe responded, "With my teeeeeeeeeeth!"

I heard of the lonely man who sent his photograph to a lonely hearts club. The club sent it back promptly with these words written across the back: "We're not that lonely!"

One man was talking about his car. "The old clunker makes a lot of noise," he said. "In fact the only things on it that don't make noise are the horn and the radio."

We are like the patient in the psychiatrist's office who says: "Lately I feel that everyone takes advantage of me." Answers the psychiatrist: "Don't worry about it. That's perfectly normal." With a sign of relief the patient says: "Really? I didn't know that. Thanks a lot. Now, how much do I owe you, Doctor?" Answers the psychiatrist: "How much do you have?"

There was a *Peanuts* cartoon once in which Charlie Brown complained to Linus about his publisher. "The publisher sent me a rejection slip," lamented Charlie.
   "So what?" said Linus. "Lots of writers get rejection slips."
   "But I didn't even submit a manuscript," cried Charlie.

We know we cannot please all the people all of the time. Sometimes we can't please anybody. A retired man tells how he always used to go to Bill Meyers Stadium in Knoxville, Tennessee, to watch the Knoxville Smokies play baseball. He says that there was an old man at the stadium who never missed a game. He would sit in the same seat each game and invariably offered the same chant. Whenever a Knoxville Smokey came up to bat he would yell, "Walk him, pitcher, walk him." If the pitcher should walk the batter, then the old man would yell triumphantly, "You walked the wrong man pitcher, you walked the wrong man."

The paratroopers were aloft for their first jump. Everything went off in perfect order, until the last man came forward to jump. "Hold it!" shouted his commanding officer. "You're not wearing your parachute!"
   "Oh, that's all right, sir," replied the recruit. "We're just practicing, aren't we?"

Luck is what enables others to succeed at something at which we have failed.

117

Someone has said there are two kinds of losers: Good *losers* and honest ones.

The poor Bible salesman reported to his sales manager, "I got two orders today–'Get out!' and 'Stay out!' "

I love the story of the man who bought a grandfather clock and was carrying it back to his car across a busy pedestrian walk. He bumped into another man and knocked him flat. The man looked up in disgust and said, "Why don't you get a wrist watch!"

One poor man to his psychiatrist: "Every time I get my act together the curtain comes down."

Every year at Southern Seminary in Columbia, S. C., the composite senior-class picture is hung in the student union. A Bible verse that best identifies the class accompanies the photograph. One professor, asked what verse might be appropriate for our class, replied, "St. John 11: 35."

Students scurried to the Scriptures to find the words he had chosen: "Jesus wept."

—Mark S. Bredholt in *Readers's Digest*

The city boys decided to become wood cutters, so both rented chain saws and started to work. The first man went deep into the woods and cut six cords the first day, eight the next and more each succeeding day. The second man tried and tried but could cut no more than half a cord of wood any day. Frustrated he went back to the rental shop to complain about the saw.

"This looks O. K. to me," said the proprietor as he pulled the starter string and kicked the saw into action.

"Hey," yelled the startled woodcutter, "what's that awful noise?"

—*Modern Maturity*

A nervous bride asked her pastor for help in dealing with anxiety about the wedding service. The pastor answered with a sure-fire formula. "As you come through the door, keep your eyes down," he advised her. DON'T LOOK A-ROUND AT THE PEOPLE. Keep your gaze fixed upon the aisle down which you will walk. When you are about half-way down the aisle, raise your eyes just a bit until you can see the altar and keep your gaze fixed there until you are nearly to the front, and then lift your gaze just the slightest bit until you see him—him who is your beloved."

The day of the wedding came. The church was full. The Wedding March began. The doors opened and there stood the beautiful young bride looking remarkably composed. People did wonder, however, as she passed them about her muttering determinately under her breath, "Aisle, altar him. Aisle, altar, him." Many young brides marry with the intention that "I'll altar him." Unfortunately it rarely works.

Folks today are in love with love. One fellow bought up every book he saw on the physical art of love. One day he was in an airport and in a little shop he saw a book with the intriguing title, "How to Hug." He was in such a hurry to catch his plane, he didn't have time to examine it before he paid for it. It wasn't until he was in the air, that he had a chance to see what he had bought—the fifth volume of an encyclopedia.

Many a husband chuckled at this one printed in **Parade** magazine recently: "There was a line of men standing in front of the Pearly Gates, waiting to get in. A sign overhead read: 'For Men Who Have Been Dominated By Their Wives All Their Lives.' The line extended as far as the eye could see. There was another sign nearby: 'For Men Who Have Never Been Dominated By Their Wives.' One man was standing under it. St. Peter came over to him and said, 'What are you standing here for?' The man said, 'I don't know. My wife told me to stand here.'"

"Marriage teaches you loyalty, patience, understanding, perseverance, and a lot of other things you wouldn't need if you'd stayed single!"

Tactful husband who forgot: "But, Dear, how can you expect me to remember your birthday when you never look any older?"

I like the story of the woman who had an artist paint a portrait of her covered with jewels. Her explanation: "If I die and my husband remarries, I want his next wife to go crazy looking for the jewels."

119

A woman was congratulated on her thirtieth wedding anniversary for holding on to the same man for thirty years. "Oh," she replied, "He's not the same man he was when I first got hold of him." That's true, is it not? Persons do not stagnate in a good marriage. They grow and mature. We are not the same persons we were twenty, thirty or forty years before.

A line from many years ago by George Gobel still gets a chuckle: "I make all the big decisions in my family and my wife makes the small ones. She decides where we go out, whether to buy a car, etc., and I make the big ones — like whether to admit Red China."

One poor pastor we heard about had some marital problems when he got back from a recent week-long conference. He couldn't understand it until his wife showed him a telegram he had sent her:
"Having a wonderful time stop wish you were her."

Having had their first quarrel, a young couple did not speak for several hours. Finally the husband decided to give in.
"Please speak to me, Dear," he said, "I'll admit I was wrong and you were right."
Sobbed the bride, "It won't do any good — I've changed my mind."

"By all means, marry. If you get a good wife, you become very happy; if you get a bad one, you will become a philosopher — and that is good for every man."
—Socrates

Grumbled the new groom at dinner: "Why can't you make bread like my mother does?" Answered his bride: "Why can't you make dough like my father does?"

A newlywed was complaining to her mother, "Marriage really is a terrible grind. I never dreamed it would be like this. You wash dishes, make the beds, tidy up the living room and then two weeks later you have to do it all over again."

"Just this morning my husband said I was a terrible housekeeper. I got so angry I ran into the . . . uh . . . what do you call it? . . . oh, yeah, the kitchen."

At a wedding feast recently the bridegroom was called upon, as usual, to respond to the given toast, in spite of the fact that he had previously pleaded to be excused. Blushing to the roots of his hair, he rose to his feet. He intended to imply that he was unprepared for speech-making, but he unfortunately place his hand upon his bride's shoulder, and looked down at her as he stammered out his opening and concluding words: "This-er-thing has been forced upon me."

"What I mean is," explained the insurance salesman to a bewildered rural prospect, "How would your wife carry on if you should die?"

"Well," answered the farmer reasonably, "I don't reckon that's any concern o'mine—so long as she behaves herself while I'm alive."

Somebody hit the nail on the head when he said, "Some men succeed because of application—that is, the one they signed for a marriage license."

CARTOON. Man consulting with psychiatrist: "Doctor, my wife has developed an inferiority complex. I want to know how to keep her that way."

Asked how he met expenses, the man explained that his wife had introduced him to them.

If your wife no longer gets suspicious when you come home late, it's later than you think.

A week after the robbery, a young wife called the police to report several valuable items missing. The investigating officer asked, "Why did you wait a week? When you found all of your bureau drawers pulled out and clothing scattered around, didn't you suspect a burglar had done it?"

"Why, no, Officer," she replied, "I just thought my husband had been looking for a clean shirt."

✦ Any man who thinks he's more intelligent than his wife is married to a smart woman.

Two friends met on a downtown street one evening. They had not seen one another for years, and they decided to sit and exchange stories of the past. They were not aware of how quickly time was passing.

They left for home, but both of them were a little fearful of what their wives would say about their coming in so late. The next day they met again. One asked, "How did your wife take your coming in so late?" "Oh," replied the other, "I explained it to her and it was all right. What about your wife?"

"Well," he replied, "when I came in my wife got historical."

"You mean 'hysterical,' don't you?" his friend asked.

"No," he replied, "I mean 'historical.' She brought up everything that has happened in the past thirty years."

I like what one farm lady said to her pharmacist:

"Now, be sure and write plain on them bottles which is for the horse and which is for my husband. I don't want nothin' to happen to that horse before the spring plowin'.

A doctor was talking to my wife about my condition when I was in the hospital for a checkup. "I don't like the looks of your husband," he said.

"I don't either," the woman said, "but I could have done worse. He has a good job and is nice to the children."

I heard about one woman whose dog had puppies. Her husband got furious with the litter underfoot. They were trying to sell the puppies, but they weren't moving. Finally, the husband issued an ultimatum. "Advertise and get rid of these puppies — either they go or I go!" Soon an ad appeared in the newspaper: "My husband says either he goes or puppies go. Puppies are adorable, fat, pedigreed. Husband is rude, fat, mixed breed. Take your pick."

A newlywed was bragging at the office how his new bride was. He said, "Every night when I get home she has everything out, the evening paper is at my easy chair, the dinner is on the stove and there's always plenty of hot water." They said, "What's the hot water for?" and he said, "You don't think she'd make me do the dishes in cold water, do ya?"

Jokes about husbands and wives are always popular. Like this One: "Last night my wife and I had a terrible argument. Afterwards she came crawling to me on her hands and knees. 'Get out from under that bed, you coward,' she screamed."

Late one night she whispered in his ear, "I hear a burglar downstairs. He's eating some of the casserole we had for supper." "Leave him alone," her husband replied, "I'll bury him in the morning."

Here's one to share with your wife. "Some wag has dubbed the Pope's latest encyclical on birth control. 'Pope Paul's Epistle to the Fallopians.' "

One wife has found the secret of a harmonious marriage. She always laughs at her husband's jokes. They aren't clever, but she is.

A Kansas cyclone lifted the house, picked up the man and wife sleeping in it, and gently set it down in the barnyard. The wife was weeping softly.
"Don't be scared," soothed the husband.
"I'm not," she replied. "I'm just so happy. It's the first time in 25 years that we've been out together."

"God help the man who won't marry until he finds the perfect woman, and God help him still more if he finds her."
—Benjamin Tillett

Which is worse—a wife driving from the back seat—or a husband cooking from the dining table?

The other day I heard a story about a salesman who came home from the office to find his house in complete disarray. His wife was usually a wonderful housekeeper, so he simply couldn't understand why everything was in such a mess. "What happened?" he asked in amazement. "Remember how you always ask, 'What could you possibly be doing all day?, " his wife replied. "Well, today I didn't do it!"
—Robert Schuller

There is a familiar cartoon about an elderly couple on a Sunday afternoon drive in their car. They are driving behind a cuddling young couple who are more interested in each other than they are in the road in front of them. The little old lady looks across at her husband behind the wheel of the car, then looks at the two young people in front of them, and asks her husband, "Why don't we sit together like that anymore?"

Quick as a flash the old man answers, "Well, dear, I haven't moved."

A husband stepped on the scales. The little card read: "You are intelligent, have a magnetic personality, strength of character; you are a leader of men, you are intelligent and handsome and attractive to the opposite sex." His wife said, "Hmph! It got your weight wrong too!"

One wife got tired of being called names by her husband. He was constantly embarrassing her by joking about her weight. One day he called her a stupid dingbat broad! He did not see her for three days! At the end of the third day he was able to open his left eye just enough to see her.

Andy explains to the Kingfish that the lodge meeting had been cancelled because, "the grand, exalted, almighty, supreme, invincible Potentate done got beat up by his wife last night."

"The evening my bride cooked her first dinner for me, I choked on a bone in the chocolate pudding."

—Woody Allen

Mrs. Smith wasn't talking with her husband much anymore and they decided counseling was in order. After six weeks the counselor was baffled and on the seventh week he asked Mr. Smith to come to the sessions with his wife. Once they were seated the counselor came over to Mrs. Smith and kissed her on the cheek. Mrs. Smith instantly came to life, hugged her husband, and told him all that had been happening over the past two months. Mr. Smith was shocked! When Mrs. Smith went to the waiting room, Mr. Smith said to the counselor, "I don't understand—what happened?"

"Don't you see?" the doctor blurted out, "your wife needs this kind of treatment Monday, Wednesday, and Friday!" Mr. Smith scratched his head in confusion and said, "Well, I can get her here on Monday and Wednesday, but I can't make it on Friday."

A Sunday School teacher was trying to demonstrate the difference between right and wrong.

"All right, children, let's take an example," she said. "If I were to go into a man's pocket and take his wallet with all his money, what would I be?"

A child in the back answered, "His wife."

As a result of receiving many irritating letters from his wife, a World War II soldier earnestly appealed, "For goodness' sakes, let me fight this war in peace!"

I know a couple who bought a new waterbed. They've been drifting apart ever since.

The golfer took off his hat as a funeral procession passed near by. "Why that's a mighty noble gesture," said his partner. "It's the least I could do," He said as he took his place at the next tee. "This Sunday we would have been married for 32 years."

Three stages of modern family life are matrimony, acrimony, and alimony.

–Virginian Pilot

"I once read of a nagging wife who hired a medium to bring back the spirit of her dead husband. When he appeared in a ghostly form, she asked, "Honey, is it really better up there?" Without hesitation, he answered, 'oh, yes, it is much better here, but I'm not up there!"

In a cemetery at Middlebury, VT., is a stone, erected by a widow to her living husband, bearing this inscription:
"Rest in peace—until we meet again."

A wife heard the voice of her husband muttering from the bathroom that his razor couldn't cut at all this morning.

"That's silly, John. Your beard couldn't be as tough as the kitchen linoleum!"

A visiting clergyman asked the young bride if she had ever cast her bread upon the waters.

"Not since my first batch," she replied proudly.

Wife to irate husband: "Normally, I wouldn't dream of opening a letter addressed to you, but this one was marked 'private.'"

A hotel reservation clerk opened one telegram and read: "Do you have any accommodation where I can put up with my wife?"

Married life ain't so bad after you get so you can eat the things your wife likes.

—Frank McKinney Hubbard

Nobody enjoys a wedding but the bride's mother — she likes a good cry.

—R. W. Kauffman

He took her hand in marriage, but made a basic blunder of letting her retain a thumb to keep him under.

There is some wisdom to the observation: "If it weren't for marriage, husbands and wives would have to fight with strangers."

GREEK WISDOM: In ancient Greece, a man getting a divorce could not marry a woman younger than his first wife.

Internal Revenue service auditor to nervous citizen: "Let's begin with where you claim depreciation on your wife."

When Sam Jones was holding his meetings in Dallas, on one occasion he said: "There's no such thing as a perfect man. Anybody present who has ever known a perfect man, stand up."

Nobody stood up.

"Those who have ever known a perfect woman, stand up."

One demure little woman stood up.

"Did you ever know an absolutely perfect woman?" asked Sam, somewhat amazed.

"I didn't know her personally," replied the little old woman, "but I have heard a great deal about her. She was my husband's first wife."

You probably heard about the newlyweds. On their honeymoon, the groom took his bride by the hand and said, "Now that we're married, dear, I hope you won't mind if I mention a few little defects that I've noticed about you."

"Not at all," the bride replied with a deceptive sweetness. "It was those little defects that kept me from getting a better husband."

I asked a Burmese why women, after centuries of following their men, now walked ahead. He said there were many unexploded land mines since the war.

—Robert Mueller

You know that story about the Vermont farmer who was the silent type. He and his wife got to their golden wedding anniversary and finally he broke into a speech, a long speech for him. He said to his wife: "Sarah, I have loved you so much that sometimes I could hardly keep from telling you."

It's doubtful if any husband is as good as his wife thought him to be before marriage, or as bad as she thinks he is afterward.

On his 30th wedding anniversary, honest John was heard to say that he'd been happily married for at least 15 years.

One poor man was short and fat; he was also bald and middle-aged. One morning he and his wife were walking down the street, when suddenly the man turned a beaming countenance to his wife and said, "Did you see that pretty girl smile at me?"

"Oh, that's nothing, "said his wife, "The first time I saw you I laughed right out loud."

Did you know the best way for a housewife to have a few minutes to herself is at the close of the day to start doing the dishes?

"Does your wife like housework?"
"She likes *nothing* better!"

Marriages may be made in heaven, but man is responsible for the maintenance work.

Changing Times Magazine

OVERHEARD: "I married her because we have so many faults in common."

Anon.

A wife complained to her husband: "Look at the old clothes I have to wear. If anyone came to visit they would think I was the cook."
The husband replied, "Well, they'd change their minds if they stayed for dinner."

Many a man in love with a dimple makes the mistake of marrying the whole girl.

—Ring Lardner

He: "Our marriage is a continual puzzle."
She: "Yeah, peace is missing."

Did you hear about the German who made his living by the sweat of his frau?

Marriage has always been a fertile ground for humorist. I get a chuckle out of the story about a couple who had been married for over seventy years. The man was one hundred and one years old. His wife was ninety-nine. One hot afternoon they sat on the front porch rocking. The old man was nearly deaf. The wife looked over at him with admiration in her eyes and said, "Zeke, I'm proud of you." He looked around and said, "What's that you say, May?" she raised her voice, "I'm proud of you!" He looked away."I'm tired of you too, May," he said.

128

I heard about another man who was crying on his friend's shoulder. "My wife deserted me," moaned the unhappy husband. "She took the car and ran off with a traveling salesman."

"Why, that's terrible!" exclaimed his friend, aghast. "Your brand new car!"

Men are not the only ones who can use humor to make a point. I just read about a thrifty young woman who became concerned over the lavish amount of money her boyfriend was spending on her. After an expensive dinner date, she asked her mother, "What can I do to stop Tom from spending so much money on me?"

Her mother replied simply, "Marry him."

Humor has been a time-honored way for us to deal with conflict between husbands and wives. Dr. I. E. Gates, former president of Wayland Baptist College, tells the little story of a blackmailer. A man received a letter from him which said, "If you do not place five thousand dollars in a hollow stump (naming the location of the stump) by six o'clock tomorrow afternoon, I am going to kidnap your wife."

To this letter the man replied, "Dear Mr. Kidnapper: I haven't the five thousand dollars to do as you requested, but your proposition does interest me."

Mark Clark, the military general, was asked what was the best advice he ever had. The general pondered for a few moments and then he replied, "Well, the best advice I ever had was to marry the girl I did. And then the young officer that asked Mark Clark that question said "Well, sir, who gave you that advice?" And General Clark replied, "She did."

Every wife recognizes the painful truth behind the way one person described marriage: "When a man makes a woman his wife, it's the highest compliment he can pay her, and it's usually the last."

Here's one to share with your spouse: One comedian said his mother had 14 children and they all put her on a pedestal.

"We had to do something to keep her away from Dad," he added.

The small cartoon, "*A Little Leary*" once said, "Marriage is when a man takes a girl off a pedestal and puts her on a budget."

Man and woman married 50 years are asked the secret of their marital bliss. "Well," drawled the old man, "the wife and I had an agreement when we first got married. The agreement was that when she was bothered about something, I was to take a walk. I suppose you can attribute our marital success to the fact that I have largely led an outdoor life."

Cecil Osborne, author of *Release From Fear and Anxiety*, relates an incident in his own life. He and his wife had been married 16 years. Every Thanksgiving they had driven 800 miles so they could spend the holidays with her parents. He had no particular desire to drive 1600 miles round trip to visit her family, but it gave her so much pleasure that he "manfully put up with the annual ordeal." Finally, on the sixteenth trip, he admitted to her how he had begun to resent the trips. She replied, "You mean you've been doing this all these years for me? Good grief, I've hated it! I thought you were the one who enjoyed it so much!"

—Rev. Dan Emmitte

My wife and I are avid sailors. When not on a boat, we're reading about boats. One day I noticed a card my wife had filled out. As a gift to me, she was ordering a subscription to a sailing magazine. On the line asking how the gift card was to be signed, she had written: "First Mate, and Last."

—Russell H Matson in *Reader's Digest*

There were two porcupines living in Alaska. It was very cold. To keep warm, they decided to draw close together, but when they did that, they needled one another. So they pulled apart. But again they got cold. And so they moved close again, and they got needled. Poor porcupines! They were continuously either cold, or else needling one another.

That's the way some people live in their homes. At a distance they are lonely and cold. But when they draw near, they needle and hurt each other. Raymond C. Orthund, *Lord, Make My Life a Miracle* (Ventusa, Ca: Regal Books, 1974).

I like the story of the wife who went to the police station with her next-door neighbor to report that her husband was missing. The policeman asked for a description. She said, "He's 35 years old, 6 foot 4, had dark eyes, dark wavy hair, an athletic build, weighs 185 pounds, is soft-spoken, and is good to the children." The next-door neighbor protested, "Your husband if 5 foot 4, chubby, bald, has a big mouth, and is mean to your children." The wife replied, "Yes, but who wants HIM back?"

Funnyman Berl Williams recalls the time his wife entered a room with her head bristled with pink plastic curlers. He claims to have asked, "What happened to your head?" Replied she, "I set it." Countered he, "What time does it go off?"

Someone has described a wedding ring as a "small gold band that cuts off your circulation."

One of the television networks put on a documentary about the Kentucky mountain folks, and they brought to New York a man who had spent his entire life in the mountains. The visitor was absolutely amazed at all he saw around him.

His eyes popped as he saw a little old lady enter an elevator in the lobby of the RCA building. The door closed, the little red light blinked, and she was gone. Then, he almost dropped dead in surprise when, a minute later, the same door opened and out stepped a gorgeous young blonde.

"You just can't beat science," he said. "If I'd a known about that contraption, I'd have brung along my old woman."

CARTOON: Couple leaving marriage counselor's office: "Now that we've learned to communicate, shut up."

Evangelist Tex Evans used to tell a joke on himself which relates that one of his youngsters asked his wife, "Mamma, if Daddy should die, do you reckon there's another man in the world just like him?" And his mother answered, "Maybe there is, son. And it would be just my luck to get him."

The minister had reached that portion of the marriage ceremony where he said, ". . . and do you take this woman for better or for worse, for richer or for poorer, through sickness and in health, in good times and in bad, in . . . "

"Please," whispered the bride almost in tears, "if you aren't careful, you're going to talk him out of it."

Ann Landers once said, "Television has proved that people will look at anything rather than each other."

"Keep your eyes wide open before marriage," suggested Ben Franklin, "half shut afterwards."

—Poor Richard's Almanac, 1738

"My wife and I have our differences. But, like a Californian after an earthquake, we always say, 'With all your faults, I love you still.' "

—Contributed

The desk clerk soothed the irate husband. "We'll put you in the bridal suite."

"Ridiculous!" the husband exploded. "We've been married for fifteen years."

"So?" commented the clerk. "If I put you in the ballroom, you wouldn't have to dance, would you?"

Only two things are necessary to keep one's wife happy. The first is to let her think she's having her own way. The second is to let her have it.

—Lyndon B. Johnson

Jim: "What's the matter?"
Slim: "I just lost three wives in three months."
Jim: "What happened?"
Slim: "The first one died from eating poisoned mushrooms."
Jim: "What about the second one?"
Slim: "Same thing. Poisoned mushrooms."
Jim: "And the third one?"
Slim: "Fractured skull . . . she wouldn't eat the poisoned mushrooms."

An alert insurance salesman called on a young man shortly after he had returned from his honeymoon. "Now that you are married," he said, "I am sure that you will want to take out more insurance on yourself."

"I don't think I need any more," the young man said. "I don't think she is that dangerous."

I asked a Burmese why women, after centuries of following their men, now walked ahead. He said there were many unexploded land mines since the war.

—Robert Mueller

In Bob Mumford's book, *Living Happily Ever After,* he relates a problem that arose between himself and his wife, and they decided to pray about it. He says, " 'O God, change that woman,' went up my impassioned plea. From the next room came an equally sincere petition, 'O God, change that man You gave me.' "

– Bob Mumford, *Living Happily Ever After* (Old Tappan, N.J.: Fleming H. Revell Company, 1973), p. 21.

The 8-year-old boy arrived home from school with a note from his teacher.
"Although your little boy is quite bright," it read, "he spends far too much time fooling around with the girls. But I have a plan which will break him of this habit."
The child's mother sent him back to school with a note addressed to the teacher. "Let me know how your plan works out," it said. "I'll try it out on his father."

Martin Buxbaum tells of two women overheard discussing marriage at a party. One of the women said, "My husband and I have managed to be happy together for twenty years. I guess this is because we're both in love with the same man."

A reporter asked Henry Ford when he celebrated his golden wedding anniversary: "To what do you attribute your fifty years of successful married life?" Ford replied, "The formula is the same I've used in the making of cars-- stick to one model!"

A Joe Mirachi cartoon (*Parade*) has a counselor tell a couple: "Quite frankly, I don't think either of you would be compatible with ANYBODY!"

A fine young man came into his uncle's office and said, "Uncle, I am deeply in love with a beautiful young lady. How can I know what she really thinks of me?"
The wise uncle said, "marry her, my boy, marry her."

The wife said to her hubby, "The two best things I cook are meat loaf and apple dumplings."
He sheepishly replied, "Well, which is this?"

A man came home from work one day to find his house in shambles. The beds hadn't been made, the kitchen sink was filled with dirty dishes, the children's clothes and toys and books were scattered throughout the house. Besides that, dinner wasn't ready.

"What in the world happened?" the man asked his wife when he saw the mess.

"Nothing," she said, "absolutely nothing. You are always wondering what I do all day long. Well, take a look. Today, I didn't do it."

I heard about one mean old mountaineer who fell sick and was thought to have died. There were no funeral directors back in the hills then, and embalming was not yet practiced. So the widow and family dressed the body and placed it in the coffin. As the deceased was being carried from the house, one pallbearer stumbled, causing the coffin to crash into a gatepost. The knock somehow revived the old mountaineer, who sat up yelling at everyone in sight.

The man lived for over a year and was as mean as ever. Then he got sick and did die. Once more the body was put in the coffin and the pallbearers lifted their burden. As they shuffled by, the long-suffering widow lifted her head and said, "Watch out for that gatepost!'

"The only person who listens to both sides of a husband-and-wife argument is the woman in the next apartment."

--Sam Levenson

An old lady tottered into a lawyers's office and asked for help in arranging for a divorce. The lawyer just didn't believe it. "Tell me," he said, "how old are you?"

"Eighty-four," she said. "And my husband is eighty-seven."

"How long have you been married?"

"Almost 62 years."

The lawyer slapped his forhead. "Married 62 years? Why do you want a divorce now?"

"Because," she said, "enough is enough."

--Ray and Ortland, *The Best Half of Life* (Waco: Word Books, 1975).

I also heard a story this week about Adam and Eve. It seems that Eve got worried that Adam had an extra woman on the side and she complained to him about it. He said, "Now Eve, you know we are alone in this garden." With that he went on to bed and to sleep. In the middle of the night he woke up and saw Eve standing there over him, and he wondered what in the world she was doing. He asked her, and she said, "I'm counting your ribs."

A group of high school seniors went to New York for their senior trip. They had engaged rooms in one of the finest hotels. When they arrived in the city they went to the hotel and registered. They were assigned a room on the 30th floor. After getting settled in their rooms they went out to see the sights. They went to Manhattan, the Empire State Building, the Statue of Liberty, etc. Finally they came back to their hotel, utterly exhausted. They went to the desk and asked for the key to their rooms. The clerk said, "I am sorry, the elevators are not running. You will have to walk up or wait until the elevators are repaired. They thought of the Beauty Rest mattresses in their room. Tired as they were they decided they would climb the thirty flights of stairs. One of them had an idea. He said, "On the way up each of us will tell the funniest story we know for ten stories." The other two agreed and they started the climb. When they reached the tenth floor they were still going strong. When they reached the twentieth floor their legs were like lead and they were panting for breath. The steps got longer and longer but they trudged on. The one whose turn it was to tell the funny stories said, "I'm sorry, I'm just too exhausted to laugh." They trudged on in silence. When they reached the 29th floor one of them began to laugh. He sat down on the steps and almost had hysterics. Finally, he said, "I have just thought of the funniest things I have ever heard of in my life." They said, "What is it? Tell us!" He said, "We left the key in the lobby."

Many of us have lost the key to the meaning of our lives . . . .

I wish that life was as easily explained as that great philosopher of the comic strips, Charlie Brown, once deduced that it was.

Lucy is saying to him, "Life is a mystery Charlie Brown . . . Do you know the answer?" Charlie Brown answers, "Be kind. Don't smoke. Be prompt. Smile a lot. Eat sensibly. Avoid cavities and mark your ballot carefully . . . Avoid too much sun. Send overseas packages early. Love all creatures above and below. Insure your belongings and try to keep the ball low . . ." Before he can get out another platitude, Lucy interrupts: "Hold real still," she says, "because I am going to hit you a very sharp blow upon the nose!"

During the early part of the Vietnam War we heard reports of "light at the end of the tunnel." That hope never materialized. A cartoon in *The New Yorker* shows a dejected man emerging from a tunnel. Why is he downcast? The caption reads, "DISCOVERING THAT THE LIGHT AT THE END OF THE TUNNEL IS NEW JERSEY."

A cartoon in *The New Yorker* shows two women who have met at a restaurant. One woman says, "Lately I've been very happy, but I don't know if it's me or vitamins."

135

A cartoon showed a mother and her little boy visiting a museum of modern art. They were standing in front of a painting entitled "Black on Black." The wise little boy exclaimed to his mother, "Oh, look, Mommy, it lost its picture!" That is constantly the temptation and the tendency of modern folks. At times we lose the picture. . .

A boy received a nice guitar for Christmas. He put his hands on the fret and held it in one fixed position while he strummed on the instrument hour upon hour. His father became vexed with him and said, "Son, you are supposed to move your left hand up and down the neck of the guitar and produce new sounds. Chet Atkins and Les Paul, the great guitarists do that." The little boy replied, "Well, Dad, they run their left hand up and down because they are still looking for it—I found it."

There's an amusing little story about vision—or lack of it—in William Marsteller's book, *Creative Management*. It's about the two old men who met every day in front of the Plaza Hotel. They would sit side-by-side and say very little for hours at a time.

Finally, one of them said to the other: "Life is like a fountain."

After a long pause, the other said, "So, why is life like a fountain."

After an even longer pause, the first one said, "Well, maybe you're right, maybe life isn't like a fountain after all!"

I like the story of the little boy who came to his father and asked him, "Dad, who made God?" The father, engrossed in the evening paper, responded, "Beats me, son." The little boy would not be put off. "Dad, why is the earth round?" The dad answered, "I don't know, son." The boy played for a minute, then asked, "Dad, is there life on other planets?" The father patiently answered, "Nobody knows the answer to that." Finally the boy asked his father, "Dad, do you mind me asking you all these questions?" The father put down his paper, "Why, not at all, son," he said, "How else are you going to learn?"

There's a cartoon strip with a picture of a little girl who sets up a psychiatric booth which says "Psychotherapy - 5 cents." In Los Angeles a chaplain at a college has set up a booth which says "Spiritual Counseling - 5 cents," and he says that one of his most frequent questions is "What is the meaning of life?" The answer to that ought to be worth at least 5 cents.

— David Brinkley, "NBC Nightly News"

Finding a Cure

Dr. John Haggai tells a story about a man who sped up
asked the druggist if he had anything for the hiccups. The
word, hit the man between the eyes and knocked him down.
up and asked again, "Sir, do you have anything for the hiccups'

The druggist replied, "You don't have them anymore, do you?"

The man replied, "No, I never did, but my wife out in the car does."

Hospitalized man to wife: "Do you have any idea what it does to somebody
to be 'W. J. Hambley, Senior Vice President' one minute and 'the gall bladder in
403' the next?"

– Burbank in *The Lion*

"Dr. Abernethy," said a patient, "I have something the matter, Sir, with
this arm. There, oh! (making a particular motion with the limb). That, Sir gives
me great pain."

"Well, what a fool you must be to do it then," said Dr. Abernethy.

– *The Memoirs of John Abernethy* (1764-1831)

"In fast time or slow,
There's no longer minute
Than the one the doctor
Will be with you in it."

Nervous patient: "Doctor, I often feel like killing myself. What shall I do?"
Doctor: "Leave it to me."

A doctor was talking to a new patient the other day. In great alarm, the
patient mentioned a rare and deadly disease of the liver and claimed to be suffering from it. "Nonsense!" protested the doctor. "You are not suffering from that.
In fact, you wouldn't know whether you had it or not. It is a disease which gives
no discomfort at all."

"That's just it!" gasped the poor patient. "My last doctor told me that. That
is how I know I have it. I feel quite well!"

"I am very sorry to tell you," said the doctor. "You are very sick and may have long to live. Is there someone you would like for me to call?"

The man grew pale. "Yes," he whispered. "Another doctor."

I still chuckle over Rodney Dangerfield's report from his psychiatrist. "You're crazy," the psychiatrist said. Dangerfield protested, "If you don't mind, I want a second opinion." The psychiatrist said, "All right. You're ugly too."

Two doctors were talking. The first said, "I operated on him for appendicitis." The second rejoined, "What was the matter with him?"

A minor operation is one performed on someone else.

After giving the woman a full medical examination, the doctor explained his prescription as he wrote it out.

"Take the green pill with a glass of water after getting up. Take the blue pill with a glass of water after lunch. Then, just before going to bed, take the red pill with another glass of water."

"Exactly what is my problem, doctor? the woman asked.

"You're not drinking enough water," he said.

— Contributed

"Doctor," called a frantic young man over the phone, "my father's at death's door!"

"Now don't get excited, son," soothed the doctor. "I'll be right over and pull him through."

Houston — *(The L. P. Times)* — The medical community was thrilled today to learn that researchers have discovered a cure for which there is no known disease.

— Dr. Laurence J. Peter

"Open wide," commanded the dentist as he began examining a new patient. "Good grief!" he said. "You've got the biggest cavity I've ever seen . . . the biggest cavity I've ever seen!"

"You don't have to repeat it," snapped the annoyed patient.

"I didn't ," said the dentist. "That was an echo."

138

One politician to another: "We must push the health program. Getting people to live longer is the easiest way to get more taxes out of them."

Conversation between doctor and patient.
"You're in bad shape. You need an operation."
"How much will it cost?"
"Eight thousand dollars."
"Gee, doc, I don't have that kind of money."
"I'll make it easy for you. Give me $3000 down and pay me $100 a month until the bill is paid."
"That's like buying a new car!"
"I am."

—The Lion

A friend of ours told a friend of hers that perhaps phenobarbital would help her get relaxed at night. "It's not habit-forming," she said. "I know. I've been taking it for twelve years."

Doctor: Have you any aches or pains this morning?
Patient: Yes, Doctor, it hurts me to breathe. In fact, the only trouble now seems to be with my breathing.
Doctor: All right. I'll give you something that will stop that.

It was a busy day at the doctor's office. One elderly patient had to wait an unusually long time. The doctor was very apologetic. Replied the oldster, "Oh, I didn't mind, Doc, but I thought you would prefer treating my ailment in its earlier stages."

Doctor: What was the most you ever weighed?
Patient: 192 pounds.
Doctor: And what was the least you ever weighed?
Patient: 9½ pounds.

"Miracle drugs won't help you," the doctor told his elderly patient. "Go to the country, get plenty of rest, eat nutritious foods and smoke only one cigar a day."
"A month later, the patient returned in radiant health.
"Your advice is wonderful," reported the patient. "I rested, ate well and did the other things you recommended, but smoking that one cigar a day was a dilly. To start smoking at my age is nearly impossible."

A sad and bedraggled man approached the most famous and expensive doctor in the city and admitted right off that he could not afford to pay his $1000 fee. The doctor was feeling mellow, so he reduced his fee to $500. "But, Doctor," begged the sick man, "I have a wife and seven kids to support," and so the fee was brought down to $250. The man sighed, "For me that's food for my kids for a week." Finally the doctor said $150 and at the stricken look on the man's face said, "I know when I'm beat — fifty dollars. Only first, tell me this: I am known as the top doctor in the city, the most expensive one in 100 miles, why did you come to me?" "Because," answered the man emphatically, " where my health is concerned, money is no object."

"How long will it take to pull my tooth?" the patient asked the dentist. "Only two seconds." "How much will it cost?" "Twenty-five dollars." "For only two seconds of work?" "Well," the dentist answered cooly, "I can pull it very slowly if you prefer."

My doctor is so polite. Just before my surgery he tapped me on the shoulder. "May I cut in?" he asked.

When the hypochondriac died at the age of 96, he had inscribed on his tombstone. "I told you I was sick."

Doctors are extremely expensive these days. A few weeks ago I fell down a flight of stairs and hurt my leg, so I went to a doctor. He fixed me right up and said "Don't worry. You'll be walking before the day is over."
Brother, was he right! . . . I had to sell my car in order to pay him!

And Charlie, who had a swinging reputation, went to his doctor for a physical checkup. As he put his shirt back on, he asked, "Well, Doc, do I have to give up wine, women, and song?"
"Not exactly, Charlie," said the doctor. "You can sing all you want to."

A young doctor was complaining to an older colleague: "Every time I go to a party, someone comes up to me wanting free medical advice. It is so annoying." The older doctor replied, "I solved that long ago with one word — undress."

A cartoon shows an affluent matron, well groomed, with an expensive fur stole, in a strange role. Walking up and down the street, she carries a placard which says, "Will Somebody Please Explain What's Going On?"
She's not the only one confused today!

PEOPLE WERE AMAZED 75 years ago when cars went 15 miles per hour . . . they still are!

Little boy to work-bound father: "Daddy, please bring me home a rat from the race today."

Sometimes it seems nothing works out right. In the part of town where you can park as long as you want to, you don't want to.

TV is good for your health. Skip it and get a good night's sleep.

Did you know — a utility pole never hits a car except in self-defense?

ON WALL OF TRAFFIC BUREAU: "Drive safely and avoid the mourning after."

A speeding lady told the traffic officer. "I was trying to get to the super-market before the prices changed again!"

Live to 90? If you want to, don't look for it on your speedometer!

Experts predict that eventually every home will have a computer, which means that our personal lives will be just as messed up as things at the office.

The story is told about a great theologian in times past who jumped into a cab and yelled at the driver, " Get going!" Ten minutes later he asked, "Are we nearly there?" and the driver asked, "Nearly where? You didn't tell me where it was you wanted to go."

Someone saw this sign in a public park: "No ball playing. No bicycle riding. No pets. No running. Remember this is your park."

I read a story about a patrolman who arrived at the scene of an accident to find a woman lying unconscious a few feet from an automobile. A small crowd had gathered, and a man was trying feverishly to revive the woman.

"Who was driving this car?" the patrolman asked.

"I was," said the man who was helping the woman.

"How did you hit her?" the patrolman asked.

"Oh, I didn't hit her," the man said. "As I approached the intersection I saw that she was trying to cross the street. So, I stopped for her to cross. She was so surprised that she fainted."

I chuckled at a story about a priest who was trying to institute some liturgical reform in his very old-fashioned parish. He was teaching them the new responses. He said to them, "When I say, 'The Lord be with you,' you will reply all together, 'And with you also.' Then I will say, 'Let us pray.' " The day came for the introduction of the new liturgy. Something happened to the microphone, and the priest was trying to adjust it. He said in a loud voice, "There is something wrong with this microphone." And the congregation responded with one loud voice, "And with you also!"

A cartoon by Michael Masline appeared in the *New Yorker* (April 6, 1981) some years back. It shows a middle-class man, in a middle-class living room, watching a middle-class television set. On the screen is a large pot, and a voice behind the pot says, "How much would you pay for all the secrets of the universe? Wait, don't answer yet. You also get this six-quart covered combination spaghetti pot and clam steamer. Now how much would you pay?"

Our horror story for the week is the one about the world's largest electronic brain, now ready for action. Twenty years to build, two stories high, a block long, 3,000,000 transistors, 7,000 miles of memory tape—and everything humming smoothly, awaiting a question. The top-ranking scientists in the world all gather together, and after hours of deliberation they settle on one question, the most difficult one they can think of: "Is there a God?" A technician feeds it into the brain and suddenly wheels begin to turn, tubes pulsate, counters click-- and three words appear on the answer tape. "There is now!"

Famous Fibs:
* I'll start my diet tomorrow.
* We service what we sell.
* Let's have lunch sometime.
* We'll keep your resume on file.
* Your table will be ready in a few minutes.
—Gene Brown in Danbury, Conn. News-Times.

Thomas Huxley, the English psychologist, jumped in a cab once and shouted to the driver, "Drive fast!" After a block he said, "Do you know where you're going?" "No," said the driver, "But I'm driving fast!"

A man was driving through a very dense fog. The only object that he could see clearly was the tailights of the car ahead, so he decided for safety sake he would follow those lights to be certain that he stayed on the road, Suddenly, without warning, the tailights ahead came to a complete stop and he ran into the driver he had been following. "Why didn't you give some kind of signal that you were going to stop?" he shouted angrily at the other driver. "Why should I?" came the reply, "I was in my own garage."

Charged with ignoring a "Don't Walk" sign, one pedestrian came up with a novel excuse—he claimed he saw the sign but thought it was an advertisement for a cab company!

An Indian on a reservation keeps sending out smoke signals. A tourist passes by. He questions the Indian: "What did you say?" The Indian: "Nothing yet. That was only the area code."

We had a smart aleck apply for a job here last week. Where the application form asked for age he wrote, "Atomic." Under church preference he wrote, "Colonial with white columns, if possible." Under marital status, he wrote, "Shaky." Where we asked salary desired, he wrote, "Yes."

Anyone who isn't confused isn't thinking clearly.

--Claire Booth Luce

Remember when it was the doctor who wanted to know if the patient had insurance?

A few years back, when there were frequent reports that flying objects of round saucer-like shape had been seen here and there in different parts of the Western World, an army parachutist was driven from the course of his natural landing in a military field where he would have been picked up by his unit. He, with others, had been engaging in maneuvers. The wind carried him over a neighboring farm. The farmer and his wife were in the yard cooking steaks over a grill. The soldier landed. As he approached the couple in his heavy garments, dragging his parachute behind him, with a green helment on his head and a light in the center of it, he inquired of the couple, "Where am I?" To which, the elderly women, in shock, I presume, replied, "Earth."
William R. Cannon, *Evangelism in a Contemporary Context* (Nashville: Tidings).

The U.S. is the only country where a housewife hires a woman to do her cleaning so she can do volunteer work at the nursery where the cleaning woman leaves her child.

—Helen Bender

It's inflation when you have to pay $5 for the $2 haircut you used to get for $1 when you had hair.

—Franklin P. Jones in *Quote Magazine*

The world has so many problems, if Moses had come down from Mt. Sinai today, the two tablets he carried would be aspirin.

Because of urban problems, many businessmen have decided to move their companies to the suburbs. One of the cities that has been hit hard in this respect is Detroit. In fact, at a recent banquet of the Detroit Press Club, a banner in the dining room read: "WILL THE LAST COMPANY TO LEAVE DETROIT PLEASE TURN OFF THE LIGHTS?"

Larry Lacour tells of the telephone executive who went to a doctor. The physician listened to the heart and reported to his patient, "All I get is the busy signal."

Author Anthony Burgess has put it this way:
"You can turn a treatise on municipal drainage into a best seller by calling it 'Odor or Sanctity' and attributing it to an unreformed prostitute."

A junior executive complained to his wife of aches and pains. This went on for two weeks. One day he returned home feeling better.
"I found out what was wrong," he told his wife. "We got some ultramodern office furniture two weeks ago, and I just learned that I've been sitting in a wastebasket."

Several years ago there was a *Hagar the Horrible* cartoon. Hagar is evidently singing a cheerful drinking tune as he lies in front of a keg of wine cradling a bag of money to his chest. The words of the song go like this:
"Oh, words of love--Oh, words divine,
The silver thought, the golden line,
Of all men's words, There's none so fine,
As these three words . . . 'I got mine.' "
A similar message was contained in a *Funky Winkerbean* cartoon strip by Tom Batiuk. The dean of the college, attired in mortar board and gown, is speaking to the graduation class. "I know we face a world of crisis," he complains, "Crucial shortages and a radical change in lifestyles. Even so, I still think your senior class could come up with a better motto, 'Get yours while there's still some left!' "

145

Said one New Yorker to another, "Can you tell me how to get to Central Park?"
"No."
"Okay, I'll mug you here."

-Henry Youngman

"Today, we're worrying about shortages of things our grandparents never heard of."

Conversation overheard on campus:
"Where's Mike today?"
"Oh, I'm not going with him anymore."
"How come?"
"He's so boring. I mean, all he talks about is relevance."
"Relevance! What's that got to do with anything?"

A Housing Development is where they cut all the trees and then name streets after them.

You may have heard about the beleaguered small businessman who was filling out his hundred-and-forty-seventh federal form of the year and came to the item, "Number of employees; broken down by sex." He pondered a bit and filled in "None so far as I know. Our problem here seems to be alcohol."

You can't fool all the people all the time. That's why we need a two-party system to get the job done.

—Mark Twain

You have probably heard a tale told by Sir Arthur Lewis, a Nobel Laureate in economics. Professor Lewis' story concerns a discussion among a sociologist, a physician, an engineer, and an economist about which is the world's oldest profession.
"Wrong." said the physician. "Since God took a rib from Adam and created Eve, surgery is the oldest profession."
The engineer wouldn't buy that at all. He said that "since God created an orderly universe out of chaos, engineering is the oldest profession.
But the economist had the last word. He asked, "Who do you suppose created the chaos?"

Dagwood turns away from his desk with a look of triumph and says to Blondie, "We finished the month with money left over."

Blondie: "Then here's some more bills I've been saving."

Dagwood, looking crestfallen, "That's the trouble with the rat race. There's never a finish line."

A terrible thing happened to me last week. I tried to live within my means and was picked up for vagrancy.

—Bob Orben

I saw a new book just this week entitled **How to be Happy Without Money.** I would have bought it, but it cost $15.

Postage rates keep rising. Stamps aren't the only things taking a licking.

One comedian says he buys things on the "Lay awake" plan. He "lays awake" each evening trying to figure out how he will pay for it.

Stephen Olford tells about a circus athlete who earned his living by displaying astonishing feats of physical strength. His show would normally conclude with a simple, but impressive, demonstration of his ability to squeeze an orange dry! After completing his act, he would then challenge his audience to produce any one who could extract even one drop of juice from the crushed fruit.

On one of these occasions, a little man volunteered. He was so diminutive that his very appearance raised a laugh from the spectators. Undaunted however, the man stepped onto the stage and took from the athlete what appeared to be nothing more than a shriveled up piece of rind. Then, bracing himself, he slowly and firmly compressed his right hand. Every eye was on him, and the atmosphere was electric! A moment or two elapsed, and then, to everyone's amazement — and not least the athlete — a drop of orange juice formed and dripped to the floor. As the cheers subsided, the athlete beckoned the man to come forward, asked his name, and then invited him to tell the crowd how he had managed to develop such fistic powers. "Nothing to it," replied the man; and then, with a grin, he added: "I happen to be the treasurer of the local Baptist Church!"

147

The salesman was trying to sell a home freezer. "You'll save enough on your food bill to pay for it," he said.

"I can understand that," the husband said, "but we're paying for our car on the busfare we save, and on our washing machine on the laundry money we save and on our house on the rent we save. Right now our monthly payments are so high that we just can't afford to save any more money."

Who can ever forget comedian Jack Benny and his attachment to money? A hold-up man demands, "Your money or your life!" Jack, with hand to cheek after a long pause, "I'm thinking. I'm thinking!"

A teacher was explaining to her class the importance of good penmanship. She advised, "If you can't write your name, when you grow up you'll have to pay for everything with cash!"

An economist went for a Sunday afternoon walk and somehow or another he encountered God on his walk. He didn't know what to say, and suddenly he remembered that as a little boy, someone had told him that a thousand years was like a minute to the Lord. So he asked the Lord if that was true. And the Lord said, "Yes, that's true." And the economist, by this time, had recovered his composure and said, "Then perhaps it may also be true that what is a million dollars to us is only a penny to you." And the Lord said, "Yes, that's certainly true." So the economist said, "Well, Lord, how about giving me one of those pennies." The Lord said, "Certainly, my dear fellow. I don't happen to have it on me, but if you'll wait a minute, I'll go fetch it."

Some persons are concerned about money almost to the point of desperation. A mail carrier tells of greeting a four-year-old boy who had planted himself firmly in front of his family's mailbox and would not budge. With his feet spread wide and his arms folded, he told the mail carrier firmly, "My mom says she can't TAKE any more bills."

A panhandler stopped a man and asked for a dime. The man said "A DIME? What can ya get for a dime? How about a quarter?" And the bum said, "To tell ya the truth, I can use it, but I don't wanna carry so much cash around with these characters on the streets."

148

"Business-expense tax exemptions are varied and profuse, but what about the cemetary plot salesman who daily records, 'Lunch with prospect?' "

One little boy asked his father if he could throw a silver dollar across the Potamac like George Washington. "Remember, son," said his father, "money doesn't go as far as it used to."

THE CYNIC WAS RIGHT. "most folk who slap us on the back expect us to cough something up."

I like the sign I saw on the front of one church: "You can't take it with you, but you can send it on ahead."

Someone described a poor fellow like this: "He's as broke as the Ten Commandments."

Red Foxx says he knew all there was to know about poverty He remembers his father saying, "The garbage man is here — better have him leave some."

Somebody put it rightly: "Almost everybody believes in tithing — a few even practice it."

Around April 15 we discover that America is the land of untold wealth.

INCOME TAX FORMS are a test of the "power of deduction."

Money still talks. Ususally it says "goodbye."

A New Yorker cartoon shows two wealthy middle-aged men looking at a cemetery from their limousine. Says one: "Kind of takes some of the fun out of being rich, eh, Hamilton?"

One man was asked, "what would you do if you had all the money in the world?" He replied, "I'd apply it to all my debts as far as it would go."

As Adlai Stevenson once put it, "There was a time when a fool and his money were soon parted, but now it happens to everybody."

E. Stanley Jones tells about a poor man who had an overnight guest, and as he showed him to his humble bedroom in the hayloft he said, "If there is anything you want, let us know, and we'll come and show you how to get along without it."

We are like the rich man who was so proud of his beautiful lawn. "I had these trees moved right here to my lawn," he boasted. "Had them set up in perfect geometrical pattern this way."
"My, my," murmured the pastor, "it just goes to show you what wonders God could perform if only He had money!"

The self-made millionaire was addressing the graduating class at the local university. He was talking about the motivational force that drove him, and he said, "All my success in life I owe to one thing—pluck. Pluck and more pluck." One of the young people came to him after the graduation ceremony was over and said, "That was a great speech, sir, but will you please tell us something about who to pluck and how?"

No subject has dominated the headlines over the past several months any more than the question of the economy. Inflation, stock market, unemployment seem to be on everyone's mind. I can sympathize with that. Do you remember the story that was popular a year or so ago about a pollster taking a survey of how much of people's income goes to different kinds of spending? The person being interviewed said, "I spend 40 percent of my income on housing, 20 percent on clothing, 40 percent on food, and 20 percent on transportation and amusement." The pollster said, "But sir, that adds up to 120 percent." the reply was, "I know it!"

A.J. Keate's cartoon wife agrees with a husband, whose arm is in a sling and total body wrapped in bandages while his leg is in traction: "You were right. Removing the cellar stairs light bulb saves us six cents a month."

150

A budget helps you pay as you go if you don't go anyplace.

A budget is what you stay within if you go without.

A New Zealand publication carried an intriguing advertisement of a "tested and proved" method for cutting household bills in half. It offered prospective customers the opportunity to get in on the secret for only $3. How could the promoters guarantee such fantastic results? That was what the police wanted to know. They found that the advertisers planned to send each customer a cheap pair of scissors.

"I don't know what I'll do with the wife asking for 50 dollars one day and 100 dollars another."
"What does she do with the money?" his friend asked.
"I couldn't tell you. I never give it to her."

Someone asked, "I wonder how much money billionaire Howard Hughes really left?" A wise friend replied, "He left it all."

A wealthy man many years ago was somewhat of a free spirit and requested a very special burial. After his death the burial took place as he had directed: donned in a sports jacket and hat, with his cigar in his mouth, he was placed in a sitting position at the wheel of his brand new red Cadillac convertible, with the speedometer set at 80 mph–then he was lowered into the tomb. A friend looked through his tears and said, "Man, that's living!"

Annoyed when a definitely intoxicated man boarded a bus at a late hour and slumped into the seat beside him, the lone passenger's apprehension increased when the drunk asked thickly, "Got any money?"
Seeking to head off a "touch," the man brusquely replied, "no."
Giving him a long look, the inebriated one leaned forward to intone loftily: "I should try to get some if I were you. You would find it very useful."

There's something to be said for people who put their money in mattresses. They have something to fall back on.

Don't knock inflation. Without it, we wouldn't be able to afford today's prices.

—Al Batt

Every morning at his office building entrance, the executive gave the sidewalk vendor a dime, but never took the pencils offered.

One day after making his usual donation, he felt a light tap on his shoulder. "I'm sorry, sir," the vendor said, "but pencils are now 20 cents."

The fellows were discussing the decline of the stock market. One asked the other, "Does it bother you?"

"Who me?" replied his friend. "I sleep like a baby! Every two hours I wake up and cry!"

Fortune-teller: "You will be poor and unhappy until you are 30."
Client: "And then?"
Fortune-teller: "Then you'll get used to it."

It requires a strong constitution to withstand repeated attacks of prosperity.

—J. S. Basford

"Pastor," said a young fellow, "I am a spendthrift. I throw my money around right and left. In this morning's service I want you to pray that I may be cured of this habit."

"Yes, my boy," agreed the pastor, "the prayer will come right after the offering."

A few years ago there was a terrible earthquake in Alaska. Anchorage was devastated. A number of people wrote to the governor and demanded that he do certain things for them. They outlined the suffering that they had endured and demanded that the state take responsibility. Later the governor appeared on television and reported that, among all the demands, he had received a letter from a boy who had written on a 3 x 5 card and had taped to it two nickels. The boy had written these words: "Use this wherever it is needed. If you need more, let me know."

A news announcer on a radio show found himself with a few minutes to spare. Slowly, in the sincerest and deepest tones he was capapble of, he said, "It is not often that such a glorious opportunity is presented to me. Ladies and gentlemen, I ask for a moment or two of your silence and attention." He then went on to read the Ten Commandments.

When he finished, there were tears in his eyes, which dried very quickly when the station-break announcer broke in with, "The opinions just expressed are not necessarily those of the sponsor."

Sam Levenson, *You Don't Have to Be in Who's Who to Know What's What* (New York: Pocket Books, 1979).

Say what you will about the Ten Commandments, you must always come back to the pleasant fact that there are only ten of them.

H.L. Menchen

There was a believer who was not everything he ought to be and he knew it! In fact, when he finally passed from this life to the next one he was deeply concerned that St. Peter wouldn't let him through the Pearly Gates. But when he got to his destination, he was welcomed with open arms. "Are you certain that you didn't make a mistake?" he asked St. Peter. "You see, there are certain parts of my life of which I'm sort of ashamed." St. Peter answered, "No, we didn't make a mistake. You see, we don't keep any records." The man was greatly relieved and overjoyed. Then he saw another group of men over in a corner beating their heads against a celestrial wall and clinching their fists and stomping their feet in disgust. "What is the matter with them?" the man asked St. Peter. "Oh," said St. Peter with a smile, "They also thought we kept records."

One businessman's motto: "You can fool some of the people some of the time, and generally that's enough to make a profit."

He who lays all his cards on the table usually ends up playing solitaire.

G. K. Chesterton, whose principles constantly got him into trouble, once said, "I like getting into hot water. It keeps you clean!"

A cartoon in *The New Yorker* magazine got it right when it showed a business meeting in progress. Everyone around the table is staring hard at one fellow who is saying: "Well, yes, of course . . . Honesty is one of the BETTER policies."

Assigned to write a story with the word "adult" in it, Freddie wrote, "Adults don't have any fun. Adults just sit around and talk. Adults don't do anything. Nothing is duller than adultery."

The Student asked: "It says here that if we study hard, don't drink, don't smoke, and don't run around with girls, we'll live longer. Is that true?" The Professor answered: "We won't know for sure until someone tries it."

A little boy and his mother were sitting in the church pew. During the service, the little boy kept scraping and scuffing his feet against the pew. His mother said, "Stop that." And he stopped for a while, but soon he was back at it. She said again, "Stop that, right now." He quit. But soon, he started it all over. Finally, she told him, very strongly that he had better stop. And to give her words authority, she nudged him with her elbow. The little boy looked up at her and said, "I would stop it if you would give me a reward, like a dime." And his mother said, "Oh, how come you can't be good for nothing like your father?"

-- Contributed

We can appreciate the plight of the editor who was weary of the abuse which followed his editorials. Finally, instead of an editorial he simply printed a copy of the Ten Commandments. A few days later he received a letter which said, "Cancel my subscription. You're getting too personal."

We are like that cartoon in the newspapers a couple of years ago that showed two natives from the bush country of Australia. One was saying to the other, "I would like to get me a new boomerang, but I can't get rid of this one I already have."

An anonymous taxpayer in New York sent a letter to the State Income Tax Division in Albany saying that he had cheated on his income tax return ten years ago and had not been able to get in a good night's sleep since. He enclosed $25 and added, "If I still can't sleep, I'll send the balance."

Suddenly called out of town to nurse an ailing relative for an indefinite period, a mother left her husband and children to run the house. After awhile she began to wonder whether she was missed. A letter from her youngest son removed all doubts. "Dear Mom: Since you went away, this is the biggest house I ever saw."

A mother of 3 boys went to the manager of the local grocery and pleaded, "Isn't there some cereal that will *sap* their energy?"

After watching several new scouts at their attempts at outdoor cooking, the scoutmaster asked, "How are you managing? Have you forgotten any essential equipment?"
"Yes, I have," answered one of the scouts.
"Oh, what?"
"My mother."

One young mother wrote home that she worked without ceasing from son-up to son-down.

The joy of motherhood is what a woman experiences when all the children have gone to bed.

Six-year-old Mary Jane was looking at photographs of her parent's wedding. Her father described the ceremony and tried to explain its meaning. Suddenly the light dawned. "Oh," Mary Jane exclaimed, "Is that when you got Mother to come to work for us?"

Mothers who scold little boys for carrying crazy things in their pockets should look in their own handbags.

Automation: a technological process that performs all the work while we just sit there. When we were kids, this process was called Mother.

A little girl was about to speak a piece in an old fashioned children's day program. When she got in front of the crowd, the sight of hundreds of pairs of curious eyes focused upon her threw her into a panic. Every line that she had rehearsed so carefully faded from her mind and she stood there frozen in her tracks unable to utter a single syllable. In the front row her mother was almost as frantic as the little girl. She gestured, she screwed up her lips as though to form the words to be spoken, but to no avail. Finally in desperation the mother whispered the opening phrase: "I am the light of the world." Instantly the child's face relaxed, a smile appeared where there had been clouds before, and with supreme confidence, she began, "My mother is the light of the world."

A subtle piece of Jewish humor makes a good point about child-rearing. Three Jewish mothers were bragging about their sons. "My son is a wealthy lawyer," said one. "For my birthday he gave me this fur coat." Said the second: "My son is a medical doctor and last winter he gave me a vacation in Miami Beach." The third thought for a moment then blurted out, "My son sees a fancy psychiatrist each week. He pays the psychiatrist $ 50 an hour. And guess who he spends his time talking about — ME!"

Perhaps our parents were overly protective. You have heard about the mother who sent a note to her son's teacher: "Georgie is very sensitive. If he needs disciplining, please do not slap him. Slap the boy next to him and this will frighten Georgie into doing right."

Beyond Every Great Man Is His Mother
    Mrs. Washington: "Georgie never did have a head for money."
    Mrs. Morse: "Sam, stop tapping your fingers on the table — it's driving me crazy!"
    Mrs. Lindbergh: "Charles, can't you do anything by yourself?"
    Mrs. Armstrong: "Neil has no more business taking flying lessons than the man in the moon."

                                      —Modern Maturity

An eight-year-old wrote about mother: "A mother is a person who takes care of her kids and gets their meals, and if she's not there when you get home from school, you wouldn't know how to get your dinner and you wouldn't feel like eating it anyhow." I think the most important part of that sentence is that *you wouldn't feel like eating it anyhow!*
—H. S. Vigeveno, *Letters to Saints and Other Sinners* (New York: A. J. Holman, Company, 1972)

Competition motivates. It is a shame that cooperation does not motivate as effectively. I heard a good story this week about a Methodist preacher and a Baptist preacher who were fierce competitors. Their churches were across the street from each other and were roughly the same size. They were constantly vying for the attention of the community and, unfortunately, the competition had caused quite a bit of tension between them. A prominent layman in the community wanted to see the two pastors get together in a spirit of cooperation and love. So he paid for the two of them to go on a hunting trip together to the Rockies. For several days they share the same small tent and cooked their meals over the same small fire. A good spirit of comraderie developed between them. Until one night they heard a giant grizzly bear clawing at their tent. They realized that the bear was angry. The Methodist preacher yelled, "Let's run for it!" The Baptist preacher protested. "You can't outrun a grizzly," he said. "I don't have to outrun the grizzly," said the Methodist. "All I have to do is outrun you!"

The saying, "It's not the size of the dog in the fight, but the size of the fight in the dog," reminds me of the story of the diminutive man who applied for a job as a stevedore. The foreman looked him over carefully and said, "You're too small." The little man was indignant. "I can do any job that your biggest men can handle. At least give me a chance to prove myself."

"All right," said the foreman. "Over there you will find a group of men loading 300 lb. anvils. You go ahead and join them. Everything went fine until all of a sudden there was a terrific splash. "Man overboard," someone cried. The foreman rushed to the side of the ship. There was the small man thrashing furiously in the water. He was gasping for air as his head bobbed up and down. "Throw me a rope," he yelled. "Throw me a rope. And hurry – or so help me, I'll let go of this anvil!"

Not long ago *Specialty Salesman* magazine told about an optimistic watch salesman. He examined the sample watch furnished him, noting the attributes inscribed rather illegibly on its back: "Shockproof, antimagnetic, waterproof, and bustproof."

This last adjective inspired him. He began demonstrating the watches with almost vicious enthusiasm. He tossed them off walls, against buildings, onto cement sidewalks. His confidence in himself, in the company and their watches, plus his vigorous demonstrations, paid off. He won a sales contest prize: $100 and one of the watches.

It was when he examined his own prize watch that the startling truth was revealed. For on the back, more clearly inscribed this time, were the words: "Shockproof, antimagnetic, waterproof and **dustproof**."

I'm sure you, too, know people who have gone a long way on *confidence*.

– John D. Yeck, **How to Get Profitable Ideas** (New York: McGraw-Hill Book Company, 1965).

Robert Short, author of *The Gospel According to Peanuts* and *Parables of Peanuts* tells how as a high school student in Midland, Texas, he became an agnostic, though he was raised in a Methodist home. He became president of a science club that caused such a controversy that his high school principal complained to his parents. He tells how he sat across from his mother who, with tears running down her face said, "I thought we raised you right. I never thought it would come to this—our son an agnostic."

Later Robert Short found a new relationship to Jesus Christ in college and felt a call to the ministry. At home he told his mother of his decision. Sitting at that same kitchen table, with tears running down her cheeks, she said, "I never thought it would come to this—my son, a religious fanatic."

I heard recently about a man who prided himself on being exceedingly punctual. He followed a very precise routine every morning. His alarm went off at 6:30 a. m. He rose briskly, shaved, showered, ate his breakfast, brushed his teeth, picked up his briefcase, got into his car, drove to a nearby ferry landing, parked his car, rode the ferry across to the downtown business area, got off the ferry, walked smartly to his building, marched in to the elevator, rode to the seventeenth floor, hung up his coat, opened his briefcase, spread his papers out on his desk, and sat down in his chair at precisely 8:00 a. m. Not 8:01, not even 7:59. Always at 8:00 a. m. He followed this same routine without variation for eight years.

Until one morning his alarm did not go off and he slept fifteen minutes late. When he did awake, he was panic stricken. He rushed through his shower, nicked himself when he shaved, gulped down his breakfast, only half-way brushed his teeth, grabbed up his briefcase, jumped into his car, sped to the ferry landing, jumped out of his car and looked for the ferry. There it was, out in the water, approximately 15 feet from the shore. "I think I can make it," he said to himself, running toward the dock at full speed. Reaching the edge of the water he gave an enormous leap out into the water and miraculously landed with a loud thud on the deck of the ferry. The captain rushed down to make sure he was all right. "Son, that was a tremendous leap," the captain said, "but if you would have waited just another minute, we would have been to the shore."

Have you heard of the Protestant boy who fell in love with and wanted to marry a lovely Catholic girl? The girl said she would marry him if he became a Catholic. Her parents insisted he must do that to have their consent. The boy began to read Catholic literature and attended Instruction classes taught by the priest. All went well until one day the mother came home and found the daughter in tears. She was sobbing her heart out. "It's . . . it's Paul," the girl wailed. "There isn't going to be any wedding!" "Whatever is the matter, dear? Doesn't he love you anymore?" "It isn't that," the daughter explained. "We've oversold him, Mother! Now he's going to become a priest!"

A professional golfer was impressed with the coordination and strength of his friend, a weightlifter who was six feet, six inches tall and weighed 265 pounds. He invited the weightlifter to learn golf. When they played together, the golfer explained how to tee up and drive a ball. On his first attempt, the weightlifter drove the ball well over four hundred yards onto the green. The ball stopped about eighteen inches short of the cup.

They walked to the ball and the weightlifter asked what he should do next.

The golfer replied, "Now you're supposed to putt the ball into that hole."

With a straight face his friend asked, "Why didn't you tell me that back there?"

—Matthew Prince, *Winning Through Caring* (Grand Rapids: Baker Book House, 1981).

A San Francisco executive posted signs reading "DO IT NOW!!!" throughout his factory hoping to inspire the employees to action. Several weeks later, a friend asked him how his staff reacted. He shook his head in disgust: "I wish you hadn't asked. The cashier skipped with $ 10,000. The head accountant eloped with the best secretary I ever had. Three typists asked for a raise. The factory workers voted to go on strike. And the office boy joined the navy!"

Zig Ziglar tells about a young fellow who was courting a girl. To reach her house the aspiring suitor had to cross a large pasture in which there was a twelve hundred pound, rip-snorting mean bull. He climbed through the fence as far from where that bull was as he possibly could and walked as quickly yet as inconspicuously as he was able. All of a sudden, though, he heard the thunderous hoofbeats of that twelve hundred pound bull heading directly for him. He knew that there was no way he could get across that enormous pasture before that bull reached him. It was even too far back to make it to the fence by which he had gained access to the pasture. With all his strength he rushed for a tree. Unfortunately, it only had one limb on it and that was about twenty-two feet off of the ground. He knew the odds were against him ever jumping that high, but he also knew that he was about to get trampled and gored by this enormous bull, so, just at that last minute, he gave this tremendous lunge upward for that tree branch. He missed it—but fortunately, he was able to catch on to it—on the way down.

I read this past week about a tourist in Las Vegas. He had no money to gamble, so he watched the games and bet mentally. According to the report, in no time at all, he had lost his mind!

A simile within a humorous story can add punch. For instance, if you are telling a story about yourself in which you felt very conspicuous, you might interject: "I felt very much like the lady who took off her shoes in a movie theater and had them stolen. There was snow on the ground outside. Her husband turned around and squatted down and said to her: 'Get on my back and try not to look conspicuous.' I mean, there are some situations in which it is impossible not to look conspicuous."

The world's stingiest man went Christmas shopping, but everything he saw was too expensive except a $50.00 vase that was on sale for $2.00 because the handle had been broken off. He bought it and had the salesman ship it by mail so that his friend would think he had paid $50.00 for it and that it had been broken in shipment.

A week after Christmas he received a thank you note from his friend. "Thank you for the lovely vase," his letter said. "It was so nice of you to wrap each piece separately."

G. K. Chesterton was once in Market Harbor, England. He telephoned his wife and said, "I'm in Market Harbor. Where should I be?"

There is an old Irish story about the man who was asked to sit up all night at a wake. Unknown to him he was being set-up by some practical joking friends, and in the dead of night the presumed corpse sat up in the coffin screaming the fellow's name. Whereupon the man carrying out this somber vigil walked over to the coffin, pushed the very-much-alive cadaver back down into the coffin, and exclaimed sternly, "If you're dead, lie down and act like it!"

I understand that at last summer's Southern Baptist Convention one brother offered thanks for the wives who had remained home to help keep affairs in order. In urging the resolution, he said, "While I am here drinking deeply from the wells of wisdom and spirituality of my older colleagues, I am bound to remember that my dear wife remains at our little church, bravely carrying on with the deacons."

A man offered a stranger a lift. The stranger accepted. Shortly afterwards, the motorist noticed that his watch was missing.

Whipping out a revolver he carried on the road, he dug it into the other man's ribs and exclaimed, "Hand over that watch!"

The stranger meekly complied as the car came to a stop and he was let out. When the motorist returned home, he was greeted by his wife.

"How did you get on without your watch?" she asked. "I suppose you know that you left it on your dressing table?"

I like the cartoon, depicting a woman shaking hands with a minister as she left the church, which had this caption: "Thank you for your sermon. It was like water to a drowning man."

The frantic father called the doctor late at night. "Please hurry," he said, "my twelve year old boy just swallowed a ball point pen."

"I'll be there in about twenty minutes," the doctor said.

"What should I do until you get here?" the man wanted to know.

"Use a pencil," the doctor said.

A man and his wife drove through a red light and were stopped by a policeman. The man's replies to the officer's questions were somewhat surly. His wife, thinking to help her husband out of the difficulty, spoke up and said, "Don't mind him, Officer, he's drunk."

He was one of these playful, middle-aged wolves. He seated himself close to a cute little brunette on the bus, leaned over and asked, "Where have you been all my life?"

"Well," she said, looking him over coolly, "for the first half of it I wasn't born."

Husband(answering phone): I don't know. Call the weather bureau.
Wife: Who was that?
Husband: Some jerk asking if the coast was clear.

One salesman we heard of was a master of diplomacy. His boss was going to send him to Ottawa in the middle of January on some business. "I would rather you send someone else," replied the salesman. "Why is that?" asked his boss. "It's too cold this time of year," the salesman answered. "Besides there's nobody in Ottawa but hockey players and ugly women." His boss sat upright in his chair. "Hold on," he protested. "My wife is from Ottawa." Without a moment's hesitation the salesman shot back, "What position does she play, sir?"

161

One little fellow got a souvenir from the Holy Land. Said his mother: "This is from the Holy Land, and it is so far away we'll never be able to go there."

Next day when showing his gift to a neighbor girl, he announced, "This is from heaven, and that's one place our family will never go."

Dr. Noah Langdale says that Dr. Charles Allen and the late Rev. Pierce Harris were dear friends who were both extremely popular and preached to great congregations in Atlanta during the 50's and early 60's. Rev. Harris had a daily column in the **Atlanta Journal,** and Rev. Allen had one in the **Atlanta Constitution.** Eventually Charles moved to Houston First United Methodist and Pierce Harris wrote some nice things about Charlie in his column. 25 of Allen's friends wrote him of Pierce's kind remarks. Allen wrote a letter of appreciation, but added that he really didn't think 25 of his friends read Pierce's article. Pierce replied that he didn't think Charles had 25 friends who could read!
(Dr. Langdale is President of Georgia State University and a great speaker.)

Boss to new employee: "I want you to know that my door is always open. Please walk by quietly."

From another ancient text:
That reminds me of the two Irishmen who landed in New York. They had not been around very much, so they decided to take a train trip. As they were riding along on the train, a boy came through selling fruit. They recognized oranges and apples, but there was a strange fruit they had never seen before so they asked the boy, "What is that?"

He answered, "That is a banana."

"Is it good to eat?"

He said, "Sure."

"How do you eat it?"

The boy showed them how to peel a banana, so each bought one. One fellow took a bite out of his and just then the train went into a tunnel.

He said, "Pat, if you haven't eaten the darned thing, don't do it. I ate mine, and I've gone blind."

Sometimes we take a result of that kind, and we go blind before we look for the cause which brought it about.

A young kindergarten teacher thought she saw a familiar face as she boarded a city bus and exclaimed to one of the passengers: "Why, how do you do, Mr. Brown!" As the man addressed evidently did not know her and looked rather dazed, she saw her mistake and hurriedly apologized, saying "Oh, I beg your pardon—I thought you were the father of one of my children."

Then everyone within hearing looked so amused that the young lady left the bus at the next stop.

If you are with a youth group telling terrible, terrible jokes, here is one that is worse than most:

Two carrots, a boy and a girl, are walking together down the street, hand in hand. As they come to a corner, the girl carrot steps down off the sidewalk into the street just as a car comes careening around the corner. There's a squeal of the car's brakes, but the car nevertheless runs right over her.

An ambulance rushes her to the hospital. The boy carrot is extremely upset. What's going to happen to his friend? Will she be all right?

In the hospital, the boy carrot sees the doctor coming towards him down the hall. With a grim look, the doctor comes up to him and says, "My friend, I've got some news for you—good news and bad news. I'll give you the good news first. Your friend is going to live, but—and I'm sorry—she's going to be a vegetable for the rest of her life."

– Natalie H. Rogers, *Talk-Power* (New York: Dodd, Mead and Company, 1982).

Preaching vigorously, the minister came to the words, "So Adam said to Eve. . . ." Turning the page, he was horrified to discover the final page was missing. As he rifled through the other pages, he gained a little time by repeating, "So Adam said to Eve. . . ."

Then in a low voice, but one which the amplifying system carried to every part of the church, he added, ". . . there seems to be a leaf missing."

In the post-office lobby, a middle-aged businessman noticed an old lady trying to write on a postcard. Her hand was shaking violently. A moment later, she caught his eye and said, "Sir, I wonder if you'd help me. Could you address this postcard for me?"

"I'd be glad to," he assured her and wrote as she directed.

"Thank you," she said gratefully. "I hate to ask, but could you write just a short message for me?"

He smiled, turned the card over and did as she requested. "Is there anything else I can do?"

"Well," she said apologetically, "there's just one other little thing. At the bottom, would you write, 'Please excuse the handwriting.' "

Chaplain Otis Rice of St. Luke's Hospital in New York tells the interesting parable of the young lion, just beginning to realize his strength, who went out on a rampage one morning, roaring and beating his chest. He approached the giraffe and cried, "Why aren't you strong and mighty as I the King of the Beasts?" The giraffe, as any normal giraffe would do, took to his heels and ran without stopping to answer. The lion then met the gazelle and asked the same question. The gazelle also turned and ran. Then the lion met the little mouse. "Why aren't you strong and mighty as I the King of the Beasts?" he roared. The little mouse stopped to answer. He looked up at him and said, "Because I've been sick."

Lance Webb, **Point of Glad Return**, (Nashville: Abingdon Press, 1060).

163

The two mountaineers were startled when the first motorcycle came through the hills. It was coming right at them. One of them grabbed his rifle and fired. "Did you hit it?" the other asked anxiously. "Nope," he said. "But I made him turn loose of the man he had."

Two cannibals met in a hut. One was tearing out pictures of men, women, and children from a magazine, stuffing them into his mouth, and eating them. "Tell me," said the other, "is that dehydrated stuff any good?"

An old lady went to a tombstone cutter's office to order a stone for her husband's grave. After explaining that she wanted no frills, just a small stone, she told him to put the words, "To My Husband," in a suitable place.

Upon delivery, to her horror, she saw the words:

"To My Husband In a Suitable Place "

Bulletin Blooper: The pastor will preach, and there will be special sinning by the congregation.

I like the story about a funeral of an elderly veteran which included a military salute at the grave. As the rifles were fired, the widow fainted, at which time one of the small grandsons screamed, "Great day, they've killed Granny!"

There's a new computer out that's so human — when it makes a mistake it blames it on another machine.

—Mickey Freeman in *Parade.*

If all the cars in America were lined up end to end, someone would pull out and try to pass.

I am reminded of a story about a young boy who had just been vaccinated. The doctor was getting ready to put a stick-on bandage on his arm.

"Please put it on the other arm," the boy pleaded.

"Why do that?" the doctor asked. "This will let everyone know you have been vaccinated and they won't hit your sore arm."

"Please put it on my other arm! Please!" the boy said. "You don't know those kids at school."

From friends in Paris I heard a story which underscores my observation. It concerns Pope John XXIII, that magnificent churchman and human being, when he was Papal Nuncio in France, the Vatican's diplomatic envoy to the French capital. At one reception where there were many well-shaped beauties, he told a diplomatic colleague: "The problem with these receptions is that if a woman arrives wearing a gown that is cut daringly low, everyone gazes not at the lady but at me, the Papal Nuncio, to see if *I* am looking at the lady!"
  —by Robert J. Buckley, Chairman and Chief Executive Officer, Allegheny International, Inc.

A fellow who'd had one too many was stumbling home through a cemetery late one frosty night. Not watching where he was going, he fell into an open grave. Pretty soon another inebriated type came along and heard the first fellow yelling from the hole in the ground: "Help. I'm cold. I'm cold."
  The second fellow peered down into the open grave. "Well no wonder," he said, "you've kicked off all your dirt."

The instructor had just concluded his lecture on parachute jumping. "Sir," asked one student, "what if the chute doesn't open?"
  "That," replied the teacher, "is what is known as jumping to a conclusion."

Mother, let me go to the zoo to see the monkeys.
  Why, Tommy, what an idea. Imagine wanting to go to see the monkeys when your Aunt Betsy is here.

A fellow says his surgeon assured him that he could have marital relations on a regular basis after his prostate surgery. "And now," says the fellow, "all my friends are saving up for the operation."
  —Quoted by Neil Morgan in San Diego *Tribune*

To cope with vicious and insulting poison-pen letters, a well-known TV star hit upon mailing the offensive correspondence back to the sender with his personal note which stated, "The enclosed letter arrived on my desk a few days ago. I am sending it to you in belief that as a responsible citizen you should know that some idiot is sending out letters over your signature. Cordially. ."

An attorney who traveled out of state to try an important case promised to wire his partner the moment a decision was announced. At long last the wire came and it read, "Justice has triumphed." His partner in New York wired back, "Appeal at once."

An officer in the South Pacific who had been overseas sixteen months received a letter from his wife telling about a prayer their four-year-old daughter made: "Dear Lord, please send me a baby brother so we will have something to surprise Daddy with when he gets home."

At the time of the last walk on the moon, a reporter asked one of the astronauts if he had been nervous when he was strapped into his seat before going into space.

"Well," he said, "of course I was. Who wouldn't be? There I was, sitting on top of 9,999 parts and pieces — each of which had been made by the lowest bidder!"

At the reference desk of the Wichita Public Library, a young man asked for a book on marriage. The librarian brought him one. When he saw the title, he seemed flustered, and said it was not what he wanted. Did we have anything else on marriage? The second book she brought, more explicit than the first, caused him to pinken. It still was not quite what he wanted. The librarian then brought him a very detailed marriage manual. Before delivering it, however, she said to another staff member, "If he can't handle this, he better give up the whole thing."

He looked through it, turned deep red and blurted, "All I want to know is—am I supposed to wear a white tie!"

—Ford Rockwell in *Reader's Digest.*

A woman who had just given birth to triplets was explaining to a friend that triplets happened once in 15,000 times. "My Lord, how did you find time to do your housework?" asked her friend.

One is tempted to say with Mae West, "Too much of a good thing is--wonderful."

166

I recall some oft-quoted words posted on the bulletin board of a church. They concerned the health of a minister whose alert secretary used the board, which regularly carried church announcements, for the purpose of communicating the state of the minister's health. But she also continued the sentence sermons, familiar to readers. One day those who passed by the church, in autos and on the sidewalk, were startled to read: GOD IS GOOD—DR. JONES IS BETTER.

There is a delightful story about a church organist who wanted to make an impression on the visiting clergyman with her musical accomplishment. She wrote a note to the old sexton who had been a little slack in his work of pumping enough air for the organ, and handed it to him just before the service started. But, making a natural mistake, the sexton passed the note on to the visiting clergyman, who opened it and read: "Keep blowing away until I give the signal to stop."

Every pastor knows the feeling that one minister had. He had been sick for a while and the chairman of his board came to try to cheer him up. He said, "Preacher, we don't want you to worry about a thing while you are here in the hospital. Last night at our board meeting we voted 10 to 9 to pray for your recovery."

A pastor who was popular with his congregation explained his success as the result of a silent prayer which he offered each time he took the pulpit. It ran thus:

"Lord, fill my mouth with worth-while stuff,
And nudge me when I've said enough."

The minister's mind suddenly went blank concerning whether the parishioner's new baby was a boy or girl. But the harder he tried to cover himself the more flustered he became. "How old is, uh, uh, the, child?" he asked. "Barely four weeks old," was the reply. "Well, uh, uh, your youngest, I suppose?"

Each of the new church buildings in town had a higher steeple than the existing ones. Soon the people in town were laughingly referring to their steeplechase.

I believe it was Zig Ziglar who said, "The salesman should not be ashamed of his calling, but rather of his not calling." Think about it.

167

A preacher's small daughter watched him all week long as he prepared for Sunday's sermon. Finally, she said: "Daddy does God tell you what to say in your Sunday talks?" "Yes, he does dear," came the reply. "Why do you ask?"

"Well, I was wondering" she said, "why you're always crossing so much of it out."

A certain curate in the course of conversation at a dinner party some time ago remarked to a friend, "I had a curious dream last night, but as it was about my vicar I hardly like to tell it." On being pressed, however, he began. "I dreamt I was dead and was on my way to Heaven, which was reached by a very long ladder. At the foot I was met by an angel, who pressed a piece of chalk into my hand and said, 'If you climb long enough you will reach Heaven, but for every sin you are conscious of having committed you must mark a rung of the ladder with the chalk as you go up.'I took the chalk and started. I had climbed very, very far and was feeling very tired when I suddenly saw my vicar coming down. 'Hullo!' I said, 'what are you going down for?' 'More chalk.' "

A suburban minister during his discourse one Sabbath morning said: "In each blade of grass there is a sermon." The following day one of his flock discovered the good man pushing a lawn mower about his garden and paused to say: "Well, parson, I'm glad to see you engaged in cutting your sermons short."

"Brother Jones is always critical of my sermon," complained the young pastor. "Oh, don't worry about him," his deacon counselled. "He's just like a parrot; he only repeats what everybody else is saying."

I can sympathize with the minister who dreamed he was preaching and he woke up and he was!

Prison chaplain: "Remember, son, the sermons you heard while you were here as you make your way in the world."
Soon to be released prisoner: "Chaplain, no one who's heard you preach would ever want to come back here."

A clergyman on a recent occasion discovered, after beginning the service, that he had forgotten his notes. As it was too late to send for them, he said to his audience, by way of apology, that this morning he should have to depend upon the Lord for what he might say, but next Sunday he would come better prepared.

Sometimes it is difficult for us to understand our parishioners' casual attitudes toward worship because we do not sit where they sit. A little boy told his mother he was going to be a minister when he grew up. "Since I have to go to church anyhow, it's a lot harder to sit still and listen than it is to stand up and yell."

Oscar Wilde reported a sign which once hung over a saloon piano in the Old West: "Do not shoot the pianist. He is doing the best that he can." Maybe that ought to hang over a few pulpits.

Ministers are expected to be community minded. One minister's son told his friend, "My dad's a Moose, a Lion, an Elk and an Eagle." "O, wow," replied the lad, "how much does it cost to see him?"

The hostess for the banquet was disturbed. Her clergyman was late and he was to offer the Grace. Finally, she asked her husband to fill in. He was visibly shaken but stood and announced reverently: "As there is no clergyman present, let us thank God."

Notice to all prophets: Avoid New York State. Section 899 of the Code of Criminal Procedure of the State of New York provides that "persons pretending to forecast the future" can be considered disorderly as defined by subdivision 3, section 901 of the code. Such disorderly people are liable to a fine of $250 and six months in jail.

"Mummy," said the little boy, "why does the minister get a month's vacation in the summer when Daddy only gets two weeks?"
"Well, son," answered Mother, "If he's a good minister, he needs it. If he isn't, the congregation needs it!"

While paying calls in his parish, the parson knocked at the door of one family. A woman's voice called out, "Is that you, Angel?"
"No," came the minister's prompt reply, "but I'm from the same department."

The preacher kept waving his arms wildly as he talked. "What'll we do if he ever gets out?" a four-year-old asked her mother.

Dr. Ralph Mohney, pastor of Broad Street United Methodist Church, Kingsport, Tennessee, told this story in his weekly column in his weekly church newsletter.

A minister was on his way to church one Sunday morning when he heard the weatherman say that it would begin to rain that afternoon and continue through the rest of the week. Monday was his day off and he loved golf!

He hated to think he would miss his game on his day off because of rain. Since it was quite early, he thought he would have time to go to the golf course, play nine holes, and still have time to get back for the 11:00 A.M. service, even if he didn't have time to make it to Sunday School.

Soon, he was on the course alone. The "old tempter" noticed the cleric there on Sunday morning and called the Lord's attention to it asking, "Isn't that one of your men?"

The Lord answered, "Yes, he is."

Tempter:"Aren't you going to do anything about it?"

The Lord replied, "Yes, I'll take care of it!"

The minister approached a par four hole in which the green was easily visible from the tee. He addressed the ball and came through with a mighty stroke. Then, the Lord took charge.

He blessed the ball and it kept going and kept going and kept going. To the minister's astonishment, the ball rolled across the green and into the cup. A hole in one on a par four hole! He was beside himself with excitement and joy!

The Old Tempter said, "I thought you were going to take care of him. Why did you let a thing like that happen?"

The Lord simply said, "I took care of it. Who's he going to tell about it?"

Years ago, I heard a similar story "that got out of hand." Holston Annual Conference was being held in Knoxville, Tennessee. One of the clergy was tempted to play gold instead of attending an afternoon session of conference.

He got a hole in one! The only time in his life–a hole in one!

The Bishop began the morning session the following day by hanging a copy of the local paper over the pulpit with the picture of the minister beneath a caption which read, "Conference Pastor Gets Hole in One!"

There is something to be said about our sins catching up with us–particularly as it relates to the presiding Bishop!

–Dr. John Bardsley

A country church had just acquired a brand-new pastor. He drove around the local area one day, calling on homes to get acquainted with the parishioners. He had been up a narrow lane to the house on top of a hill, not far from the highway, finding no one home, he proceeded back down the hill to where the lane opened onto the highway.

Not at all familar with the roads in the area, he came upon the intersection more suddenly than he expected and almost crashed into another car entering the narrow lane. The woman driving the other car grumbled to herself, "Reckless driver–I should've got your license number and reported you."

Reaching her home on top of the hill, the woman parked the car and was nervously trying to unlock the front door when she noticed a note attached to the door. "Sorry I missed you this time," it said. "Will try again soon.–The new pastor." Daniel Scott in *The Saturday Evening Post*

The chaplain of a mental hospital was taken aback by a patient who stood in the middle of the service and complained, "I can't stand this nonsense any longer." Commented the patient's doctor, "First rational statement he's made in years."

A noted evangelist was speaking at two different churches in a large city in the same week. A reporter was present at the first service. After the sermon the evangelist pleaded with the reporter not to publish in the local paper any of the stories the evangelist had used that night since he was going to use the same stories the following night at the other church. The next morning the reporter published an excellent review of the evangelist's message and concluded with these words: "Rev. Jones also told many stories which we cannot publish."

Here's good advice for every preacher: "To make a sermon immortal, you don't have to make it everlasting."

"Is it true?" she asked with a sneer, "that before you entered the ministry you were a veterinarian?" Replied he, "Why do you ask? Are you sick?"

The following word of warning is from Oliver Wendell Holmes. "I might have been a minister myself for aught I know, if a certain clergyman had not looked and talked like an undertaker."

A former priest tried to explain why he left the ministry. "Were you defrocked?" someone asked. "No," he replied, "just unsuited."

Another pastor was to offer the benediction following a message by a dynamic evangelist. Afterwards, he used these words from I Kings to describe his experience: "After the whirlwind, a still, small voice . . ."

An Indian was asked by a tourist what he did for a living. "I'm a preacher," came the reply.
"Oh," the visitor continued. "Do you mind telling me how much salary you get?"
"Fifty dollar a month."
"Why," exclaimed the tourist, "that's pretty poor pay!"
The Indian shrugged. "Me pretty poor preacher!"

171

A little boy asked his father a question. The father was a pastor and the little boy said, "Daddy, before you preach, why do you bow your head and put it down into your hands?"

"Well," said the pastor, "I am praying. I am asking God to help me with the sermon."

"Then why doesn't He do it?" asked the little boy.

Someone asked the church decorator what she did with the flowers after the services. She replied innocently, "Oh, we take them to the people who are sick after the sermon."

I cannot praise the preacher's eyes,
I never saw his glance divine;
For when he prays, he shuts his eyes,
And when he preaches, he shuts mine.

"Preacher," said the chairman of the board of deacons, "I am sorry to hear that you are planning to leave us for another pulpit." "Oh, you have nothing to fear," the pastor replied, "I am going to recommend a successor who will probably be a better man than I." "That's what worries me," said the chairman, "your predecessor told us the same thing."

A truly eloquent person had been preaching for an hour or so on the immortality of the soul.

"I looked at the mountains," he declared, "and could not help thinking, 'Beautiful as you are, you will be destroyed, while my soul will not.' I gazed upon the ocean and cried, 'Mighty as you are, you will eventually dry up, but not I.'"

"I see that at your church convention," said an old farmer to the preacher, "you discussed the subject — 'How to get people to attend church.' I have never heard a single address at a farmer's convention on how to get the cattle to come to eat. We spend our time discussing the best kind of feed."

—National Health Federation Bulletin

It's not easy to be a true prophet today, as Samuel Butler once noted. "The lions would not eat Daniel. They would eat almost anything, but they drew the line at prophets."

You may know the story of the congregation in the small town church where there was a young bride whose husband was an usher. During the Sunday morning service, she became terribly worried that she may have left the roast cooking in the oven. She wrote a note to her husband and passed it to him by way of another usher. The latter, thinking it was a note for the pastor hurried down the aisle and laid it on the pulpit. Stopping abruptly in the middle of his sermon to read the note, the astonished pastor was met with the following message: "Please go home and turn off the gas."

Every rural pastor can appreciate this little verse:

To raise a garden requires
much time and labor
I had rather live next door
to a gardener
And cultivate my neighbor.

Dramatically inclined, a clergyman had a dove in the high gallery during a service of worship. On the cue, "The Holy Spirit descended like a dove" by the minister, the janitor was to throw down the dove into the unsuspecting congregation. At the proper time the preacher gave the cue—three times! After the third cue, everybody was shocked to hear the janitor say, "The cat ate the Holy Spirit. Do you want me to throw the cat down?"

A young minister wanted to marry a certain young lady, but her father balked. "I don't want my daughter marrying a preacher." The following Sunday the father went to hear the young man speak. After the service he had changed his mind. "It's all right, son. You're sure no preacher."

"Dr. Jones can dive deeper into the truth than any preacher I ever heard," said one layman. "Yes," replied another, "and come up drier than any I've heard."

Assigned to a town in which the local post office provided the community gossip, a minister had the feeling for about six weeks that people were laughing at him secretly. Finally he asked — and discovered that the source of the humor was a postcard from a member of his former parish who had written: "This new preacher is okay, but he doesn't hold me the way you did."

173

One Sunday morning my wife was teaching her class of small girls the subject of patience.

She asked, "What is patience?"

One little girl raised her hand and said, "Patience is when you are sitting in church and the preacher is preaching. You're just sitting there and he is preaching. He keeps preaching and you keep sitting there. That's patience."

– Bob Norton

An elderly woman who had suffered a multiple hip fracture asked her doctor: "How long must I stay in bed?" His answer: "One day at a time."

Grabbing Winky by the arm the mother in *"The Ryatts"* warns, "STOP that fighting this minute . . . I've just about had it with you kids!" Holding his newspaper in his hands, the father enters to ask, "Where's your patience, Sue?" She surprises him: "I'm saving it for a rainy day!"

Patience is not one of our shining virtues, is it? You remember that situation years ago that was reported in the *Reader's Digest* in which a car at a crowded intersection, while waiting for the traffic light to change, stalled, holding up a line of other vehicles behind it. Obviously flustered, the lady who was driving the car hurriedly got out and lifted the hood to investigate. As she did, the driver of the car behind began honking his horn.

The honking continued until the driver of the stalled car, still unsuccessful in discovering the trouble, went over and spoke to the impatient motorist behind her. "If you will fix my car," she said calmly, "I'll be glad to keep blowing your horn for you."

"It will be two weeks before I can get your car running again," said the mechanic. "Two weeks?" protested the owner. "It only took the Lord six days to create the world!" "Yes," replied the mechanic, "But have you looked at the condition of the world lately?"

One zoo keeper we heard about apparently had ushered in the new age. In the same cage he kept a lion and a lamb. Someone asked him how he did it. "Oh, I just put in a fresh lamb each morning."

The cartoon section of your newspaper is one of the best sources of humorous illustrations. And as many others have noted, the best of the best for religious speakers is probably the "Peanuts" cartoon. For example, in one cartoon Linus is twanging a bow and arrow. His sister Lucy is most irritated by it all.

"Oh, good grief! Now he's Robin Hood. If he sees a movie about skin diving, he plays skin diver for weeks! Or mountain climbing, then he's climbing up all the furniture!"

Charlie Brown: "Why don't you take him to a movie about Albert Schweitzer?"

A very vivid cartoon was published sometime back. A man and a boy are standing in the middle of a "bull's eye" around which there are three signs:

The first sign says: Ground zero – 1 megaton warhead, you are vaporized.
The second says: 2 miles – you are very dead.
And the third adds: 5 miles – you are cooked.

The man, holding the little boy's hand, asks: "So, what do you want to be when you grow up?"

The boy's reply was, "Alive--if it's not too much trouble."

The only way we can win the arms race with the Soviets is if they go broke first.
– Art Buchwald

Disarmament is like a party. Nobody wants to arrive until everyone else is there.
--Changing Times

A *Wall Street Journal cartoon* (9-6-77) shows a toy department salesman making his pitch: "It's not a war toy, madam. It's a cease fire toy."

A young girl was working so diligently at her homework that her father became curious and asked her what she was doing.

"I'm writing a report on the condition of the world and how to bring peace," she replied.

"Isn't that a pretty big order for a young girl?" her father asked.

"Oh, no," she answered, "and don't worry. There are three of us in the class working on it!"

In the cartoon, *Archie*, Moose is brought to the principal's office.

The principal says, "Moose, tell me what you've learned in school about settling disputes."

Moose grins and replies, "Uhhh . . . I used to settle disputes with my fists, but now I use this!" He points to his head.

The principal grins, satisfied, "I see. You mean you use your brain?"

Moose, "Uhh. . . Naw . . . I butt 'em with my head."

The *Rotarian* carried a Campbell cartoon of a cleaning woman wiping a world globe as she holds a large container of "Global Solution."

Sometimes life is just a matter of holding on. As someone put it — "The giant oak is just an acorn that held its ground."

It's good to be reminded every once in a while about the frog that fell in the bucket of cream and just kept churning his feet until he walked out on fresh butter.

The world's most frustrated man? It's the fellow who must always find a short cut, but discovers he is on a straight road.

We can all profit from the experience of a musician on the streets of New York City who asked a hippie: "How do I get to Carnegie Hall?" The reply: "Practice, man, practice."

One pastor has a plaque over his desk with the following inscription:
Don't worry if your job is small
And your rewards are few,
Remember that the mighty oak
Was once a nut like you!

Sometimes we can set somewhat unrealistic goals for ourselves. We are often like the lady who stepped into an elevator and told the lad who operated it: "The eleventh floor, please." He asked politely, "Whom did you wish to see on the eleventh floor?" She snapped back, "That's none of your business, young man." "I'm not being nosy lady, it's just that this building only has eight floors." We can make the same mistake; we can set unrealistic goals for ourselves. But the real question that confronts us is whether we are willing to pay the price to achieve what we know in our hearts we can achieve.

Chuck Swindoll tells about a farmer who was continually optimistic, seldom discouraged or blue. He had a neighbor who was just the opposite. Grim and gloomy, he faced each new morning with a heavy sigh.

The happy, optimistic farmer would see the sun coming up and shout over the roar of the tractor, "Look at that beautiful sun and the clear sky!" And with a frown, the negative neighbor would reply, "Yeah--it'll probably scorch the crops!"

When clouds would gather and much-needed rain would start to fall, our positive friend would smile across the fence, "Ain't this great--God is giving our corn a drink today!" Again, the same negative response, "Uh huh . . but if it doesn't stop 'fore long it'll flood and wash everything away."

One day the optimist decided to put his pessimistic neighbor to the maximum test. He bought the smartest, most expensive bird dog he could find. He trained him to do things no other dog on earth could do--impossible feats that would surely astound anyone.

He invited the pessimist to go duck hunting with him. They sat in the boat, hidden in the duck blind. In came the ducks. Both men fired and several ducks fell into the water. "Go get 'em!" ordered the owner with a gleam in his eye. The dog leaped out of the boat, walked **on** the water, and picked up the birds one by one.

"Well, what do ya think of that?"

Unsmiling, the pessimist answered. "He can't swim, can he?"

– Charles R. Swindoll, *Three Steps Forward, Two Steps Back* (New York: Bantam Books, 1980).

"Zig" Ziglar has motivated many people to dream bigger dreams. I like what he said about David and Goliath. He writes:

One night as I was reading the story of David and Goliath I was injecting some extra embellishments to clarify the story and bring out additional lessons. I pointed out that David's brothers were negative and afraid, that they figured Goliath was "too big to hit." David was positive and knew that Goliath was "too big to miss." They compared Goliath's size to their own which made Goliath awfully big. David compared Goliath to God, which made Goliath awfully small. Quite a difference!

–Zig Ziglar, *Confession of a Happy Christian* (New York: Bantam Books, 1982).

A little Japanese boy called at a gentleman's home and offered to sell some pictures for ten cents each.

"What are you going to do with the money?" he was asked. "I am raising one million dollars for the earthquake relief," he answered gravely, and he was so tiny and the sum he named was so large that everyone laughed.

"One million dollars!" they said. "Do you expect to raise it all by yourself?"

"No," he replied, "there is another little boy helping me."

Seeking to emphasize the Christmas story of the Star in the East compared with other stars in the sky, the Sunday School teacher asked the class to count the number of stars they could see at night. Reporting answers the next Sunday as varied as 190 to "too many to count," the pupils were fairly much in agreement. That is, all except Bobby who answered positively, **three**. "But, Bobby," asked the teacher, "how is it that you saw so few stars when the other children found so many?" Bobby thought a minute. Finally he answered: "Well, our backyard is awfully small."

A man lived on the border between Wisconsin and Minnesota. He assumed he lived in Minnesota, but a new survey showed that he lived in Wisconsin. "Thank goodness," he exclaimed, "I never could bear those cold Minnesota winters."

I like the perspective of one little fellow I heard about. He was most excited that he had pulled a cornstalk out by its roots. When his father congratulated him he beamed. "And just think," he said, "the whole world had hold of the other end of it."

Subjective time is relative. As one scientist put it, if you sit on a hot stove, a minute seems like an hour. If a pretty girl sits on your lap, an hour seems like a minute.

In the window of a locksmith's shop was a sign: "Keys Made While You Wait." Business was slow and he tried to figure out what the problem was.
He finally decided that people just don't like to wait. So he changed the sign to read: "Keys Made While You Watch."

Don't forget about the little fellow who put on his application for a lumberjack's job that he had learned his trade in the Sahara Forest. The employment manager said with a smile. "You mean the Sahara Desert." The little man struck out his chest and said, "Sure, now it is."

The young boy was showing off to his father what a hitter he was; three time he tossed the ball into the air and swung at it and missed each time. At the third miss he said, "Boy, what a pitcher I am!"

179

George W. Mallone tells the story about the youngest son in a family who was asked to say the blessing at breakfast one morning. With his head bowed and his eyes tightly shut, he prayed in a clear, loud voice: "We thank Thee, God, for this beautiful day and for our food. Amen."

Everyone at the table glared at him. The day was not beautiful. It was a miserable day—cold, damp, and dark. His father said sternly, "You must never pray insincerely like that."

An older brother muttered, "What a jerk! Trying to be smart."

And his mother asked, "What do you mean, 'A beautiful day!'?"

As the youngster reached for the strawberry jam, he simply said, "You can't judge a day by its weather."

I like that. "You can't judge a day by its weather." We can choose.

I like the attitude of the coach of a school boxing team. Some of the new boxers were good, some not-so-good. One of the latter, after trying hard for a couple of rounds, asked the coach, "Have I done him any damage?"

"No," said the disgusted coach, "but keep on swinging. The draft might give him a cold."

I like the story about the man who was applying for a life insurance policy. He was surprised to learn that the medical history of his mother and father played such a big role in his insurability.

The medical examiner put him on the spot. He told about his mother's death at forty-three of tuberculosis. The doctor frowned. At what age did his father die, he was asked. "A little past thirty-nine." "What cause?" "Cancer," the man answered truthfully.

"Bad family record," said the doctor. "No use going further," and he tore up the entry blank. Determined not to make the same mistake twice, the man applied for a policy at another company. "What was your father's age at death?" he was asked. "He was ninety-six," the man replied this time. "And what did he die from?" asked the doctor. "Father was thrown from a pony at a polo game," was the reply. "How old was your mother at death?" the doctor asked in a matter-of-face way. "She was ninety-four," the man answered. "Cause of death?" asked the doctor. "Childbirth," answered the man.

It's kind of like the young fellow who was walking near a draft board during the Vietnam war. A neighbor said, "You had better stay away—you are liable to get drafted." The young man said, "Well, I always figure I have got two chances: I might get drafted and I might not. And even if I'm drafted, I still have two chances: I might pass and I might not. And if I pass, I still have two chances: I might go across and I might not. And even if I go across, I still have two chances: I might get shot and I might not. And even if I get shot, I still have two chances: I might die, and I might not. And even if I die, I still have got two chances!"

I like the story about the man in Budapest who goes to his rabbi and complains, "Life is unbearable. There are nine of us living in one room. What can I do?" The rabbi answers, "Take your goat into the room with you." The man is incredulous, but the rabbi insists. "Do as I say and come back in a week."

A week later the man comes back looking more distraught than before. "We cannot stand it," he tells the rabbi. "The goat is filthy." The rabbi then tells him, "Go home and let the goat out. And come back in a week."

A radiant man returns to the rabbi a week later, exclaiming, "Life is beautiful. We enjoy every minute of it now that there's no goat—only the nine of us."

Some of us have a basically negative attitude about life in general. E. Stanley Jones told about a little girl whom he knew who started out one day on an orgy of self-expression, in other words, she was naughty. Her mother said to her, "You do this, my child." And the child answered, "I don't want to." The mother, being very busy, said, "Alright, then you do what you want to do." The little girl heaved a big sigh and said, "I don't want to do what I want to do."

There is a *Peanuts* cartoon strip which goes like this: Snoopy the dog is feeling great. He comes dancing into the first frame saying to himself: "Sometimes I love life so much I can't express it!" In the second frame he continues to dance: "I feel that I want to take the first person I meet into my arms, and dance merrily through the streets." Then, in the third frame, he meets very grumpy Lucy: Snoopy is silent. In the fourth frame, he is dancing again: "I feel that I want to take the second person I meet into my arms, and dance merrily through the streets."

Earl Nightingale tells about a man running toward a large river. As he reached the dock he increased his speed and when he came to the end he threw himself as high and as far out as he could before hitting the water, landing about ten feet from the dock. As soon as he surfaced he swam back to the land and tried it again, over and over again. A friend asked him, "What are you doing?" He said, "A friend of mine has bet me a million dollars to one that I can't jump across the river and after thinking over those odds, I couldn't help at least trying."

An important part of prayer is LISTENING TO WHAT GOD WOULD SAY TO US. But sometimes God does not say what we want to hear. A favorite story is about an agnostic who fell off a cliff. About halfway down he caught hold of a bush sticking out of the cliff. There he was hanging, momentarily spared, but still too far from the ground to let go! He begins to pray: (Note: this story is most effective if the speaker exaggerates his voice here) "Is any body up there?" A voice answers, "Yes, this is the Lord." The man yells frantically, "Help me." There is a moment of silence. Then the Lord answers: "Let go of the bush and I will save you." There is another silence as the man looks down at the ground far below. Finally he yells: "Is there anybody else up there?"

Why is it that God so often says to us things we do not want to hear? Could it be because most of the problems you and I have are not on the outside, but on the inside? Our situation is only part of our problem. Our inward condition is our greater problem.

Mrs. Finch—a sweet, elderly widow—bowed her head to pray. For the last week her prayer had been the same—that God would send her some bread. This dear lady lived in poverty and she realized that she would run out of food soon. Her only prayer was for bread to nourish her a few more days.

One day, two mischievous boys heard her prayer as they were passing her cottage. They quickly devised a scheme to surprise the old lady. The next day the boys arrived at the woman's prayer time and climbed on her roof. When she made her request for bread they dropped a loaf of bread down her chimney.

Upon opening the package and seeing the bread, she began to dance around, shouting praises to God. The two pranksters slid off her roof and rapped on her door. Upon opening it, the laughing boys told her that it was they, not the Lord, who supplied the bread. Smilingly she replied, "I asked God for bread and He gave me bread, even if he did let the devil deliver it."

An overweight business associate of mine decided it was time to shed some excess pounds. He took his new diet seriously, even changing his driving route to avoid his favorite bakery. One morning, however, he arrived at work carrying a gigantic coffeecake. We all scolded him, but his smile remained cherubic.

"This is a very special coffeecake," he explained. "I accidently drove by the bakery this morning and there in the window were a host of goodies. I felt this was no accident, so I prayed, 'Lord, if you want me to have one of these delicious coffeecakes, let me have a parking place directly in front of the bakery.'

"And sure enough," he continued, "the eighth time around the block, there it was!"
                                                                    Jim Grant in *Reader's Digest.*

It is said that one of President Reagan's favorite stories is the one about the minister's son who was taken out camping one day. His companion warned him not to stray too far from the campfire because the woods were full of wild beasts of all kinds. The young boy had every intention, really. of following that advice but inevitably he was drawn by curiosity and wandered farther and farther from the fire. Suddenly, he found himself face to face with a very large and very powerful looking bear. He saw no means of escape and seeing the bear advance rather menacingly towards him, the minister's son did what he had been taught to do. He knelt down to pray for deliverance. He closed his eyes tightly, but opened them a few moments later and was delighted to see the bear was also kneeling in prayer right in front of him. And he said "Oh, bear, isn't this wonderful! Here we are with such different view points and such different lives and such different perceptions of life and we're both praying to the same Lord." The bear said evenly, "Son, I don't know about you, but I'm saying grace."

We are so shallow in our understanding of prayer. Many of you may follow the delightful cartoon series, *"The Family Circus,"* by Bill Keane. In one of them, the older brother leans on a crushed football and says, "I need a new football. I don't know if I should send up a prayer, write a letter to Santa Claus, or call Grandma."

I think prayer meetings were killed in a lot of churches by the same people praying the same monotonous prayers week after week. You might remember the story of the old fellow who prayed every Wednesday night at his prayer meeting, "O Lord, for the wings of a dove that I might fly away and be at rest." Every prayer meeting night it was that same prayer. A younger member of the group could no longer bear it. One night he muttered under his breath just as the fellow had finished praying that same prayer for the hundredth time, "Lord, stick another feather in him and let him fly."

A priest and a parishioner are golfing together, and the latter noticed that every time the priest was about to putt he crossed himself. And every putt went right in! After four holes of that the parishioner asked, "Father, does that really work for you?" "Oh, yes indeed!" the priest replied. So on the fifth green the parishioner crossed himself, drew back the putter, tapped the ball, and missed the hole by a good foot and a half. "I thought you said it works," the frustrated golfer complained, "Ah, it does," the priest replied, "but you also have to know how to putt!"

Charlie Brown, that widely known theologian of the comic strip, once reported to Lucy as he knelt beside his bed for prayer, "I think I've made a new theological discovery. If you hold your hands upside down, you get the opposite of what you pray for."

Will Rogers once said that the history of North America would be written in three phases: The passing of the Indian, the passing of the buffalo and the passing of the buck.

Bishop Kennedy tells a good little story about a mother who heard the family cat yowl in pain. She knew where to look: she looked for her son Tommy, and said, "Tommy, stop pulling his tail." Replied Tommy, "I'm not pulling his tail. I'm just standing on it. He's doing the pulling."

Comments the bishop: "So we put the blame on the cat, or on the poor, or on the White House, or on the union. This is the age of the alibi. Where does one find an honest facing of the facts and a true picture of the situation? Only in the church."

Little Emily, the minister's daughter, ran into the house, crying as though her heart would break.

"What's wrong, dear?" asked the pastor.

"My doll! Billy broke it!" she sobbed.

"How did he break it, Emily?"

"I hit him over the head with it."

A candidate for a job was asked what he would do if he saw two trains approaching from opposite directions on a single track. He pondered for a moment and replied, "I would call my brother." "Why," he was asked. "Well," he replied thoughtfully, "he hasn't ever seen a train wreck."

E. Stanley Jones tells about a visitor to a mental hospital who saw workmen hauling materials for a new building. Among them was a patient with a wheelbarrow, but turned upside down. When the visitor asked him why he had it upside down, he replied: "Do you think I'm crazy? If I had it turned up, they would fill it."

The questionnaire included a space to give the reason he left his last job. His response: "Done all the work."

He had also served in the Army, and to the question, "Why did you leave the armed services?" he answered, "Won the war."

"Slippery ice, very thin pretty girl tumbled in. Saw a boy upon the bank—gave a shriek, and then she sank. Boy on bank heard her shout, jumped right in—helped her out. Now he's hers — very nice; but she had to break the ice."

We are like the old lady who sued her boyfriend for slander twenty years after he called her a hippopotamus. The judge asked her why she didn't sue him sooner. "I just found out what a hippopotamus looks like," she said.

Writing a composition on Ben Franklin, one student informs us: "Benjamin Franklin was a poor boy. He went to Philadelphia to live. He didn't have many clothes. One day he walked down the street and saw a pretty girl. She smiled at him he smiled at her. Before long they were married and he discovered electricity."

No matter how lovesick you may be, don't take the first pill that comes along.

"High heels," said Christopher Morley, "were invented by a woman who had always been kissed on the forehead!" In other words, if you are going to make good connections, be sure to start on the level.

A friend asked a young minister why he resigned from his former pastorate. The young pastor answered, "Because there were 15 single women there, all trying to marry me."
"But don't you know there's safety in numbers?"
"Not for me" the minister laughed, "I found mine in Exodus."

As we move closer to Valentine's Day, we start to think about the meaning of love in our lives. You may know the story about the little boy who wanted to spy on his sister and her new beau. He knew they liked to sit under a certain tree, so before the young suitor arrived, the little boy climbed high up in the tree and hid himself.
Soon he heard the amorous young couple down below. The fellow was evidently trying to make his first advance and impress the girl at the same time. He looked up at the night sky and said with a loud voice, "Little star up above, should I kiss the girl I love?" Boy, was he surprised when he heard a voice from above answer, "Sixteen-year-old down below; pucker up and let her go!"

Whenever a fellow opens the door of a car for his wife, you can either assume that the car is new or the wife is new. There is that tendency to take one another for granted, and we husbands need to be aware of that. Somebody once said, "Before a man gets married, he lies awake in bed all night thinking about what his beloved said. After they are married, he falls asleep before she has finished saying it." I suspect that many of you can identify with that. There is that continuing need for romance in marriage.

Forgetfulness can have tragic consequences in any profession, but probably no more than in the ministry. One day, a retired pastor was giving a seminary graduate advice on how to conduct his first wedding ceremony. Finally, the senior minister concluded with this instruction: "If, in the middle of the ceremony, you should forget the words, just quote the first passage of scripture that comes to mind." Sure enough, during his first wedding, the young pastor lost his place and forgot what he was suppose to say next. Remembering the elder's advice, he quoted the first verse that came to mind: "Father, forgive them: for they know not what they are doing!"

I will never forget the story of a famous bishop who spoke at a theological seminary. He repeated Jesus' story of the wise and foolish maidens. Then he looked those seminarians in the eye and challenged them, "Young men, would you rather be in the light with the ten wise maidens or out in the dark with the ten foolish maidens?" I am not certain the bishop was able to finish his message. For those who stand in the shadows there is the grudging obeisance to religion, but there is also that nagging suspicion that we would rather be out in the dark with the ten foolish maidens.

Dr. Peter Rhea Jones tells the story about a trapper out in the woods. He had his wife out there in the far wilderness and they had a little baby son. After the child was born, unfortunately, the wife abandoned the boy and her husband and left them out in the wilderness and returned to life in a more civilized setting. The father and the son continued to live out in the far wilderness. They never went into town. But the man became increasingly bitter toward women. He never told his boy about the opposite sex and the boy never saw any girls. Finally at age twenty the necessity came for them to travel some distance to a city to buy some goods. As they were coming into the city that boy began to notice something he had never seen before: all those pretty girls. And he said, "Paw, what are those?" His father, who was hostile toward women, said, "Aw, son, they are just silly gooses." They went on doing their work and buying their supplies and they were ready to go back home, and the father generously said, "Son, we're going to go back and won't be returning for a long time. I'll buy you anything you want." He said, "Paw, how 'bout one of them gooses?"

Matt Prince tells about the daughter of a fashionable couple from a large eastern city who went to Africa as a Peace Corps volunteer. She had been to finishing school and her parents had made every effort to see that she was properly prepared to occupy a place in their social strata.

When the young woman's term on the field was over she sent a telegram announcing that she would be bringing her new husband home with her. Her mother and father waited with excited anticipation at the airport gate. Their daughter emerged from the plane on the arm of a man about seven feet tall who was adorned in feathers, beads, skulls, tigers' teeth, and assorted pouches of magical potions around his neck. He even had a bone through his nose and rings in his ears. The mother fainted. As the father held his now unconscious wife, he shouted to his daughter, "No, no, dear. We said we wanted you to marry a rich doctor."

I heard that one of our young people went out on a date the other night. He said to his girlfriend, "If I try to kiss you, will you yell for help?" And she said, "Only if you think you need help." I heard about another young man who went out on a date and was out parked on a hillside with a young lady, and he asked the same question, "May I kiss you?" And she said, "It's kind of stuffy here in the car. If you could lower the top on your car, then you could kiss me." He was telling one of his friends about this, and he said that it took him five whole minutes to get the top down on that car. And the friend said, "Well I can take the top down off of my car faster than that." And the young man said, "Yes, but you have a convertible."

Gene Yasenak in *Family Weekly* once wrote this little humorous line, "Kissing is a means of getting two people so close together that they can't see anything wrong with each other."

Romantic love is one of God's greatest gifts to us. Every survey of what makes people happy shows that the happiest people are those who have love in their lives. Conversely, the greatest pain in this world is the pain of rejection. We know how the fellow felt who confided to his old friend that life was now empty because the women he loved had refused to marry him.

"Don't let that get you down," said the friend, "A woman's 'no' often means 'yes'."

"She didn't say 'no,' came the reply, "she said 'phooey.' "

An Indiana pastor illustrated the importance of timing in most colorful language. It's like a boy and girl planning to take a romantic walk in the moonlight, and one says, "If you get there first, go right on, don't wait for me."

– Lyle E. Schaller, **Parish Planning** (Nashville: Abingdon Press, 1971).

Bob Roberts tells a story that appeared in the newspapers sometime back about a mother of eight in Darlington, Maryland. She had been visiting next door, and went into the living room, she saw her five youngest children huddled in the center floor, on her new carpet very much involved with something wiggly and squirmy. On closer examination, and to her total dismay, she discovered that the children were gathered around a family of skunks. In her horror she screamed, "Run, children, run!" Whereupon each child grabbed a skunk and ran.

That may be a parable of our lives. We may be horrified at that part of our lives that is selfish, sinful, neglectful, and even cruel. Yet we cannot leave it behind anymore than those early disciples could escape from their sinful nature.

And then there was the little girl whose voice rang out above the others as she sang, "Just as I am, without one flea."

Here's one of my very favorites: One mother had been sick in bed for several days, and so her daughter decided to make her some hot tea to make her feel better. The six-year-old brought the tea into the room and then waited as her mother drank it, so that she could be properly congratulated for her good deed. Her mother drank the tea, and then asked the little girl how she went about making it. "Just like you do, mommy," replied the girl. "First I took the tea leaves and boiled them, then I strained them" she went on. "What did you use to strain them?" her mother asked. "Oh," replied the girl, "I couldn't find the strainer, so I used the fly swatter." Sensing that she had said something wrong, the daughter tried to put her mind at ease and said, "Oh, not the new fly swatter — I used the old one."

The sick feeling that mother must have had in her stomach is the feeling I get when I see some of the things that happen in this world. . .

A guy got a job painting a yellow line down the highway. After three days, the foreman complained: "The first day you did great — you painted that yellow line three miles. The second day wasn't bad — you did two miles. But today you only painted one mile, so I'm going to have to fire you."

On his way out of the foreman's office, the guy looked back and said: "It's not my fault. Each day I got farther from the paint can."

Someone put it this way concerning our relationship with God: "If we are not as close to God as we used to be, who moved?"

It was the brilliant Oscar Wilde who made famous that much-quoted line, "I can resist everything except temptation." In another connection he said, "The only way to get rid of temptation is to yield to it."

I like the story about the battered old man who got up one night during a revival meeting and said: "Brothers and sisters, you know and I know that I ain't been what I ought to of been. I've stolen hogs and told lies, and got drunk, and was always getting in fights, and shooting craps, and playing poker, and I've cussed and swore; but I thank the Lord there's one thing I ain't never done: I ain't never lost my religion."

A pastor tells about visiting a little black church in Southwest Virginia. An elderly man was teaching a Sunday School class to a group of young people. That elderly man put it this way: "If you're driving down the road and you see Satan standing by the road trying to catch a ride, don't you dare stop the car, don't you dare open the door, don't you dare let him in, 'cause it won't be long until he'll want to drive."

Or the story of the little girl who cut off a large portion of her hair. "But how did you know, Mommy?" she asked, "I hid the hair that I cut off very carefully? How did you know?"

We are told that Phillips Brooks' preaching was fired by a glowing personality. He loved Christ. He loved people. Especially did he love little children.
They tell this story on him. One April Fool's Day, as he was walking down a Boston street, he saw a little fellow trying in vain to reach a door bell. True to his love for children, Brooks went up the steps saying, "Let me help you, my little man!" Brooks rang the door bell. The little boy scampered down the steps shouting back to Brooks, "Now, run like the devil."

Maybe you heard about the little boy who went to kindergarten the first day. The teacher asked him his name. He replied, "Willie don't." Obviously that is what he heard all the time at home, so he thought "don't" was his middle name. I suspect that some of us grew up in the church thinking that our name was "Christian Don't."

We modern folks don't like to talk about our sins. If we do, we don't call them sins. We call them weaknesses, mistakes, frailties. If we should call them sins we do it with a snicker. Like the couple who was visiting a new church one Sunday, arriving a few minutes late. The congregation was praying a prayer of confession. As they walked in, the minister and the congregation were reading aloud: "We have left undone those things that we ought to have done, and we have done those things which we ought not to have done." The visiting man nudged his wife and whispered, "That's us. We're in the right crowd this Sunday."

189

Writer Bill Reel of the *New York Daily News* did a story this summer on a New York Mets reserve player named Clint Hurdle. Hurdle was telling several hundred people sitting in the parking lot of the Salem Evangelical Free Church in Staten Island, N.Y. of the change that Jesus Christ had brought in his life. Faith in God, he said, had made him a happy man.

"I dreamed last night I died and went to Heaven," said Hurdle. "St. Peter showed me around. He took me into a room filled with clocks. I wondered what all the clocks were for. St. Peter said there was a clock in Heaven for everybody on earth, and that when anybody sinned, his clock jumped ahead on hour."

"I found the clocks of my Christian friends on the Mets," Hurdle continued. "There are a lot of Christians on the team—Gary Carter, George Foster, Sid Fernandez, Mookie Wilson, Ronn Reynolds, Terry Leach, Roger McDowell, coach Bill Robinson, manager Davey Johnson—and I began watching their clocks.

"Every time one jumped ahead, I'd get self-righteous and say, 'Gary, I know what you're doin', or 'George, you better straighten out.'

"I watched their clocks for a while, jumping ahead an hour with each sin, and then a thought occurred to me. I asked St. Peter, 'By the way, where's my clock?

"And St. Peter said, 'We keep your clock in the kitchen and use it for a fan.' "

One man, after listening to a list of the ten commandments remarked, "Well, at least I've never made any graven images."

A father had just given his reckless teen-age son a lecture on his wild behavior. "Do you know what happens," he concluded, "when you break one of the Ten Commandments?" "Sure, Pop," was the youth's calm reply, "You have nine left."

An Army sergeant sought to lead an Episcopal worship service in the absence of the base chaplain. He read the Call to Worship, the invocation, led the men through the Prayer of Confession, then read the Absolution of Sins. It was then that he noticed in small print in the prayer book that only an ordained minister could give the Absolution. He knew that he was not ordained. He was stumped for a minute. Then he remembered that he was a sergeant. He faced them squarely with chest out and chin in and sounded off, "As you were, men. As you were."

A department store ran this advertisement in a newspaper: "For sale at reduced prices—shirts for men with minor flaws."

A man, much the worse for wear, was standing before the court. The judge eyed him menacingly. "You are accused by your landloard of being drunk and setting fire to the bed."

"It's a lie, Judge," cried the man indignantly. "That bed was on fire when I got in it!"

A down-and-out derelict stood on a street corner one day and watched a big limousine bearing a boyhood friend drive by. With a philosophical shrug he sighed: "Ah, there but for me, go I."

You may know Schiller's story of the time when the Emperor Frederick the Great visited Potsdam Prison. Each man he interviewed proclaimed complete innocence. They were victims of a frame-up. Someone else was to blame. But at last, one poor fellow with his head hanging down, never looking up, said, "Your Majesty, I am guilty and richly deserve my punishment." Frederick bellowed for the warden, "Come and free this soul, and get him out of here before he corrupts all the noble, innocent people in this prison!"

A little girl came home from school with pride over what she had learned that day. She was eager to tell someone. "Daddy," she exclaimed eagerly, "I learned what the earth does every twenty-four hours." "What does it do, honey?" dutifully asked her father. "It revolts on its abscess," was the quick answer.

During his ordination examination a seminary classmate of mine was being asked a series of doctrinal questions by an elderly minister. He came to this question: "Do you believe in the Doctrine of the Total Depravity of the Human Soul?"

The candidate brought down the house with his immediate smiling reply. "Yes, but I find it very difficult to live up to!"

Kendrick Strony, **All the Master's Men** (Chappaqua, NY: Christian Herald Books, 1978).

A man was going to a Halloween party dressed as a devil. On the way it began to rain, so he darted into a church where a revival was in progress. At the sight of his devil's costume, people began to scatter through doors and windows. One lady got her coat caught on the arm of a pew. As the man came closer, she begged, "Satan, I've been a member of this church for 20 years, but I've really been on your side all the time!"

191

I can appreciate the story of a little boy named Bobby who badly wanted a new bicycle. His plan was to save his nickels, dimes, and quarters until he finally had enough to buy a new 10-speed. Each night he took his concern to the Lord. Kneeling beside his bed, he prayed, "Lord, please help me save for my new bicycle and please Lord, don't let the ice cream man come down our street tomorrow."

There is a joke about how the various nationalities view lovemaking that will make you laugh or will make you cry. The woman says afterwards:
   French: C'est magnifique, Henri, magnifique!
   British: There, Sydney, I hope you feel better now.
   American: What did you say your name is?

In the cartoon *Ebb and Flow*, Ebb notices that Flow has returned home from a shopping trip with several packages: "Flow, I thought you were only going window shopping!"
   Flow replies: "I was--but the Devil tempted me!"
   Ebb: "Then, why didn't you say, 'Get behind me, Satan!' "
   Flow: "I did!–But then he whispered over my shoulder: 'Honey, it fits so beautifully at the back!' "

There was a cartoon several years ago in the *Saturday Review of Literature* in which little George Washington is standing with an axe in his hand. Before him lying on the ground is the famous cherry tree. He has already made his smug admission that he did it–after all, he "cannot tell a lie." But his father is standing there exasperated saying, "All right, so you admit it! You <u>always</u> admit it! The question is, when are you going to stop <u>doing</u> it."

You may be familiar with the story of a man who discovered his little daughter praying for him out loud. Afterwards he said to the little girl, "Honey, I appreciate you praying for me, but did you have to tell God that I have a hangover? Couldn't you have said just a headache?"

Here is a subtle but salient piece of humor. A priest was on a mission of mercy in the middle of the night. As he passed an alley a figure with a gun stepped out and demanded: "Give me your money." The priest told the gunman: "My billfold is in the pocket of my coat." He opened his coat to get it, revealing his Roman collar. "Oh, I didn't know you were a priest," stuttered the holdup man. "Pardon me, Father. Keep your money." In grateful relief father offered him a cigar but the fellow shook his head: "No thanks, Father, I'm not smoking during Lent."

192

I was speaking at a women's organization, and they asked if I would mind standing in a reception line following the meeting. The program chairperson was quite persuasive, so I agreed to do so. The speech must have gone well, because the ladies coming through the line were saying nice things to me, and smiling as they shook my hand.

Pretty soon I noticed a little boy standing in front of me. He looked straight at me and said, "Your speech stunk!"

Well, there were more ladies coming through the line so I just ignored him. But a little while later he came through the line a second time. Again, he placed himself directly in front of me and said, "We heard all your jokes before—and they weren't even very funny."

That bothered me a bit, but there were still people in line, so I continued shaking hands and greeting the ladies. Then I noticed that this young boy was in line for a third time. He got up to me, and this time he said, "You'll never be invited back here again!"

At this point I really didn't know what to do. I figured he was too little to hit, and I was too big to cry—so I shrugged it off as an occupational hazard and continued greeting the ladies.

Wouldn't you know it, a little while later I noticed, out of the corner of my eye, this bratty little kid in line for a fourth time.

At this point his mother must have noticed him too; because she came running over to me, leaned over my shoulder, and said, "Oh, Mr. Woerpel—that's my son, Billy. Please don't pay any attention to him. He's only five years old. You know, he's just at that age where he repeats everything he hears."

–Dwayne R. Woerple, Manager, Public Communications Standard, 10.1, (Ohio).

My father gave me these hints on speech-making: Be sincere . . . be brief . . . be seated.

– James Roosevelt

Or as someone else has put it:
    Stand up to be seen,
    Speak up to be heard and understood,
    And shut up to be appreciated.

An author was due to deliver the first speech of his lecture tour. "I'm such a miserable speaker," he confessed to his agent, "that I know they'll all walk out on me before I finish." "Nonsense!" retorted the agent. "You are an excellent speaker and will keep the audience glued to their seats." "Oh, I say," cried the author, "that is a wonderful idea! But do we dare?"

Any of you who have ever tried speaking in front of people will appreciate the predicament that Dr. Ralph D. Nichols of the University of Minnesota found himself in. He was addressing a high school commencement when suddenly a child began to cry. Then another child added his loud voice. A small boy galloped up and down the aisle, chased by another. With the sinking feeling only a public speaker knows, Nichols realized he had lost his audience.

Nichols tried every trick of the speaker's trade. He spoke more loudly, told a funny story, walked around the stage, peered intently and disapprovingly at the area of disturbance. But all was to no avail.

Then he tried his last desperate trick. He found one good listener—an elderly gentleman in the first row who was looking up, smiling, and nodding his head approvingly. Concentrating all his attention on this one listener, the speaker gradually salvaged the situation and the speech.

During the refreshment period that followed, Nichols asked the school superintendent to introduce him to the old gentleman who had sat on the front row.

"Well, . . . I'll try to introduce you," said the superintendent, "but it may be a little difficult. You see, the poor old fellow is stone-deaf."
– John W. Drakeford, *The Awesome Power of the Listening Heart* (Grand Rapids: Zondervan Publishing, 1982).

"I am the most spontaneous speaker in the world because every word, every gesture and every retort has to be carefully rehearsed."
—George Bernard Shaw

Well, here we go with what I hope is a lively speech. Did you hear of the man who was at the speaker's table and went to sleep, due to the boring talk? The speaker flew into a rage, took the gavel, and hit him over the head. The sleeper awoke, took one look at the speaker, and said, "Hit me again. I can still hear you!"

Al Davis, the head coach of the Oakland Raiders, was guest speaker at a football dinner. As he rose to his feet, a news photographer started jockeying for a good angle. The toastmaster, fearing that Al would be annoyed, snapped at the photographer: "Don't take his picture while he's speaking. Shoot him before he starts."

Toastmaster (to after dinner speaker): "Would you like to give your speech now, Mr. Jones, or should we let 'em enjoy themselves a bit longer?"

When Yogi Berra was playing baseball for the New York Yankees, someone asked him if there was anyone he envied in baseball. He responded that he was jealous of a particular teammate's ability to bat either right-handed or left-handed. Yogi then issued one of his delightful quotes: "I'd give my right arm to be ambidextrous."

"That's quite a slice you had on that golf ball," said the angry policeman to the sheepish duffer. "It curved clear off the course and broke the windshield of my squad car. Just what do you intend to do about it?"

"Well," said the golfer, "I was thinking that probably the best thing to do would be to try moving my thumb a little farther up on the club."

– The Lion

Jim Murray, the sports columnist, spoofed the tendency towards "jargonese" with this idea: "No longer can a Jack Dempsey explain his loss to Gene Tunney with, 'I forgot to duck.' If Dempsey talked like one of these graduate school boys, he'd say, 'I failed to come to terms with my environment.' "

A fisherman was lugging a large fish when he met another fisherman with half a dozen small ones on a string.

"Howdy," said the first fisherman, dropping the huge fish and waiting for a comment.

The fellow with the string of small ones stared and stared. Then he said calmly, "Just caught the one, eh?"

– Contributed

I'm like the guy who had only been playing golf for a month.
But it took him four years to learn.

Executive: A person who follows his work schedule to a tee.

– Family Weekly.

There is the story of the man who was watching his fourth football game of the weekend when his wife stepped in front of the television and said, "You love football more than me."

He gently pushed her aside, stared back at the set and said, "Yes, dear, but I love you more than basketball."

Factory bulletin: "Anyone desiring to attend the funeral of a near relative must notify foreman before 10 a.m. on day of the game."

GOLFER: A man who drags 30 pounds of equipment for miles but has his wife bring him an ash-tray!

A new arrival was stopped at the pearly gates. "I'm sorry," explained Saint Peter, "but you told too many lies during your time on earth. I'm afraid you'll have to go you-know-where."

"Ah, come on now, Saint Peter," begged the newly arrived one. "Have a heart. After all, you were once a fisherman yourself."

An Englishman watching his first American football game was asked, "How do you like it?"

"Not a bad game, except for all those committee meetings they hold before each play," he answered.

"Ability is the art of getting credit for all the home runs that somebody else hits."

-- *Casey Stengel, the old Perfessor*

Young man: "Well, I went to the football tryouts today."
Girlfriend: "Good! Did you make the team?"
Young man: "I think so. The coach took one look at me and said, 'This is the end.'"

It's easy to understand why Americans love pro sports. Where else do you get a chance to yell terrible things at millionaires?

– G. G. Crabtree

Eddie Arcaro claims a Western horse owner raced an eight-year-old that had never raced before. Although an old horse with no record attracts no bets, this one galloped home first with a good margin to spare, an 80 to 1 shot. Naturally suspicious the stewards asked the owner. "How come you never raced this horse before?" Retorted the one under inquisition: "Well, to tell you the truth, gentlemen, we couldn't catch him until he was seven!"

Sports do not build character. They reveal it.   – Heywood Hale Broun

There are two kinds of fishermen—those who insist that they fish for the sport, and those who catch something.

– Arnold H. Glasow

I heard a story the other day of a Roman Catholic priest who was a weekly golfer. One day he needed an eagle in order to win the game. (An eagle, as you may know, is hitting the ball and getting it in the hole two strokes under par.) So the priest took a big swing, but it was an awful slice. Just as the ball was spinning out of control there was an enormous clap of thunder. As lightning struck the ball, it hit a tree and bounced off, angled off a fence, hit another tree and landed in the sandtrap. But then it bounced out of the sandtrap, rolled onto the green, curled twice around the hole and rolled in for an eagle. The pious priest looked up toward heaven, and said, "Thank you, Father, but I'd rather do it myself."

– Robert Schuller

Rodney Dangerfield: "I went to a fight the other night and a hockey game broke out."

If you think fishermen are the biggest liars in the world, ask a jogger how far he runs every morning.

When a coach was asked if all the praise heaped by the press on a star athlete would not go the young man's head, the coach said, "No, he can't read."

I like the story of the fisherman in Alaska who was having no luck fishing through the ice. Next to him was a man pulling them in left and right. He asked him how he did it. The successful fisherman mumbled something unintelligible. The unlucky man asked him again, explaining he couldn't understand. The successful fisherman put his hand to his mouth, spat something into it, and then said, "You've got to keep your worms warm."

The ancient Aztecs had a tradition. In any athletic contest the leader of the losing team was sacrificed to the sun. Fortunately none of our college athletic departments have thought of that yet.

For the parent of a Little Leaguer, a baseball game is simply a nervous breakdown divided into innings.

—Earl Wilson

Tryouts for the school boxing team were being conducted. Some of the new boxers were good, some not-so-good. One of the latter, after trying hard for a couple of rounds, asked the coach, "Have I done him any damage?"

"No," said the disgusted coach, "but keep on swinging. The draft might give him a cold."

A harried husband in Detroit, greatly depressed: "Everything has gone wrong. I see no hope. My house just burned down, my daughter eloped with a scoundrel, my wife has left me, the bank is foreclosing on my mortgage, and the Tigers lost two to three in the ninth. Imagine that! . . . two to three in the ninth!"

There are a lot of football fanatics around our city. I was seated next to one — a lady — at a football game not too long ago. There was an empty seat beside her. "It was my husband's," she explained. "Oh, I'm sorry," I said. Then as an after-thought I asked, "Isn't there someone else in the family who could use the ticket?" "No," she replied, "They are all at the funeral."

Bing Crosby used to tell a story about a priest friend that has a lot of theology to it. His friend, Father Kelly, was an avid golfer. One day on his favorite course, he had a most difficult shot to make. "I guess I'll just have to swing and pray," he said to his caddy. When the ball landed in a sandtrap, Father Kelly exclaimed, "Well, I guess the Lord didn't hear." "Maybe so," said the caddy, "but in our church we keep our heads down when we pray."

A priest went with one of his parishioners to a baseball game. "Watch No. 21 out there," said the padre proudly, "he always crosses himself before he steps up to the plate." Tell me, Father," asked his companion, "Does that help him get on base?" Replied the cleric wisely, "It does if he is a good hitter."

One comedian said a goalie from a professional hockey team took his son and himself out to dinner. "There we sat," he said, "Father, son and goalie host."

A testimonial dinner was being given for the town's leading citizen. He was called upon to tell the story of his life. "Friends and neighbors," he said in a shaking voice, "when I first came here thirty years ago, I walked into your town on a muddy dirty road. I had only one suit on my back, one pair of shoes on my feet, and all my earthly possessions were wrapped in a red bandana tied to a stick I carried over my shoulder.

"This city has been good to me. Today I'm chairman of the board of the bank, I own hotels, apartment buildings, and office buildings. I own three companies with branches in forty-nine cities. I am on the board of all the leading clubs. Yes, friends, your town has been good to me."

After the banquet, an awed youngster approached the great man and asked, timidly, "Sir, could you tell me what you had wrapped in that red bandana when you walked into this town thirty years ago?"

I think, son," he said, "I was carrying about $500,000 cash and some $900,000 in government bonds."

Quizmaster: "How many successful jumps must a paratrooper make before he graduates?"
Contestant: "All of them."

It took me fifteen years to discover I had no talent for writing, but I couldn't give it up because by that time I was too famous.
—Robert Benchley

Big shots are little shots who keep shooting.

You cannot climb the ladder of success with your hands in your pockets.

Two shoe salesmen went to Africa to open up new territories. Three days after their arrival, the first salesman sent a cablegram: "Returning on next plane. Can't sell shoes here. Everybody goes barefoot." Nothing was heard from the second salesman for about two weeks. Then came a fat air-mail envelope with this message for the home office: "Fifty orders enclosed. Prospects unlimited. Nobody here has shoes."

Living With a Ten-Inch Frying Pan

An excellent sermon starter is Robert Schuller's famous story of the fisherman with the ten-inch frying pan. It is found in his book, **You Can Become the Person You Want to Be**:

A tourist walked down a pier and watched a fisherman pull in a large fish, measure it, and throw it back. He caught a second fish, smaller this time, he measured it, and put it in his bucket. Oddly, all the large fish that he caught that measured ten inches or more he discarded. All fish smaller than ten inches he kept. Puzzled, the curious onlooker questioned, "Pardon me, but why do you keep the little ones and throw the big ones away?" The old fellow looked up and without blinking an eye said, "Why, because my frying pan measures only ten inches across!"

The ten-inch frying pan can represent our dreams and goals. With young people it might represent their physical, mental and spiritual capacities. We often limit our ability to live life abundantly because all we have is a ten-inch frying pan.

Just as there are two prevalent attitudes toward life, there are basically two types of personalities in this world as illustrated by the following story. Two men decide to go on a safari in Africa. The first makes little preparation and shows up at the airport with a minimal amount of the appropriate jungle gear. The second has spent months getting ready. He has every item he could conceivably need: cameras, a rifle, mosquito netting, guidebooks, camping equipment, etc. Arriving in Africa they travel by jeep to their campsite. At the campsite the first man proceeds immediately into the jungle to explore the terrain. The second dutifully sets up the tent and makes preparation for the evening. Suddenly the first man comes upon a ferocious tiger. The man heads for the campsite with the tiger in hot pursuit. Reaching the tent he swings around the center post and heads back out again closing the tent behind him, Meanwhile he shouts to his friend, "Here's your tiger, now I am going back for mine."

Dr. Roy Angell tells about a country preacher in Texas many years ago who went one night to preach his first sermon at a new church. While he was preaching, some mischievous boys took the wheels off his buggy and swapped them around — putting the smaller front wheels on the rear and the larger rear wheels on the front. It was quite dark when he came out after the service and rode over to the home of a deacon who lived nearby. The next morning at breakfast he remarked to his host that there was quite a hill between the church and the deacon's home. The good deacon replied that there was no hill — the ground was absolutely flat.

The preacher protested: "I know there was a hill. I could feel my horse straining and the buggy tilted." Later the two men shared a good laugh when they discovered the source of the mysterious 'hill.'

Some of us have turned life into an uphill struggle. We have our rear wheels in back. Because we have our priorities out of order, life becomes more complex, more difficult. It becomes uphill all the way.

In helping us to be thankful, we need to be reminded Who it is that is the source of all that we have. A popular story tells this well:

The radio had predicted heavy rains for many days. Now the flooding was beginning. Rescue teams were sent out to tell people to evacuate their homes. One gentleman noted for his piety refused to go with the rescue team that came to take him by car to higher ground. "The Lord will take care of me," he said with conviction. Soon the water began covering his front yard. This time would-be rescuers came in a motor boat. "The Lord will take care of me," he announced. A day later the house was filled with water and the man was stranded on his roof. Again a rescue team came — this time in a helicopter. "The Lord will rescue me," he said in refusing their help. Soon the water was up over the man's waist even on top of the house. He was getting worried. "Lord," he prayed with great earnestness, "When are you going to rescue me?" The Lord replied, "What do you mean when am I going to rescue you? I've already tried three times."

The four-year-old was asked how she liked her Thanksgiving dinner. "I didn't like the turkey much, but I sure loved the bread it ate."

We're not very good at saying "Thank you," are we? We're like a little boy I heard about. On his return from a birthday party, his mother queried, "Bobby, did you thank the lady for the party?"

"Well, I was going to. But a girl ahead of me said, "Thank you," and the lady told her not to mention it. So I didn't."

A family was entertaining guests for dinner on a hot, blistering day. When all were seated, the man of the house turned to his six-year-old and asked him to say grace. "But, Daddy, I don't know what to say," he protested. "Oh just say what you've heard me say," the mother chimed in. Obediently he bowed his little head and said, "O Lord, why did I invite these people here on a hot day like this?!"

Each of us has a different list of things for which we are thankful. A Sunday School teacher asked her class to make such a list and one little boy wrote down that he was thankful for his glasses. The teacher was impressed by that. Some young people resent wearing glasses. Here, obviously, was a young man mature enough to appreciate what wearing glasses did for him. "Johnny," she said, "I see that you put your glasses down at the head of the list of things for which you are thankful. Is there any special reason?" Johnny answered, "Yes, ma'am. My glasses keep the boys from hitting me and the girls from kissing me."

201

A noted astronomer found a bishop seated next to him on a plane. In the course of conversation, the astronomer said, "I never had much interest in theology. My religion can be summed up in 'Do unto others as you would have them do unto you.' "

The bishop responded, "Well, I've had little time for astronomy. My views are summed up in 'Twinkle, twinkle, little star.' "

—Lois Maw Cubel

George Bernard Shaw was once asked by a pastor's wife to what particular denomination he belonged. Shaw is said to have answered forcefully: "Madame, I am an atheist — and I thank God for it."

It stumped the prospective employee when he ran across this question on the employment application: "Have you any religious views?" He thought for a minute and then wrote: "No—but I've got a couple of nifty shots of Niagara Falls by night."

The parson should have known better when he said to the old farmer: "You and the Lord have done a fine job of clearing that rocky field." The old farmer replied: "You should have seen it when the Lord had it all to himself."

Perhaps you have heard the revealing story about the young wife who always cut both ends off of a ham before she cooked it. It bothered her new groom whenever she did it. One day he could take it no longer. "Please tell me, honey," he said, "why do you always cut a piece off of both ends of a ham before you cook it?" "I don't know," she answered, "that's just the way my mother always did it." One day he bravely asked his new mother-in-law why she cut both ends off of a ham before she cooked it. "I don't know," she answered, "but that's the way my mother always did it." Finally he asked his wife's grandmother why she always cut both ends off of a ham before she cooked it. "Oh," she said, "it's because I only had one pan to bake with, and it was too small for the whole ham."

There is a story of a Sunday School teacher who held up a portrait of Christ and explained to the class that it was not an actual photograph but an artist's conception of what Christ looks like. "But," said one little girl, "you've got to admit it looks a lot like Him."

Bishop Gerald Kennedy tells this story:

The late Bishop Francis J. McConnell was once president of DePauw University. He always liked to be on the land, and after retirement he lived on a farm in Ohio. When he was at DePauw he had a small acreage where he raised chickens. He said that everything went all right except in the middle of the night the rooster would start to crow and wake everybody up. He could not understand the behavior, so he stayed up one night to find out the trouble. He said that along about two o'clock in the morning, the interurban train coming out from Indianapolis would swing around a curve, and the headlight would shine into the chicken house. The rooster, thinking it was the sun, would begin to crow. And the bishop said, "It is not only roosters that mistake headlights for dawns." Indeed it is not! If men can sometimes bring the darkness, so sometimes in their pride and in their limited knowledge they can promise dawns which never come, and bring disillusionment.

A. Craig Baird, ed., **Representative American Speeches**: 1956-1957 (New York: The H. W. Wilson Co., 1957), p. 185.

Now many of us nowadays do not like to think of God as a God of Judgement. We want a God who is all sweetness and light. We are like the little boy who drew a picture in Sunday School which shows a long, black limousine, a chauffeur in the front with a little stick coming out of his head with a halo on it and, in the back seat, a man and woman dressed in nothing but leaves. Underneath it is the caption: "This is a picture of the Lord driving Adam and Eve out of the Garden of Eden."

If God drove Adam and Eve out of the garden of Eden, He surely drove them in a limousine. God could not possibly throw anybody out of a party for not wearing the right clothes. Or could He?

When Daniel Webster was asked to relate to a group the most profound thought he ever had, he replied simply: "The most profound thought that I have ever had has been my accountability to God."

A Sunday School teacher tells the story of the day and mentions the wonders of creation. For interest, she asks the children to identify some of God's creatures as she describes them. "What's a foot or so long, has a bushy tail, climbs trees and saves nuts?" was one of her questions. None of the little children would answer. Three times she repeated the question, and pleaded for the obvious answer. Finally one little boy got enough courage to reply, "It sounds like a squirrel to me, but I guess it's Jesus." How often the pat and easy and obvious, even trite little Sunday School answers represent our faith.

In one of the *Peanuts* sequences Lucy is frightened because it has been raining and raining. She wonders if there may be a repetition of Noah's flood. But Charlie Brown tells her about God's promise and the meaning of the rainbow. Much relieved, Lucy says, "You've taken a load off my mind." To which Charlie replies, "Good theology has a way of doing that."

203

A visitor to the 1964 New York World's Fair was attracted by all the machine-operated panels at the Baptist exhibit. By just pressing a button, one was able to see data on missions, social outreach, and other items of interest. Just as this visitor reached to press the button, for one of the panels, he noticed a small sign, "Out of Order."

He jokingly told a friend, "I wanted to find out what the Baptist believed, but they were temporarily out of order."

The visitor added seriously that he got to thinking how often Christians of all denominations might have to label their beliefs: "Out of Order."

Said a California playwright to a friend who enjoyed dabbling in new religious fads as the friend was leaving for a vacation abroad: "Perhaps while you're away you'll pick up a new religion." Then he added facetiously, "Be careful when you come back; some things are hard to get through customs, you know."

"Ah, that's all right," was the reply, "new theologies have no duties attached."

Many cults are springing up because, while they make no demands for holy living, they provide no power. They appeal to those who have played church but have found no personal relationship with a living Lord.

See Marcus Bach, **Strangers at the Door** (Nashville: Abingdon, 1971).
Horton Davies, **The Challenge of the Sects.** (Philadelphia: Westminster Press, 1961).

A group of students at Harvard once tried to fool the famous professor of zoology Agassiz. They took parts from a number of different bugs and with great skill attached them together to make a creation they were sure would baffle their teacher. On the chosen day they brought it to him and asked that he identify it. As he inspected it with great care, the students grew more and more sure they had tricked this genius.

Finally, Professor Agassiz straightened up and said, "I have identified it." Scarcely able to control their amusement, they asked its name. Agassiz replied, "It is a humbug. "

– Billy Graham, *How to Be Born Again* (Waco: Word Books, 1977).

It is difficult for any pastor to deal with the Holy Spirit in this day and time. There is so much confusion. We are like the two-year-old who had been to visit his cousins for the day. And when his mother came to pick him up, he was all excited about what they had done. "We played games," he said. "We had peanut butter and jelly sandwiches," he said. "And guess who we saw on TV? Casper, the Holy Ghost!"

The story is told of a judge who stared at a case-hardened criminal. "Because of the gravity of this case," he said, in mellow, earnest tones, "I am going to give you three lawyers."

"Never mind three lawyers," replied the experienced defendant. "Just give me one good witness."

In the younger days of railroading, every main railroad crossing had its crossing guard who was to signal with a lantern that a train was coming. One night, a crossing guard fell asleep in his shack, but woke up and ran out with his lantern seconds before the train came. There was a terrible accident. At the investigation he was asked "Were you present at your job?" "Did you have a lantern?" The crossing guard was exonerated of any blame. He later said, "No one asked me whether or not the lantern was lit."

A lady owned a canary which she greatly valued and to which she was affectionately devoted because it sang so beautifully. Mellow and trilling were the cheery notes with which the lovely little creature brightened her day.

A neighbor boy had caught a sparrow and placed it in a cage, hoping to keep it as a pet. Then the lady and the lad thought it would be a good idea to try to teach the sparrow to sing like the canary.

So they placed the cages side by side, hoping that the glorious songs of the canary would be a "good example" to the sparrow whose musical repertoire was more limited.

Well, it just didn't work out that way. After three weeks, not only did the sparrow fail to sing like the canary, but our yellow-feathered friend was capable of only a mild "cheep, cheep."

"Good" is not always a stronger influence than "evil."

The night porter of the house where artist Pablo Picasso, the extreme modernist, was staying in Paris, helped the gendarmes catch a burglar by remembering the man's appearance and then sketching it.

Picasso was impressed, so when his place was robbed soon after, he observed the bandit who bound him with rope, and later did a painting of the man which he handed to the gendarme. Guided by the sketch, they promptly rounded up 200 people, a house, a hearse, a pair of old boots and a can opener.

S. H. Simmons, *New Speakers Handbook*

In an old Flip Wilson routine. Someone asked Flip about his religion and he answered, "I am a Jehovah's Bystander." "A Jehovah's Bystander?" remarked his friend. "I never heard of a Jehovah's Bystander." Flip looked coy and said, "Well, they asked me to be a witness but I didn't want to get involved."

A man dreamed that he had died and had found himself in a vast expanse where he was exceedingly comfortable. He rested for a while and then, becoming bored, shouted out, "Is there anybody here?"

In a moment, a white-robed attendant appeared and asked, "What do you want?"

"What can I have?" was the answer.

"You can have anything you want," replied the attendant.

"Well, bring me something to eat."

"What do you want to eat?" asked the attendant. "You can have anything you want."

And so they brought him just what he wanted, and he ate and slept and had a glorious time. He went on getting everything he wanted whenever he asked for it, but at last he grew bored and summoned the attendant and said, "I want something to do."

"I am sorry, but that is the only thing we cannot give you here."

And the man said, "I am sick and tired of it all. I'd rather go to hell!"

"Where do you think you are?" exclaimed the attendant.

When told that the company to which he was applying for a job was already over staffed, one fellow replied, "That's all right. The little bit of work I do wouldn't be noticed."

One applicant noted that he was good at working crossword puzzles. The personnel manager said, "But we want someone who is good during working hours." The applicant replied, "This was during working hours."

Work is essential to our self-esteem. During World War II industrialist Henry J. Kaiser was brought to Washington, D.C. to testify concerning his ship building activities. He had claimed to be able to build a ship a day. He was being cross-examined by a somewhat hostile young lawyer who said, "So you think you can build a ship a day," goaded the questioner, "you know Rome wasn't built in a day." Henry J. Kaiser looked the young lawyer squarely in the eye and answered, "I wasn't there."

Employer's tactful recommendation: "He worked one week for us and we are satisfied."

While money isn't everything, it does keep you in touch with your children.
—*Changing Times*

The pretty but not-quite-smart sophomore in college was seated next to a famous astronomer at a dinner party and asked him what work he was engaged in.

"I study astronomy," said the scientist.

"My goodness, I finished that last year," said the young woman.

A stage is what many a teen-age girl thinks she should be on when actually it's something she's going through.

—**Earl Mathes**

Three men were discussing what most people wanted in a new car.

"Dependability," said one fellow.

"Styling," declared another.

"Economy," said the third.

Just then a fourth man, who recently had bought a new car, entered the room. They decided to pose the question to him.

"What is the thing you'd like most to get out of your new car?" they asked.

"My teen-age son," he replied.

Weary of the constant disorder in her son's room, a mother laid down the law: For every item she had to pick up off the floor, they would have to pay her a nickel.

At the end of a week, the boys owed her 65 cents. She received the money promptly—along with a 50-cent tip and a note that read, "Thanks, Mom; keep up the good work!"

Modern Maturity

Nowadays, when you tell a teenager to shift for himself, he things you're going to buy him a sports car.

"Do you know what caused your fainting spell?"

"Yes. My son asked for the keys to the garage and came out with the lawnmower."

A boy returned from 2 weeks at his first summer camp. He showed his mother two ribbons that he had won: 1 for making improvement in swimming, the other for naming the most birds on a nature hike. His mother asked him about a third ribbon in his pocket. "Aw," he said, "I got that blue thing for having the neatest packed bag when we were ready to come home." "I'm proud of you," his mother said.

"It was easy," replied the lad. "I never unpacked it."

"Mother, what's the name of that boy I met on my vacation?" the teener asked.

"Which one?"

"You know, the one I couldn't live without?"

As the mother said goodbye to her son who was returning to school after spring vacation, she reminded him to write often. Another woman standing nearby heard the plea and gave this advice. "The surest way to get your son to write home is to send him a letter saying, 'Here's 50 dollars, spend it any way you like.'"

"And that will make my son write home?"

"Yes indeed. You forget to enclose the money."

Some of these teenage singing groups — they look like they've cut more throats than records.

—Robert Orben

Someone has noted that adolescence is that time in life when we have to apologize to our friends for our old-fashioned parents.

A parent is a person who has to give a lecture on nutritional values to a kid who has reached six-foot-six by eating hamburgers.

Children grow up so quickly. One day you look at your car's gas gauge showing empty and realize they're teenagers.

"My son," the father was telling his neighbor, "wants to be 'doing his thing.' The trouble is, he doesn't have a thing to do."

There is a story about a freshman at a state university who was about to experience her first blind date. Her roommate, who was making all the arrangements, asked whether she preferred southern boys or northern boys. The freshman was from a little town in the Midwest and innocently unaware of such subtle distinctions. She asked, "What's the difference?"

Her worldly wise roommate answered, "Southern boys are more romantic. They will take you walking in the moonlight and whisper sweet nothings in your ear. Northern boys are more active. They like to go places and do exciting things."

The girl pondered the contrast and then asked wistfully, "Could you please find me a southern boy from as far North as possible?"

Mr. Jones' pretty, twelve-year-old daughter came screaming around the corner of the house, with the neighbor's boy in hot pursuit. Mr. Jones leaped out of his hammock and halted the two. "Why are you chasing my Gwendolyn?" he asked the boy. "She pinched me," he complained. Mr. Jones turned to Gwendolyn. "Why did you pinch him?" he demanded. Gwendolyn answered demurely, "So he'd chase me."

I like the story about the high school English teacher who was telling her high school English class how to expand their vocabulary. "If you make use of the same word at least ten times," she said, "it is yours forever." At the back of the class one young woman was heard muttering under her breath, "Bob . . . Bob . . . Bob . . . ."

Society's values are strange. Notes comedian Berl Williams: "We spend thousands of dollars for school buses so our kids don't have to walk to school, then spend thousands more to build a gym so the kids can get some exercise."

Television is not only replacing radio—it's doing a pretty good job on homework too.
— Robert Orben

Someone has laughingly said that the peak years of mental activity must be between the ages of four and eighteen. At four we know all the questions; at eighteen, all the answers.

The college boy received a sports car from his parents when he graduated. On the steering wheel was this note: "Best wishes from Mama and Pauper."

In America, the young are always ready to give to those who are older than themselves the full benefit of their inexperience.

—Oscar Wilde

I am not young enough to know everything.

—James Matthew Barrie

A college professor congratulated a man on his daughter's brilliant paper on the influence of science on the principles of government.

The father exclaimed, "Good! Next I want her to begin to work on the influence of the vacuum cleaner on the modern carpet!"

Charles Schultz's cartoon character Linus — blanket in hand — once said: "There is no heavier burden than a great potential."

Clemson University economist Bruce Yandle collects graffiti for his own enjoyment and for use in his lectures. When Yandel is in the doldrums, his spirits are lifted by one of the finest pieces of graffiti he collected. Beneath the question "Where will you spend eternity?" someone had answered, "The way things look now, in German 201."

Instructions written on the inside front cover of a textbook: "If found by person, return in mail; if found by male, return in person."

"Has your son's college education proved of any value?" asked a neighbor. "Yes, it has," was the reply. "It cured his mother of bragging about him."

Earl Wilson quotes John J. Plomp saying: "It is not too easy to get a college education. The boy we buy our magazines from has been coming around for 20 years."

"Pop, what does 'college-bred' mean?"
"They make college bred, my boy, from the flower of youth and the dough of old age."